Also by J. A. Graffagnino

"The Taxi," a horror short story (Necrology Shorts)

The Journey of Mary / Ma Li (Dreams Publishing Company)

Fantasy & Horror Short Stories (AuthorHouse)

THE FIX IS IN

The Deutsche Bank Building Fire Conspiracy

J. A. GRAFFAGNINO

authorHOUSE®

AuthorHouse™
1663 Liberty Drive
Bloomington, IN 47403
www.authorhouse.com
Phone: 1 (800) 839-8640

Published by AuthorHouse   07/19/2016

ISBN: 978-1-5246-1884-1 (sc)
ISBN: 978-1-5246-1882-7 (hc)
ISBN: 978-1-5246-1883-4 (e)

Library of Congress Control Number: 2016911478

Print information available on the last page.

This book is printed on acid-free paper.

Interior Graphics/Art Credit: JB Nicholas, J. A. Graffagnino and FDNY

This book is dedicated to all first responders, construction workers, and innocent bystanders who have been injured, maimed, or killed in construction accidents.

To those investigative journalists who fought to expose the truth and who suffered because they tried to perform their jobs honestly. A special thanks and appreciation to Wayne Barrett, Tom Robbins, and Brian Kates, who lost their jobs because of their dedication, bravery, loyalty, and honesty.

To my family, my son's family, and his friends, who continue to suffer from the loss of his life. He will remain in our hearts, in our souls, and in our memories.

Image Credits

Front and rear cover and those same photos and two more by JB Nicholas on pages 13 and 14

Photos by New York City Fire Department on pages 15–26 and 28

Diagram by New York City Fire Department on pages 18, 27, and 29

Photograph of Battalion Chief John Plant provided by John Plant

Photograph of Acting Battalion Chief Neil Cronin provided Neil Cronin

Photograph of Captain Simon Ressner authorized by Simon Ressner

Photograph of Lieutenant Gary Iorio provided by Gary Iorio

Photograph of Firefighter Jay Bangash provided by Jay Bangash

Photograph of Firefighter Kenneth Fulcher Jr. provided by Kenneth Fulcher Jr.

Photograph of Firefighter Francis McCutchen provided by Francis McCutchen

Diagram of Deutsche Bank building 2005–2012 relationships

All profits from the sale of this book will be donated to the FDNY Burn Unit and the New York City Police and Fire Widows' and Children's Benefit Fund.

About the Author

The Fix Is In is J. A. Graffagnino first non-fiction book. He's published a novel, *The Journey of Mary / Ma Li*; a collection of short stories, *Fantasy & Horror*; and a horror short story "The Taxi."

The story of the Deutsche Bank building fire needed to be told, and Graffagnino had the right qualifications. A tough, no-nonsense investigator and outraged father, he had no intention of quitting until *The Fix Is In* was completed and he could recant all the chilling details of what really happened on August 18, 2007, the worst day of Graffagnino's and his family's lives.

J. A. Graffagnino lives in Brooklyn, New York, with his wife.

His website is www.jagraffagnino.com.

Contents

Part III: The Game of Hide the Guilt

Part IV: Aftermath

Acknowledgments

I wish to acknowledge the following individuals for their contributions to this book:

Officers and firefighters of the Fire Department of New York City (FDNY)
The FDNY officers and firefighters interviewed
Former US Representative Michael Grimm
Former Manhattan Borough President Scott Stringer
Senator Tony Avella
Senator Marty Golden
Assemblyman Peter J. Abbate Jr.
Councilman Vincent J. Gentile
Wayne Barrett, former senior editor and investigative reporter, *Village Voice* newspaper
Thomas Feeney, former editorial research assistant, Village Voice Media
Dr. Stuart "Qui Tam" Goldman
Eileen Long-Chelales
John Meringolo, attorney
Sally Regenhard, activist for 9/11 victims and their families
Former FDNY Deputy Chief James Riches
Norman Siegel, civil rights attorney
Robert Spencer, Director of Media Services for the Organization of Staff Analysts
Martin J. Steadman, journalist, Public Relations Director for the Uniformed Fire Officers Association
Bob Weinstein, journalist, syndicated columnist, author, and editor

I extend special gratitude to my daughters—Maria, Theresa, and Linda—and my grandchildren, whose love and support continue to inspire me. I am also especially grateful to my wife, Rosemarie, whose love, faith, and strength have carried me through these dark times.

Prologue

All truths are easy to understand once they are discovered; the point is to discover them.

—Galileo Galilei

On September 11, 2001, 19 militants associated with the Islamic extremist group al-Qaeda hijacked four airliners and carried out suicide attacks against targets in the United States. Two of the planes were flown into the twin towers of the World Trade Center in New York City. The first airplane struck 1 World Trade Center (North Tower); minutes later a second airplane struck 2 World Trade Center (South Tower). Within minutes of each other, both towers imploded and came crashing down. The South Tower struck the Deutsche Bank building at 130 Liberty Street, creating a huge gash in its side. Before the day was over, World Trade Center buildings 4, 5, 6, and 7 crashed or burned, and more than 3,000 people lost their lives in New York City alone. A third plane hit the Pentagon just outside Washington, DC, and the fourth plane crashed in a field in Pennsylvania. It was one of the worst days in America's history.

It has been eight years since the Deutsche Bank building fire. For me, it seems like it was yesterday. There is no accepting the loss of your child. There is no moving on. Neither money nor time erases the loss from my family's lives. It is as painful now as it was then. But when you know that the tragedy could have been prevented if just one person had done their job, the pain and anger is even more excruciating. I wrote *The Fix Is In* because I want you, the reader, to know the truth. I want to expose the people who benefited from the catastrophe and place blame where it belongs.

I will never forget Saturday, August 18, 2007, when a fire was reported in the middle of the afternoon at the Deutsche Bank building on 130 Liberty Street in Lower Manhattan. What initially seemed like a routine fire rapidly escalated into a roaring, out-of-control seven-alarm inferno.

I was led to believe that the fire was an accident and that high-level decision makers, along with their direct reports in several government agencies, had done their jobs properly. Like most people, I wanted to believe that our elected officials were telling the truth and that the conclusions of their investigation about the causes of the Deutsche Bank building fire were accurate.

I was wrong. Call it intuition, an unsettling cold feeling in the pit of my stomach. I sensed that I, as well as all New Yorkers, was being misled—no, lied to. I decided to find out for myself, to investigate and gather all the information I could about the fire and about the key players with a direct or indirect part in the fire, including the landlord of the building; contractors; and various city, state, and federal agencies. I simply wanted to find the truth.

To tell the story as it unfolded, I had to keep my emotions in check and avoid making assumptions. Most of the information was out there. It just had to be found and interpreted. Much of it was public record; the rest I found by spending countless hours interviewing eyewitnesses—firefighters and their commanders and civilian observers.

After eight years of digging and gathering information, I realized that my gut feeling was correct. This feeling was confirmed by information I'd uncovered and by the media's investigative reports, which contradicted the official version released by New York City officials and the district attorney's office. It was particularly painful to discover that city, state, and federal agencies stood by and allowed a series of harmful and ultimately lethal decisions to be made. They failed to protect the brave men and women who had dedicated their lives to keeping New York City's citizens safe.

In the chapters ahead, the facts speak for themselves. You'll learn the details behind state and federal prosecutors' investigative reports of the Deutsche Bank building fire and discover how top government and private industry decision makers were negligent and ultimately responsible for the death trap conditions hundreds of firefighters unwittingly walked into. They encountered unforeseen barriers that prolonged the fire and created insurmountable obstacles that led to the unnecessary deaths of three firefighters.

"The Deutsche Bank building fire was preventable," said FDNY Captain Simon Ressner. "Preventive measures were deliberately sidestepped in the name of ambition and in the name of money." When all is said and done, due to conditions at the Deutsche Bank building before the fire, all efforts to quell the raging inferno were in vain. There isn't a firefighter in the United States, especially in New York City, who doesn't remember the event.

This book is not based upon a conspiracy theory, opinions, or undocumented rumors but upon confirmed facts from reliable sources that prove there were no accidental deaths or injuries resulting from the Deutsche Bank building fire. While the facts are indisputable, this tragic event will always remain a blight on New York City's history.

The brave firefighters who responded to the Deutsche Bank building fire knew they were battling perilous odds. Yet they performed their jobs as best they could as their situation worsened. As smoke and flames enveloped them and their lives dangled by a fragile thread, the firefighters fought on for greater than seven hours, until victory was eventually theirs.

Part I

What Happened?

~1~

The Fire

I remember looking at that building, and I saw that it was breathing smoke. Kicking that dark, gray smoke out and then sucking it back in fast. The fire reminded me of a fire-breathing dragon. I have never seen anything like that. Just by looking at that building, I knew it was going to be a different type of day.

—*Firefighter Jay Bangash*

Saturday, August 18, 2007

New York City, Lower Manhattan (former World Trade Center area)

When the Saturday work shift ended, between 3:00 and 3:30 p.m., most demolition construction workers had left the Deutsche Bank building, but several remained.

At 3:25 p.m., a female worker on the 18th floor of the contaminated building at 130 Liberty Street smelled smoke. She followed the burning scent until she was able to see smoke coming from the floor below. She reached for her walkie-talkie and broadcast the smoky condition to her fellow workers and supervisors, but no one responded.

By 3:30 p.m., an anonymous caller contacted the firehouse across the street from the Deutsche Bank building. Ladder 10 and Engine 10 responded to the building in less than one minute.

At 3:34 p.m., the worker who smelled the smoke remembered she had her cell phone with her and quickly dialed 911 to report the smoky conditions.

The fire started on the 17th floor, on the south side of the building in the decontamination area. The Fire Department of New York City

(FDNY) dispatcher was notified by telephone at 3:36 p.m. Within the next minute, two engines and two ladder companies along with a battalion chief were notified. Five minutes after the first notification and as the fire rapidly enveloped the building, additional FDNY units were assigned.

Other calls to 911 by area residents quickly followed. Two minutes after arriving, an officer from Ladder 10 called in a second alarm. The officer told the dispatcher that the scaffolding was on fire and that the fire had spread to other floors.

Just prior to 4:00 p.m., Battalion 4 spoke with the building engineer at 130 Liberty Street about the building's standpipe system. (A standpipe is a type of rigid water piping that is built into multistory buildings in a vertical position or into bridges in a horizontal position, to which fire hoses can be connected, allowing manual application of water to the fire. Within the context of a building or bridge, a standpipe serves the same purpose as a fire hydrant.) The engineer told the FDNY officer that the standpipe system was operational.

As the minutes ticked away, additional FDNY units arrived at the scene. They discovered that the building's standpipe was not functioning—there was no water. FDNY firefighters scrambled to find open standpipe outlets. At the same time, they closed section valves. They checked several floors hoping to find standpipe water, but the pipes were all dry.

Fire command reported that a building engineer had told them that the standpipe system was operational in the B stairwell. Several standpipe valves in stairwell B were checked. They too were empty.

Fewer than 10 minutes after the first fire truck arrived, the fire had billowed out of control. Instead of just burning upward, the flames had also descended lower into the building. To their surprise and concern, firefighters noticed that the fire had dropped to the 15th floor.

Meanwhile, firefighters continued to search for water to extinguish the fire. All attempts failed. Firefighters were forced to retreat to the 14th floor. Units dispatched to the 17th floor to find the fire's origination point were forced to evacuate onto the building's north-side scaffold.

At 4:12 p.m., the situation was desperate. For the third time, the building's engineers and construction workers said that the building's standpipe system was functional, that both the automatic and the manual water pumps in the building were operational, and that they would activate both water pumps. The water pumps were never activated, and the building's engineers were not heard from again.

At this point, firefighters decided to try to string together sections of fire hose and run it down the outside of the building to connect to street fire hydrants. It was a long shot because there was no guarantee that the fire hydrant would have enough water pressure to pump water up to the 14th floor, but it was worth a try. Inside the building, a firefighter jumped on the roof of the only working elevator hoist and uncoiled the connected fire hoses to the ground. Outside, firefighters on the ground tried to connect the extended hose lengths to a nearby hydrant. But when they went to the spot on Liberty Street where the hydrant should have been, they found that it had been removed. The next closest hydrant was covered in a wooden box and could not be connected.

As they scrambled to find a functional hydrant, a firefighter found a sign glued on a plywood door: "STANDPIPE BEHIND DOOR". The firefighters broke the lock on the plywood door. When they tried to push open the door, they found that it was blocked by wooden barriers. They sawed through the barriers so the door could be shoved open. Inside, a crudely painted sign directed them down a narrow walkway, which led to a plywood-covered column, where they found yet another hand-painted sign that said, "STANDPIPE HERE".

The firefighters had to cut through the plywood to reach the building's Siamese fire-hose connector. They quickly hooked up their hoses and started pumping the lifesaving water into the building's standpipe system.

Eventually the firefighters hooked up to Siamese connections on three sides of the Deutsche Bank building and started pumping water into it. Each connection was pumping 700 gallons of water per minute at 200 pounds of pressure. At that rate, the entire 26 floors of the building standpipe should have been charged in less than three minutes.

After 15 minutes, with no water in either of the two standpipe systems, the firefighters searched for reasons why. They found it in the basement when they discovered that 42 feet of the building's standpipe had been removed. The basement was filled with water; the building standpipe was broken in three locations in both standpipes, rendering them useless.

An FDNY super-pumper high-water-pressure truck was called in because it had greater water pressure required to push water up to the 14th floor. The super-pumper's hoses were unfurled and carried to a working fire hydrant. As soon as the firefighters began unleashing water, the building's windows began to explode and shatter with bomb-like force as sections of the building's wall flew in all directions at bullet speed.

The fire rapidly consumed the building, fueled by combustible materials that included diesel drums, gasoline cans, PCB drums, propane tanks, and acetylene canisters, which were turned into exploding bombs and missiles. Debris tumbled from the burning building, cutting into the hose that carried the only water supply to extinguish the fire.

Meanwhile, firefighters inside the building found themselves in total chaos. On the outside of the building, smoke and flames ascended higher. But in the interior of the building, the opposite happened; smoke and flames crept lower and lower into the building. Despite all efforts to get the raging fire under control, the firefighters faced an untenable situation. Even though they faced a losing battle, they had no intention of retreating. That's not what they were trained to do.

Thick, black smoke triggered by heavy plastic sheeting, wood, glue, and other combustibles, combined with toxic asbestos dust and other contaminants, enveloped the lower floors of the building. Firefighters found themselves trapped in a maelstrom they weren't prepared for. Worse still, the all-consuming toxic fumes made the men choke and gag, making their jobs even more difficult.

Firefighters faced one obstacle after another. Inside the burning, crippled building, lighting was poor because of inefficient bulbs further hindered by hanging plastic sheets, plywood, and plastic covering the windows. Virtually every part of the contaminated building was a minefield, strewn with building materials, equipment, and debris.

As hard as they tried to grope their way through the poorly lit building, the firefighters, swallowed up in a smoke- and fume-filled labyrinth, struggled to get their bearings. As the dense smoke made navigating the maze of plywood walls, building supplies, equipment, plastic sheeting, and the piles of debris almost impossible, many firefighters became disoriented and got lost in the dark.

According to the city's building codes, materials and building supplies should have been fire retardant. Instead, the combination of wood, glue, and plastic barriers became lethal incendiary devices, accelerating the fire along its destructive path. Firefighters also discovered that the concrete-and-metal fireproof floors had been pierced, creating holes that allowed the burning debris, wood, and plastics to drip into the ceiling of the floor below, where more combustible substances fueled the fire.

Large sections of the ceiling between the floors caught fire. Within that small space, fire raced from one end of the ceiling to the other. The ceiling panels burned, and the aluminum frames warped, causing what remained of the ceiling to collapse.

Firefighters never know what to expect when they enter a burning building. But the building at 130 Liberty Street offered seldom-encountered surprises, the biggest of which was the lack of firefighters' most critical firefighting deterrent: water.

These highly trained firefighters were in a death trap, where problems mounted by the second. The raging fire used the holes in the compromised fireproof concrete floors as air tubes to travel both up and down. When it reached flammable debris and supplies, it was like lighting, a fast-burning dynamite fuse, further igniting and fueling the burning process all over again. With the smoke defying gravity and the laws of physics by descending deeper into the building, firefighters found themselves in total darkness.

An FDNY officer reported high heat and zero visibility on the 15th floor. Another firefighter reported that all the stairwells and landings were securely boarded over; only one floor below was accessible. They could neither go up nor down more than one floor. The retreating firefighters sought refuge in the one place in the building they knew was safe: the fireproof building stairwells. But when they reached the stairwell areas, they found that the fireproof walls and doors had been removed and the staircases (the only means of escape) had been covered over with heavy wooden planks and six-millimeter thick plastic, which covered all sides of the stairwell and was glued to the floor. With thick, choking smoke pouring over them and the fire's flames engulfing them, the men, whose initial thoughts were riveted on extinguishing the fire, now thought only of survival.

By 4:20 p.m., the maydays crackled into fire command at an alarming rate. Firefighters had used up the air in their portable air cylinders. They were lost, exhausted, and scared.

Rescue companies were immediately dispatched to find and rescue lost firefighters. Some of the rescue companies' firefighters also lost their bearings in the rapidly burning death trap building.

The hoist elevator was ordered to the 15th floor for evacuations. Roll calls were ordered to identify firefighters' locations and to determine whether they were able to function.

By 4:30 p.m., maydays screeched nonstop, interrupted by requests for more air tanks, fire hoses, and manpower. In a matter of minutes, 14 maydays and 19 urgent calls were recorded.

Within seconds, the situation turned from dire to desperate. Firefighters screamed for the water to be turned on. As a last-ditch effort, they tied ropes to each other as they continued to search for standpipe valves and lost firefighters.

As the tragedy intensified, conditions became more critical. Firefighters throughout the building struggled to find a safe place to regroup. They used axes and knives to cut through the thick plastic and plywood that covered the windows. As the seconds ticked away, they used whatever they could find to break the large ceiling-to-floor windows. Many took running leaps onto the exterior building's scaffolding four feet away. With so many firemen leaping to escape the burning building, many feared the scaffolding would collapse under their weight. The men were no longer trying to stop a raging, out-of-control fire; they were fighting for their lives.

At approximately 4:45 p.m., a water-pressured fire hose reached the 14th floor outside the B stairwell, manned by a squad from Engine Company 24, headed by 18-year veteran Lieutenant John (Jack) Garcia. Robert (Bobby) Beddia, a senior man with 20-plus years' experience, controlled the hose nozzle. James Martin, detailed from Engine 255 firehouse, was in the backup position directly behind Beddia. Joseph Graffagnino, my son and an 8-year veteran, was at the control position, making sure the hose didn't get tangled. The four men were stationed in the stairwell between the 14th and 15th floors.

Garcia went onto the floor to find additional lengths of fire hose and to locate the fire so he could lead his team to the best position to direct the water hose onto the flames. But by the time he started to search for the fire, it had rapidly become an uncontrollable inferno. Impenetrable, thick, black smoke made it impossible to see inches ahead. Enshrouded in smoke and intense heat, Garcia became disoriented. He lost his bearings and couldn't find his way back to his team. Running low on air, he issued a mayday while trying to exit the building. Picking up the mayday call, his team tried to radio their location. Garcia didn't respond, or if he did, his team didn't hear him in all the confusion.

Putting his life on the line, Beddia searched for his missing lieutenant. In this desperate long-shot gamble, Beddia got lost. Knowing he was running out of air, he tried to make it last by turning his air valve on and off. To get to a safe place, he realized he had to ration the small amount of air that remained in his canister.

Meanwhile, heat and smoke forced the remaining team members to retreat back into the stairwell. Graffagnino and Martin, now on the 14th floor landing, discovered that their escape route was blocked by a sealed-shut staircase and remained at their post. As conditions worsened, the two men realized that they had the only functional water line in the building.

Beddia and Graffagnino also called in maydays because they were almost out of air. Their confusion and utter desperation escalated, confirming the hopelessness of their situation. Their maydays were mixed with dozens of other maydays and urgent distress radio calls. The command center couldn't hear all the calls, because they were coming in so rapidly. Many calls were blocked by the building's density. But other firefighters managed to pick up many of the mayday calls and relay them to the command center.

While waiting for reinforcements to arrive, Graffagnino's air tank ran out of air. Seeing his buddy gasping for air, Martin tried to share his air mask. By then, Graffagnino was disoriented. When Martin removed his air mask to begin buddy breathing, he too was instantly overcome by the heavy, acrid smoke. As conditions worsened, Martin and Graffagnino struggled in vain to see what was ahead. The choking smoke, lack of visibility and exhausted air tanks made it impossible to control the indefensible conditions.

Virtually all coordination efforts were hampered by crippling conditions, including lack of air, acerbated by the looming terror of exploding contaminants scattered randomly throughout the building like minefields hidden by a black curtain of thick, blinding smoke.

When a disoriented Graffagnino attempted to stand up, Martin— acting on instinct and experience—tried in vain to yank his buddy to the ground in order to place his head under the smoke. When Graffagnino resisted, Martin lost his grip and fell. As he struggled to his feet, he found a cable (conduit section) on the floor. Meanwhile, Graffagnino fell back toward the stairs. Martin followed the cable until he could see daylight.

At 4:50 p.m., Martin called in another mayday, this time alerting command that Beddia and Graffagnino needed immediate help near the 14th floor stairwell. Picking up the maydays, firefighters on the ground notified command center.

Miraculously, Martin groped his way to the Q decking area and notified the firefighters that his team was inside the building and out of air.

By 5:00 p.m., Garcia managed to find his way to the elevator hoist and make it down to the command center.

At 5:01 p.m., an unconscious Graffagnino was found in the corridor, just outside of the north stairwell area of the 14th floor. In less than five minutes he was placed on a stretcher and brought down on the hoist that was 100 feet away. All the while, he received cardiopulmonary resuscitation (CPR). As soon as Graffagnino reached ground level, brother firefighters rushed him to the ambulance where EMS took control of his care and rapidly transported him to Béekman Downtown Hospital.

At 5:10 p.m., an unconscious Beddia was located in the corridor between the north and south turnstiles on the 14th floor and taken to the elevator area, a distance of 125 feet. CPR was immediately administered and continued in the ambulance.

Only moments after the ambulance arrived at the hospital, the emergency room physician was notified that both firefighters needed to be treated for exposure to potential carbon monoxide and cyanide toxicity.

At 6:09 p.m. and 6:10 p.m., respectively, both Beddia and Graffagnino were pronounced dead at Beekman Hospital. The medical examiner's official report said that the cause of death was cardiac arrest caused by smoke inhalation.

The casualty count was high. Out of a total of 224 firefighters dispatched to the Deutsche Bank building fire, 105 (or 48 percent) suffered injuries.

Three firefighters died because of the Deutsche Bank building fire. Along with Beddia and Graffagnino, three and a half years later Garcia also died. Garcia's cause of death was attributed to mental anguish triggered by the fire. Considering the enormity of the fire—not to mention the unforeseen obstacles the firefighters had to contend with— it's a miracle there weren't more fatalities. Yet many of the firefighters suffered emotional and physical trauma, some worse than others.

Most of the firefighters that responded to the Deutsche Bank building fire had also been at the 9/11 disaster. Many of them still suffer from survivor's guilt and post-traumatic stress disorder (PTSD). For the remainder of their lives they must endure the pain and sorrow of losing not just coworkers but brothers, friends in the truest sense of the word because their lives depend on each other.

The fire raged upward through nine floors of the high-rise building, from the 17th to the 26th floor. But the fire also traveled down to the 16th through the 14th floors, the 12th and 5th floors. In total, 15 floors were ravaged.

By 9:54 p.m., the firefighters stopped asking for more fire companies to fight the fire.

At 10:39 p.m.— 7 hours and 14 minutes after it started at 3:25 p.m.—FDNY command announced that the fire was under control.

On September 7 at 8:24 p.m., the FDNY watch line ended. (A watch line is where an FDNY fire company is at the building continuously (24-7) because of arson, a criminal investigation, or a possible flare-up of a new fire at the building. FDNY companies are rotated every three hours.)

FDNY Kept in the Dark

The FDNY knew surprising little about the Deutsche Bank building prior to the fire. Its Critical Information Dispatch System (CIDS) card contained specifics of the building, which were relayed by the FDNY dispatcher. The dispatcher said that the building was a hazmat (hazardous materials condition) because the sprinkler system didn't work and that a functional standpipe was in stairwell A.

Most of the firefighters had no knowledge of the interior layout of the building since the 9/11 terrorist attack six years earlier. The last building inspection conducted by the local firehouse searching for obvious fire-code violations had been completed a year and a half earlier.

After observing the building's exterior, firefighters quickly concluded that the building was constructed of concrete and steel and was originally a high-rise office building, 41 stories tall (reduced to 26 floors in recent demolitions), that occupied an entire city block. The building had two stairwells located in the center of the building. The A staircase was on the south side, and the B stairwell was on the north side. The sprinkler system had been destroyed when the World Trade Center's Twin Towers collapsed into the Deutsche Bank building. The sprinkler system had never been repaired and so was inoperable.

The fire was believed to have begun in a trash can that was against the wall of a 26 foot-by-26-foot plywood decontamination enclosure. There were also plywood shanties that held construction tools and equipment.

Photos of the Deutsche Bank building taken ten minutes after the workday ended on August 18 show smoke billowing from the top five floors on the south side of the building. Fifteen minutes after the fire started, the flames were huge.

When the firefighters reached the building, the only entrances were stairs and the external elevator hoist on the north side of the building, which were used by the construction crews. The south-side elevator hoist was already engulfed in flames. The firefighters went up the outside elevator hoist to the 15th floor because they wanted to approach the fire from two floors below where it had started. This would enable firefighters to establish a base area to investigate the vicinity in order to verify that no personnel remained and to search for stairwells and standpipe locations to fight the fire.

Access corridors, constructed of plywood walls covered in polyethylene plastic, had been built between the clean and contaminated building zones. Polyethylene plastic sheets were used as curtains to restrict air flow from the contaminated areas. There were also large, aluminum, accordion-type tubes throughout the floor. Firefighters had no idea what they were used for.

When the first responders reached both staircases and tried to ascend to the 16th floor, they found the way blocked by wood and plastic barriers. Many of the concrete (fire-proof) sides of the stairwell had been removed by the contractors.

In order to get to the fire, firefighters requested portable saws and axes from the FDNY Command Center so that they could cut their way through. Once through the barrier, the firefighters were told of a small hatchway that was part of the barrier. This hatch access door over the stairwell, however, was too narrow for a firefighter in gear to crawl through.

By then, other firefighters began pouring into the building as the fire raged into a second alarm and then third alarm, followed by a fourth, fifth, sixth, and finally a seventh alarm, summoning engine and ladder companies from surrounding areas.

Firefighters from different companies used the outside elevator to get to the higher floors to look for any remaining workers and to determine the extent of the fire. They weren't able to stay long, because the fire was growing stronger with each passing minute. But they were able to determine that the stairwells were blocked by wood, plastic, and foam barriers to prevent asbestos and other harmful contaminants from leaving the building.

To fight a fire you need water. When the FDNY officers first responded to the fire, they asked the contractors and building engineers what type of water system the building had and whether it was functional. The water system was identified as a dry standpipe, a system where the outside fire hydrants had to be connected to the building's Siamese connectors located in several locations on the external building structure. In this type of system, the water travels from the fire hydrant into the FDNY engine truck and passes through into the Siamese connector, which connects to the building's standpipe system, which goes to every floor in the building.

More than 200 firefighters were sent to battle a raging holocaust that never conformed to normal conditions, refused to succumb to defeat, and actually attacked the firefighters, forcing them to run for their lives.

The official statement from DA Robert Morgenthau stated that the fire was caused by a discarded cigarette. Several experts in building and fire safety, along with veteran firefighters, said that they didn't think a lit cigarette could have caused that amount of damage in such a short time period. According to many of these experts, when the FDNY can't positively identify a direct cause of a fire, the catchall fire starter is a lit cigarette.

However, firefighters did discover the reason the fire and smoke traveled lower in the building: the EPA's requirement that toxic contaminants remain in the building. To control toxic contaminants, the EPA had the contractor install 25 large internal circulation fans on floors 13, 14, 15, 16, and 17 to contain airborne toxic contaminants. However, the fans had no central or automatic cutoff switches, which meant that each fan had to be individually shut off by pulling out its electric plug. After the fire, the FDNY hired Exponent Engineering PC to develop a heat-and-smoke computer model analysis of the impact the internal fans' air flow had on the fire. The report mentioned the John Galt Corporation's fan implementation plan, which was approved by the EPA, the Lower Manhattan Development Corporation (LMDC), and Bovis.

However, the fans were not installed as per their approved locations. Instead of uniformly placing the fans around the building's interior walls, the fans were clustered mainly on the north side of the building on every floor. The impact of this fan placement drew the fire, smoke, and hot gases rapidly across the length and width of the floor while also thrusting it into lower floors, forcing the smoke to hug the floor below. As soon as the hot gases reached the fans, the intake of fresh air ignited the gases, which caused a flashover that exploded the fire back across the floor, burning everything in its path.

For some unexplainable but calculated reason, the Exponent Engineering report was released more than seven years after the fire.

The FDNY and the Department of Buildings (DOB) found that the Deutsche Bank building had the following code violations and fire safety issues:

- Permits issued by the DOB for minor floor alterations were inadequate.
- No permits were issued for building demolition.
- The sprinkler system was inoperative for six years, and the DOB had not granted any variance to exclude a working sprinkler system.
- Building standpipe systems, in both stairways, were broken in multiple places.
- The standpipe did not have two functional fire pumps (one automatic and one manual).
- Both means of egress (A and B stairways) were blocked by sealed wooden platforms on even-numbered floors.
- Stairway enclosures had been compromised or removed at several locations. Fireproof stairwell enclosures were completely removed from both stairwells on floors 16 and 17 and were partially removed on floor 14 in both stairwells. These removals allowed smoke and heat to enter the stairways, preventing firefighters from using them as areas of refuge.
- Stairwell width was reduced from 54 inches to only 25 inches because of the plywood walls. The wooden platforms and hatches were completely covered, both top and bottom, and totally sealed shut, in both the A and B stairwells. The hatches were not visible from above or below. An expandable foam sealant had been used to fill gaps or cracks that would have allowed air to pass through. In stairway A those wooden platforms blocked access on floors 4, 5, 6, 10, 12, 14, 16, 18, 20, 22, and 24. Hatches on floors 5, 14, and 16 were completely sealed shut. In stairway B access was blocked by the wooden platforms on floors 6, 10, 12, 14, 16, 18, 20, 22, and 24. The hatches were completely sealed on floors 14, 16, and 20.

The standpipe's manual fire pump, which can pump water at a rate of 750 gallons per minute (GPM), and the automatic pump, which pumps water at a rate of 500 GPM, were both out of service. The standpipe supply pipe had three sections missing in the basement area for the A stairway. In stairway B the riser pipe was disabled. The hose outlets were removed and capped. There was a 42-foot section of the riser pipe removed at the mezzanine level, with additional sections removed on the 16th and 21st floors.

Several times, the building engineers said that there was water in the standpipe system and that they were going to start the building's water pumps. However, the only water in the building was for a garden hose. In the standpipe riser for the B stairway, firefighters found a one-inch brass fitting attached to the riser for garden hose access.

Building Conditions

Fire conditions on south side, Deutsche Bank building.

Building interior floors ablaze.

The inferno raging.   *Fire burns scaffold and netting.*

The roof scaffold and netting on fire.

Only functional fire hose from 14th floor to street fire truck.

Fire trucks responding to seven-alarm fire.

Locked door with sign indicating standpipe.

Door, reverse side, blocked by wood barriers.

Beyond wood barrier, redirecting sign.

Standpipe behind plywood;
when water went
in, it was dumped in the basement.

Fire hydrant covered in wood.

When opened can't access the hydrant.

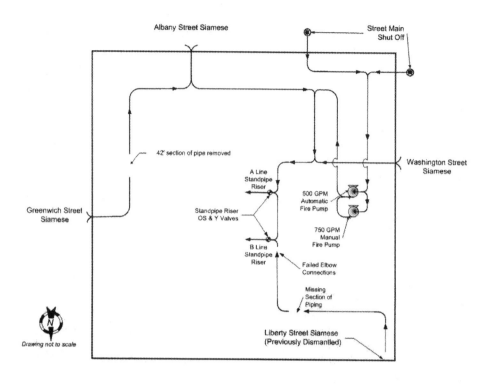

Sub-Level A Standpipe Piping Schematic

Standpipe junction valve cracked.   *Two sections of standpipe missing.*

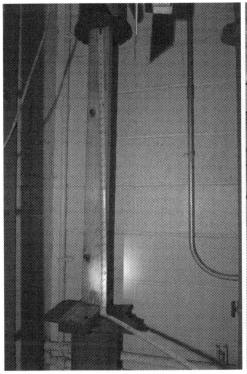
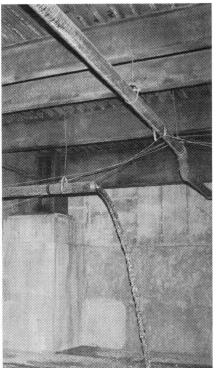

Wood placed in missing standpipe piece.   *Water pours from broken standpipe.*

Scaffold 4 feet from building.

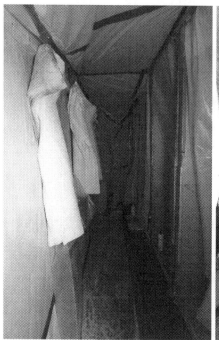

Passageway for decontamination area.

Flammables stored in shanty.

Fifty five gallon drums of PCB's.

Diesel fuel containers on 7th floor.

Gasoline canisters on 7ᵗʰ floor.

Propane tanks on 7ᵗʰ floor.

Acetylene canisters removed from floor post fire.

Four pallets of asphalt primer & mastic remover on 7ᵗʰ floor.

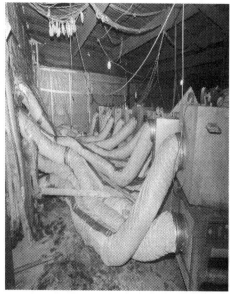

Fan cluster with tubing.   *Opposite side of fans, intake side.*

Staircase sealed in plastic, wood, tape.   *Stairwell fire proof walls partially removed.*

Hatch forced open in sealed stairwell, no walls.

FF trying to get through egress hatch.

Sealed staircase - topside.

Sealed staircase – underside.

Holes in solid, fireproof floor.

Drop ceilings provided pathway for fire.

Fire burned down from drop ceiling.

Most of floor reduced to ashes.

Gutted floor strewn with debris.

Ceiling fire burned down from floor above.

Fire's intense heat buckled support beams.

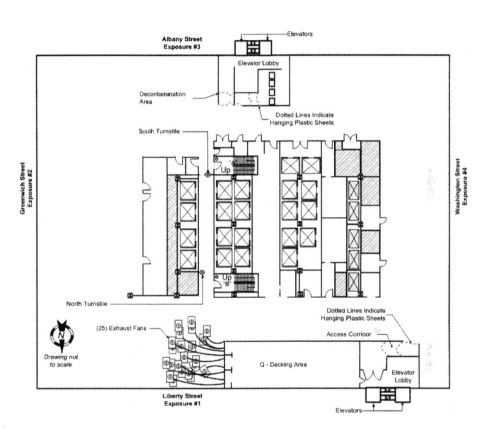

14ᵗʰ Floor Layout

14th floor facing scaffolds.

14th floor opposite side.

FF Graffagnino found outside of 14th fl B stairwell.

FF Beddia found on 14th fl between turnstiles.

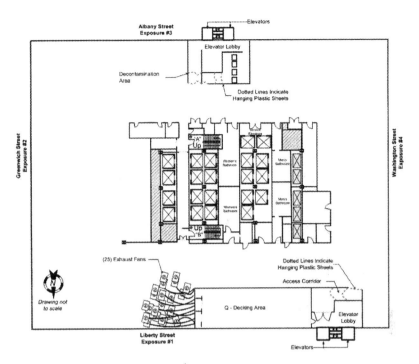

15th Floor Layout

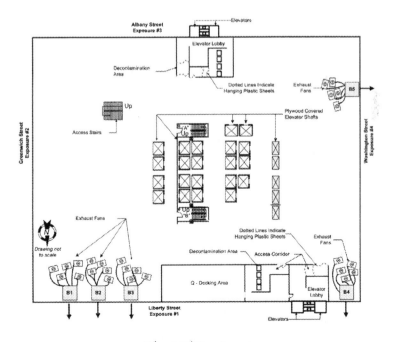

17th and 16th Floor Layout

~ 2 ~

Firefighters' Eyewitness Accounts

So many regulations were broken; it was obvious that no one checked this building at any time. The fire department should have been in that building on a regular basis. There were multiple agencies that were supposed to have been in that building every day and yet no one saw or did anything. Where was the Building Department? Where was OSHA? Where were Site Safety LLC and the fireguards? OSHA showed up afterward to give out fines for violations. This building was being worked on for years. If it was a private building, they would have been crawling all over it. They showed up after the fire is out, and we have two dead firefighters and 105 more injured.

—Firefighter Francis McCutchen

To present a variety of perspectives along with eyewitness accounts of what happened on the day of the Deutsche Bank building fire, I interviewed a deputy chief, battalion chief, two captains (one was an acting battalion chief), a lieutenant, and three firefighters.

To help the reader understand the command structure, I presented the viewpoints of different levels of FDNY officers. This is not to pin blame but to present a clear picture of what happened before, during, and after the fire. The text is interwoven with facts explaining the roles and responsibilities of city officials and contractors in charge of and responsible for the demolition and abatement of the Deutsche Bank building.

Deputy Chief
(This FDNY officer asked that his name not be used.)

While Gilbane was the general contractor, the FDNY was actively involved in the emergency planning with the emergency-management group for the Deutsche Bank site. The Environmental Protection Agency stepped in and demanded major changes for toxic containment within the building. Gilbane left, and Bovis took over the abatement/deconstruction project. The FDNY was not heard from again. Why?

First, I would like to say that the 1st Division was not among those actively involved in emergency planning for the Deutsche Bank site. Division 1 was not brought into that process. I am familiar with the time frames, 2005–2006, that you're talking about. After the fire on August 18, 2007, I went and looked into the history of what happened. Did you see the memo that was printed in the *New York Post* that was forwarded to me by Battalion Chief, at the time, Bill Siegel? Just to supply you with some background. I knew him then and still know him, because we are friends. When he first came to the 1st Battalion, we talked, and he asked me what he could do for a work project. This was in 2005. I told him to take a look at the Deutsche Bank building because I heard that things were going on there.

I didn't know exactly what was happening there other than talk that the building was in transition that they'd possibly deconstruct or demolish it. Bill Siegel went to the building around January 2005, and I visited the building also around that time frame, perhaps a month earlier or later than he did. I believe that mine was an informal visit, which I do not have a record of. When I visited the Deutsche Bank building in 2005, it was essentially an empty office building, and nothing had been done to it structurally. I was told that it was in various stages of decontamination.

I was able to get inside, escorted by a construction supervisor. The only areas that we accessed were considered clean areas (i.e., not contaminated with hazardous materials). We took an elevator to one of the upper floors. We got out of the elevator and went to a doorway that led from the elevator lobby to the floor area. We couldn't get into the main floor area, because there was plastic sheeting hanging in the doorway isolating the contaminated area from the clean area. I was told that the isolated floor area was contaminated with asbestos. There was a decontamination chamber between the contaminated and clean areas. I was able to enter the staircase and view the standpipe, which appeared, from that point of view, to be in working order. The floor appeared to be that of a normal office building, other than the fact that it was unoccupied.

In the FDNY's search for human remains, did the search parties wear protective asbestos garments with respirator masks?

I do not have any direct knowledge of the hazmat protocol for that particular operation. I must assume that they did wear hazmat protection.

Why would the FDNY go into a building if no one was in it?

I should answer this question from my perspective, if I were the responding Deputy Chief. Any response to a building fire requires an initial assessment. From my understanding, a second alarm was transmitted shortly after arrival at the Deutsche Bank building. This was based on heavy smoke and fire coming out of the building on an upper level. Construction workers met responding units and led them to the exterior elevator for access to the upper floors. This encounter would have provided initial information about possible occupants and location of fire, as well as other preliminary information, including possible hazards.

In this case, first responding units would try to get to a location where they could make an assessment and commence operations. The first priority would be life—i.e., rescuing and evacuating any people in the building who were in danger. The second priority would be to confine the fire to the area of origin. This could be achieved by closing doors and putting defensive hose lines in position. The third priority would be to attempt to extinguish the fire. It is my understanding that these procedures were followed.

To summarize, since the building was apparently undergoing some kind of construction/demolition work, there was always the possibility that someone was present in the building. That is the number one reason.

Another reason is, if the fire was not contained or extinguished, fire could spread from floor to floor, or the intense heat of an uncontrolled fire could cause various degrees of collapse, endangering anyone in the building and even people on the street below or in adjoining buildings. The best outcome is for the fire to be extinguished, if possible.

DOB engineers were in the building on a daily basis, but the FDNY was never in the building. Yet no one from the DOB was penalized or indicted. After reading the responses of the DOB people, it sounded like the answers were coached or written by lawyers. I say this because when the firefighters were going to testify before the grand jury, they were asked to appear before the general counsel for the city. The lawyers for the city wanted to put questions to the firefighters first, before they went to the grand jury and were interviewed by the District Attorney's office. The City of New York paid for all the legal fees; why not speak with City of New York general counsel? It is my opinion that if you're going to do this for FDNY personnel, you'd follow the same procedure for DOB personnel. They had five inspectors and three officers from the DOB, and all of their responses sounded similar. For example, a DOB inspector doesn't know what a standpipe looks like? This is inconceivable. The firefighters refused to meet with the city's general counsel. Any idea as to why?

The firefighters interviewed did not want to be coached by "legal," because they knew that New York City's legal council was only interested in promoting the agenda of the City of New York.

My opinion is that it was more beneficial, from a political point of view, to bring New York City fire officers, in uniform as scapegoats, as opposed to someone who wears a suit and tie that works for the Buildings Department. Symbolically it was probably more effective for them to blame higher-profile people in uniform than civilians. The standpipe system: To have an inspector look at the standpipe to determine a breach is almost impossible. Only a plumber, or other trained person, could really determine if that standpipe was in service by doing a pressure test. Based on one of the city's 33 recommendations they now require pressure gauges and alarms on standpipes in buildings under construction/demolition.

I understand that, prior to the Deutsche Bank fire, there was a person, an inspector from the Buildings Department, that wanted the standpipe tested, but when he brought it up to his bosses, he was transferred to the Bronx ... It was Aaron Williamson. I found out about this from reading about it in the *New York Times*. This indicates to me that there were people that didn't want anyone to get in the way of this building coming down.

Why would the LMDC [Lower Manhattan Development Corporation] deliberately go to the DOB and ask for an alteration permit and not a demolition permit? Everyone at the DOB knew the building was coming down and not being repaired.

I do not know what their motivation was. I can only interpret it as a way to avoid the requirement for notifying the FDNY. If a demolition permit were issued, as opposed to an alteration permit, the Buildings Department would have been required to notify the FDNY. If that had happened, there may have been other required steps and approvals in the process that might have caused Fire Prevention, Fire Operations, or 1st Division units in the FDNY to be notified. As far as I know, they were never notified.

Why would the LMDC go to such lengths to keep the FDNY out of that building?

I do not know the answer to that question. I can only assume that having the FDNY involved in the process would have presented an extra approval process and possible roadblocks in bringing the building down quickly.

The federal EPA and the NYC Department of Environmental Protection (DEP) came in with regulations that required covering the stairwells. They put heavy plastic over windows, doors, and stairwells and used fans to keep the toxins from escaping the building. OSHA and the State Department of Environmental Conservation were also involved, and all of their decisions were in direct violation of New York City building/fire codes and regulations. Why?

To my knowledge it was the federal EPA that was going around inspecting all the floors and everything else for asbestos. Apparently, it was their job to determine if the asbestos was properly contained and removed. That was one of the issues that they had with the section of standpipe in the cellar that had been cut away and removed from the building some time prior to the Deutsche Bank building fire. I read in the newspapers that it was the inability to clean the pipe to EPA requirements that drove the contractors to cut and remove that section of pipe.

Internal fans: Why didn't anyone, including the District Attorney, mention them?

That's a good question. I am not aware of any regulations on those internal fans. I don't know of any part of the building code that mentions internal fans, especially prior to the Deutsche Bank building fire. Those fans were a major factor in the spreading of that fire. In a normal building fire the smoke and flames go up and out. It is conceivable that fire and smoke could go down due to the so-called stack effect or if you have an HVAC system, due to recirculation of air within an HVAC zone. Smoke can spread to other floors but never to the extent that it happened in the Deutsche Bank building. The fire started on the 17th floor, and the fans moved the air around in such a way that it brought the fire and smoke downward till it hit the 13th floor. It made that fire travel down four floors! I don't know if the district attorney was aware if there was anything illegal about those fans. It was mentioned in the Fatal Fire report that exhaust fans were operating on the 13th to 17th floor. There was no remote shutoff for these exhaust fans. Exponent Inc., an independent testing company, was hired to determine what effects the exhaust fans had on fire and smoke movement during the fire. At the time of the printing of the Fatal Fire report, the result of Exponent's analysis was not yet available.

The Fatal Fire Report apparently drew no conclusions regarding the extent that the exhaust fans contributed to smoke spread. Based on my experience in the fire service and my background in engineering, I have drawn my own conclusions, and I assume that you have as well.

I do know that remote shutoff switches are now required for such systems and that FDNY policy is to shut them down before commencing fire operations.

Was there a plan for how to fight high-rise building fires, and if so, was it used at this fire?

FDNY has high-rise firefighting procedures in our plans. The procedures we use are based on fighting a fire in a building that is compliant with the law. This building was not in compliance with the law. That was one factor that made it extremely difficult to fight this fire. I must point out those firefighting procedures address basic predictable operations at a building fire. As you know, every fire is different, and the Deutsche Bank building fire was one of the most "different."

While procedures and plans offer general guidelines, many decisions must be made on the fire ground, based on conditions encountered. That is why so much is written in the firefighting literature about unusual situations and how to deal with them. If fighting fires was just a matter of following a plan, it wouldn't take a knowledgeable, highly trained, highly experienced chief to run them.

Multiple small fires were constant. Between 10 and 12 were extinguished by a safety person using a fire extinguisher or garden hose, yet no one called FDNY. Why?

I can only speculate on that based on my experience. My assumption is that it would have been a problem for them to have the FDNY in the building because it would have slowed down or stopped their operations. I have never seen the Bovis fire plan, but the one developed by Gilbane had an emergency plan back in 2004–2005. It was stipulated that the FDNY must be called for any fire in that building; even a fire they put out with fire extinguishers. As far as I know from reading about it in the newspapers, they never called the FDNY or 911 when any of these small fires occurred.

Battalion Chief John Plant

For a major or minor demolition permit, FDNY must be notified. But for the Deutsche Bank building the only permit issued was for alteration, which does not require an inspection of the building by the fire department. An alteration permit was insufficient for the work they were doing in that building.

When I would inspect a building under my jurisdiction that was being demolished or major renovation, I would bring my men into the building so they would become familiar with the building. I would also bring a video camera with me to record what the building looks like so we can review it and also have a video of any violations that we find so that we know what to look for when we return for verification the violation was corrected. I would not have inspected that building (130 Liberty Street), because it was contaminated. We would have to put on protective suits and then be decontaminated afterwards. I was not aware of those fans. There is nothing in the FDNY manual that states how to operate with these fans. There is no procedure for operating with those fans.

Did the FDNY know anything about the Deutsche Bank building prior to the fire?

The only information that I knew was that it was badly damaged, had a lot of mold, and that they were going to take it down.

Why weren't the firefighters ordered to leave the building if there was no water to fight the fire?

When the FDNY officers asked the workers leaving the building if there was water in the building and they answered yes there was, it is possible that the workers were thinking of the garden hose or decontamination shower and not the standpipe. Also when the men are in there trying to find a working standpipe or water supply, they are being radioed that water should be coming up any minute. Any minute, any minute, any minute led to over an hour. The firefighters continued to search for the water supply, and when they used the fire trucks, the water was being dumped into the basement because of the broken standpipe.

Another problem was with the radios. Everyone there could speak to each other, but with so many radios going on at the same time conversations and request calls were interfering with each other, so it was very difficult to hear and differentiate the callers' requests. You try to have a command channel and a tactical channel, but with so much going on at the same time, a lot was missed because of overwhelming radio calls on the tactical channel.

The FDNY officers must rely and trust the safety people, site-safety supervisor, fire-safety director, or building engineers in the building to tell us truthfully what and where in that building the fire department needs to put out the fire. I was very upset from what I read in the safety report. The responsible building people on the scene misled the fire department, which delayed us for over an hour in getting water to fight the fire. If we had water initially, that fire would have been very easy to put out.

How did the DA not hold those people accountable for lying and misleading the fire department as to the water supply system in that building? That is absolutely incredible. Those safety people failed in their job, because that information means life or death to anyone in that building. They knew the standpipe was broken, and they did nothing to fix it. Why didn't they fix it? How difficult could it have been to fix it? That is absolutely criminal to me.

The sprinkler system never worked, and the standpipe was broken for over a year. Why were the FDNY, DOB, and EMA [Emergency Management Agency] kept in the dark?

That is the site-safety supervisor, building engineer, or fire-safety director's responsibility. They are supposed to check that every day. They knew it didn't work. That was very upsetting to me because we need to have a certain trust with them and they betrayed us. They knew about the standpipe coming down because there was asbestos around the joints of the standpipe, so they just removed the joints, and the standpipe came down. They never said anything about it. That was desperate for them to do that.

There were multiple small fires, 10-12 over several months that were extinguished by a fire watch or someone using a fire extinguisher, garden hose or water bucket, yet no one ever called the fire department. Why?

They were told not to; that's why. Why wouldn't they want the fire department in the building? The building was being demolished, so what difference would it make if the fire department familiarized themselves with the building, such as where the standpipe was, the Siamese connection, etc.

The internal fans' function was to keep contaminants in the building. Why didn't anyone, including the DA, mention them?

I never knew about the use of fans to keep toxins within the building. I never heard of it before. Now we have procedures in place so that if internal fans are being used we can shut them down right away.

Most of the fires were in areas where there were piles of debris and fire accelerants, gas canisters, and propane tanks. It was rumored that the cause of the fire was arson.

Fire marshals investigated the fire, so they can tell you better than me. I really don't know. In speaking to an FDNY officer who was there—and he told me that it was originally a small fire that should have been put out easily—I would have to say maybe not. It may not have been arson. I believe that the fire could have started because of carelessness and neglect and not arson. They did have polyurethane and plastics. Plastics burn at twice as much BTUs and produces 500 times the amount of smoke.

The DA stated that regular plywood, rather than fire-retardant plywood, and flammable, heavy plastic sheeting were used in the stairwells. Why?

This is why they never wanted the fire department in that building. We would have seen these gross violations, and we would have returned every day to make sure the violations were corrected.

There were photographs of steel girders used for building support that were sagged and melted from the fire. It's hard to believe that a rubbish fire would produce intense heat capable of melting steel girders.

Normally that is correct, but if you have a fire burning out of control for over an hour, where did it get all that heat from? It was from the plastics and plywood and other combustible items lying around. With no water to put the fire out, it generates a tremendous amount of heat. If the sprinkler system would have worked, it probably would have put out the fire.

Has the FDNY created procedures to prevent this kind of scenario from happening again?

The Fire Department has instituted changes so that fires like the Deutsche Bank building fire will never happen again. One of the things I inquired about was, why can't the fire department make these fire-safety reports part of our books when we have our tests? I believe that safety reports are so well done that any firefighter would benefit from reading those reports. If they were used as study material for career advancements, it could prevent other similar catastrophes from happening. You need to have young lieutenants, captains, and chiefs reading about these reports to learn about what happened at the Deutsche Bank building fire and all these other fires over the years to learn from it. I wish this was part of the tests for promotion. I know at the Fire Academy they go over all of these fires, what happened and why.

They named the Fire Prevention Program for Officers in honor of firefighters Joseph Graffagnino and Robert Beddia.

Acting Battalion Chief Neil Cronin, Engine 24, Battalion 2

If there was no water to fight the fire, why weren't the firefighters ordered to leave the building?

I don't know. We moved the guys on my floor to the elevator, but we kept being told that we were going to get water. The engineers were working on it; they were going to get us water. When we hear that the building engineers are saying this, we believe them. The building engineers are very hands-on, very knowledgeable about the building, and we rely on them more so than a fire-safety director. The building engineers know it's their building, and they have great pride in their building, so when I hear the building engineers are working on it, I believe it. They're not "suit guys."

Captain Bosco was in charge of the firehouse closest to 130 Liberty Street. He was penalized for not conducting 15-day rule inspections of that building. Why didn't Captain Bosco perform building inspections?

I don't know why he didn't do it. But in my career I have never done a 15-day inspection.

Isn't it a regulation that when a floor is demolished the standpipe is required to be tested and capped at a floor below/above?

Yes, tested at the floor below. This obviously wasn't done.

Internal fans—why didn't anyone, including the DA, mention them?

I don't know. The internal fans were why the smoke came down lower into the building. I saw them there that day, but I didn't know what they were.

As the FDNY went into Deutsche Bank building, the remaining workers stated that the water system worked in the building, when they knew it didn't, because of the standpipe breaks. Why did they lie?

I have no idea. I got there, and I went right up. I was the acting chief that day. I checked the command board, and I didn't have any of that information. I don't know why they would have said the water system was working if it wasn't.

What was the situation like for firefighters in the building?

Well, it was a nightmare; the stairs were blocked, and plastic was all over, and I am amazed to this day that we didn't lose more men. I was one of the last officers off one of the floors when we came across a firefighter from Rescue 1. Those guys have much more experience than regular firefighters, and I thought we were losing him also. After we found him, I said that we were done. Everybody was off the floor that was under my supervision. I really didn't know what was going on there.

I heard most of the maydays, and I acknowledged either Joey or Bobby's maydays. I asked command if Engine 24 had given a mayday, and command inquired. That was when I dropped down a floor; I was on 15 and they were on 14. I dropped onto the outside scaffolding and went down to 14, via the scaffold staircase, where I found Rescue 1 and Rescue 2 looking for them. I remember them pulling them both out. I couldn't get on 14 because the scaffolding did not allow entrance back into the building from alternate floors. There was no walkway. I could stay on the scaffold on 14 to give directions, but I couldn't get on that floor. I could have entered the building on 13 but not on 12.

We were told the fire was on 17, so we took the elevator to 15, but we never got higher than 15. Captain Morse from Rescue 1 got a little higher, and he said that we had fire on 16 and 17. I stayed on 15 because we had fire on two floors above us.

You must have been taken by surprise when you realized the fire started moving down?

I didn't know, at that point, that the fire was coming down. We thought the fire was going up. We didn't know what was going on. But with all the maydays, that was my main focus; I was dealing with nine maydays. I didn't have my aide with me, because we got separated and he thought I went to 14. Now he had to get to 15 because he had to get his gear on, and I had my gear on already. All we kept hearing from command was that the engineers are going to get you water, and I trusted the Division Chief in Battalion 1 because he was my Battalion Chief. I worked every day with him, and we trusted the building engineers that they were going to get me water. I moved the guys to where the construction area was, and I told command that was where we were. I told them I moved everybody back towards the elevators, and I received a 10-4 acknowledgment.

A firefighter near me stated that the shanty was on fire. Now a shanty is as big as a house, and we were still trying to get above to the next floor. The shanty was big because it had the decontamination area for the employees, and that was on fire. I rounded up everybody to get to the construction elevator area, and I knew Rescue 1 was coming down from the floors above me, and as I turned, I started coughing on the smoke—it changed that fast. It changed that quickly before I could get back. They were holding a metal basket, and I was banging into it because I couldn't see it; that was how quick it changed.

I witnessed Rescue 2, when they were searching for Joey and Bobby, come out to the scaffold area, take off their face masks, throw up, put the face masks back on, and go back in to continue the search. On the scaffolding you probably didn't need your face mask, but they were going deeper into the building, so they would come out and change their air-tank cylinder at the construction elevator area.

You mentioned that firefighters would sometimes tie off. What's a tie off?

I saw the Rescue 1, Squad 1, and another company take their search rope, and as soon as they got a couple of feet into the building where the smoke started getting a little heavy, they tied off their search rope to a piece of metal so they could find their way out through the door we came in and they went in. This was around 4:15 p.m.

Captain Simon Ressner

When Gilbane was the general contractor, the FDNY was actively involved in the emergency planning of the Deutsche Bank site. The Environmental Protection Agency stepped in and demanded major changes for the toxic containment within the building. Gilbane left because it didn't want to comply with EPA mandates, because it was too expensive, and it also questioned the necessity of strict compliance. Bovis then took charge of the abatement and deconstruction of the Deutsche Bank building, and the FDNY dropped out of the picture until the fire. Why?

I have no idea as to why. I can tell you that it was common knowledge that the site was loaded with many contaminants, and not just asbestos. There were heavy metals; there were worries about mercury from the fluorescent light fixtures that were smashed up during 9/11; there were worries about the ground-up glass from 9/11, and it was common knowledge not to be in that building because of all those contaminants.

What did the FDNY know about the Deutsche Bank building prior to the fire?

I don't know what knowledge the Fire Department had about that building. I do know that it was common knowledge within the First Division, which was Lower Manhattan, that there had been a lot of problems at that building, such as the debris that fell on the firehouse across the street from 130 Liberty Street. There was common knowledge that the building was a toxic site. Firefighters were not to enter the building without some type of special protection. It was also common knowledge that there were ongoing issues with the site management because of the damage done to the firehouse.

Could you explain what you meant by "damage done to the firehouse"?

The main issue was when a piece of piping fell from the building, it fell from such a high height and at such a speed that it pierced the roof of the firehouse. It was amazing that no one was killed. It was considered a major construction accident. This incident put everyone on notice that the building was not being managed properly. I had no direct knowledge of what the fire department specifically knew about the building in terms of field inspections or meetings with construction supervisors.

Why would the FDNY go into a building if, let's say, no one was in it?

First let me state that FDNY procedures aren't solely based on if someone is in the building. We are trained to get inside the building, locate victims, locate the fire, and put it out. The only time that changes is if the chiefs and officers have an overriding concern that there is a structural hazard that might cause a building to collapse because of the fire. Then we would not enter the building, or we would withdraw if we already had firefighters inside. Second thing is I don't believe that the firefighters thought that everyone was out of the building. This is because there were so many different people working at different parts of the building. Third thing is that it is part of the fire-extinguishment procedure to try to extinguish the fire from the point of origin of the fire.

So a high-rise building that is occupied, the tactic is to locate the floor that the fire is on, verify that you have the correct floor, proceed to the floor below the fire, hook up hoses to the standpipe system, and extinguish the fire if possible. If not possible, contain the fire to prevent people from being trapped on other floors. It is part of our standard operating procedure to try to extinguish the fire even if no one is in the building unless we can be relatively sure that there is some other major hazard that would keep us out of the building.

Why weren't the firefighters pulled out if there was no water to fight the fire?

Initially when they didn't have water, there was an ongoing effort to try to deliver water via other means. This is also part of our standard training that frequently we could have a Siamese connection that is blocked; a fire pump may not work because of a power failure; a pipe is not working. So we would try to connect our water supply and get water to the hose line from another location. I believe that in this case, as the fire accelerated, it became a cycle that we had to commit more people because we had more people getting trapped and the best way to get them out was to put the fire out. We kept trying alternate means of getting water, but ultimately they all failed because pipes had been removed, so water could not be delivered to where the fire was.

Why didn't Captain Bosco perform building inspections? There were no inspections performed once he took command.

I have no idea why he didn't, but I also know it was not unusual not to follow through on the 15-day-rule demolition inspections, in part because there was no system establishing where construction was other than if you were lucky enough that when driving through your response area you would see it. It's possible that an inspection was done under the title of a different type of inspection. There were many types of inspections that firehouses are responsible for, in addition to the 15 day-rule inspection. Some types of inspections overlap other types, so he may have done a similar inspection that covered the same items or issues as the 15 day-rule inspection. This is only a guess on my part.

Why did the FDNY blame those seven officers?

All I can provide is my opinion. My opinion is that the department was under pressure to show responsibility. The understanding among other officers I spoke with in the First Division was that this was a scapegoat effort to divert attention. Under the circumstances it was easy for the FDNY to accept responsibility for the loss of our own. This was because we were the responding agency, we were the agency in control, we were the agency partly responsible for inspections, and we had the 15-day-rule inspection requirement.

    Why was it those seven officers? It was everyone's feeling that I spoke with that it was as high as they, the government, could go to accept it as enough responsibility. To be on the record about it, everyone also feels, especially in Chief Fuerch's case, that it was unjust. He was not negligent, and he never had a reputation of being cavalier or negligent or uninterested in fire safety. It was simply a by-the-book enforcement without any due process, without a hearing, without any kind of fact-finding into the incident.

The sprinkler system never worked, and the standpipe was broken for 12 – 18 months, yet the FDNY, the Department of Buildings, and the Emergency Management Agency weren't kept abreast of these critical developments. Why?

This I can talk about with some authority. Because of the level of complexity of the standpipes in that high-rise building, in order to determine if either of them worked, certain tests would have had to be done. The field units don't do those tests. They don't have the equipment, they don't have the expertise, they don't have the time, and they can't commit that much equipment while still being available for calls. The Buildings Department has the responsibility for any work that is done on fire-protection systems. Any permits go through the Buildings Department whether it's for installation, for demolition, or for maintenance. The only thing that the Fire Department has responsibility for is for witnessing periodic testing of the standpipe system and/or the sprinkler system. The responsibility for getting those tests scheduled and actually done rests on the owner.

Could you reiterate what you mentioned about whose responsibility it is to schedule those tests?

It is the responsibility of the owner to hire a licensed plumbing contractor or a fire-suppression contractor to schedule and perform those five-year pressure tests. The other system tests are maintenance tests, and they are scheduled through the Buildings Department inspection unit and filed by licensed fire-suppression contractors with the Buildings Department. The building code did, and still does, cover the design and installation of fire-suppression systems. The only thing the Fire Department controls is the periodic testing.

When a floor is demolished, is it true that regulations require the standpipe to be tested and capped at a floor below?

I don't remember if it is a regulation for it to be tested. It definitely is a regulation that during demolition the standpipe can be progressively demolished as demolition proceeds from the top down and that [it] has to be available and serviceable at the floor below the uppermost floor.

Regarding the tests, is there a difference between a demolition and an alteration?

Absolutely. There are specific rules for standpipe maintenance that are delineated in the building code's chapter covering demolition. There is a section in the codes, in effect at the time, where it specifies demolition of building standpipes. One section of the code states that if there are two standpipes, you may remove one of them from service. The usable standpipe must be serviceable on every floor outlet up to the floor below the floor to be demolished.

The internal fans: Why didn't anyone, including the DA, mention them?

I don't know why the DA didn't mention them, but my belief, from what the Fire Department saw, [they] weren't installed or operating in any violation of any procedure. They contributed because of how they were set up and how they operated, and were a big factor in the problem. Our understanding of how smoke and fire operate is that it's vertically upward. By having the fans operate the way they did, they reversed that expected flow path, and the fire was pulled downward. Firefighters were in a position that they thought was safe, and it turned out to be completely unsafe.

Allow me to be clearer in my understanding of the fan system. The fans were part of the asbestos-abatement system. They were set up to draw fresh air from outside the building into the contaminated space and then exhaust it after filtering out any asbestos particles. Since a standard abatement is done prior to demolition, the windows on other floors of the building are in place while a space is being abated. Deutsche Bank building was the only time that I know that demolition and abatement were being done at the same time. As part of that process and because of the damage done during 9/11/2001, there were no windows to isolate one floor from another. So, until that fire, I don't think anyone realized the impact the fans would have in drawing the fire down from above. I'm not sure if it would have occurred to me either. If the fans could have or would have been shut down early on, it may have limited the downward flow of the fire. All the questionable aspects of this disaster came down to allowing simultaneous abatement and demolition. And my opinion is that it all stems from the drive for this operation to move fast—so fast that safety measures accepted in previous operations were dispensed with.

Why didn't the DA's [office] mention that the stairway enclosures were removed, why didn't they mention the sprinkler being out of service, and why didn't they mention the blocked exits? The prosecutors' view was that these conditions were well known throughout all the agencies; they knew they were there, they witnessed these things, and therefore there was a certain tacit acceptance of the condition it [Deutsche Bank building] was in because it was visible to everyone. The standpipe was the one thing that was not apparent to everyone working at the site. The blocked exits were in effect for a long time, the removed stairwell protection was removed for a long time, and the internal fans were in effect for a long time. Thus, in the prosecutors' view, everyone was aware of that; therefore, there was no negligence in that. The negligence was in the dismantling of the standpipe, and no one was made aware of that.

When you state that "they" were aware of it, do you mean that everyone working inside the building was aware of it or that the agencies were aware of it?

Yes, the people working inside the building were aware of it. Obviously the agencies were not aware of it; at least the Fire Department was not aware of it. The Buildings Department had people on site that were available, and they were monitoring the work going on at the site. They had a trailer, and they had people present on a daily basis. I think it was the DA's view that there were enough workers and agencies aware that there was no sprinkler system and that the floors had all-wood barriers—essentially readily apparent—but that it was likely that no one except the two Galt people and the Bovis site-safety guy were aware that the standpipe segment was removed.

Was there a plan for how to fight high-rise-building fires, and if so, was it used at this fire?

There was and is a plan and an explicit method for fighting fires in high-rise buildings. It is very thorough and comprehensive. There is a very clear command structure and a clear communications structure and a fire-attack structure. The problem was there was never anything revised, changed, or applied for a building undergoing demolition. There were factors in a demolition that were completely different than what you would expect in a standard high-rise fire. As an example, not having windows changes the air flow from a building that does have windows. Not having a working standpipe, not having stairwell enclosures in place, and blocking the exits were completely different than what should have been in a normal high-rise-building fire.

All four of those things [standpipes, sprinklers, stair enclosures, and proper exits] give us the ability to save our own lives because there are systems in place that give us a place of refuge or allow us the ability to get out or allow us the ability to put water on the fire or allow us to control the air flow in the building. All of those elements were gone. The procedures do exist for fighting high-rise fires. I never read the operational section of the report; however, that operational section should explain that we did correlate with the published high-rise procedures.

Multiple small fires were constant at the Deutsche Bank building. 10 or 12 were extinguished within several months by a fire watch or safety person using a fire extinguisher or garden hose, yet no one called the FDNY. Why?

I can't say definitely, but based on what I saw at the site, based on the knowledge that the Fire Department has in responding to fires, reporting the fires would delay the project, and there were huge financial pressures on the contractors and construction manager, because of the millions of dollars in bonuses to bring that building down quickly. It is part of the story that Bovis would get $6 million if the building was down by

December 31. My opinion is the Fire Department wasn't called because they would have been at risk of having the job shut down because of the numerous fires and ensuing investigations that would have resulted from those fires.

On the day of the tragic fire, some observers said that accelerants were used together with large piles of debris. Arson was suggested. What are your thoughts?

I have no knowledge of any arson portion of the investigation. I would say that the volume of fire certainly based on photographs and the movement of the fire and the color of fire can't be explained alone by just the wood shanties. It would seem to me that the volume of fire and the rapid movement of the fire could have been helped by accelerants, but I have no idea or knowledge of what the arson investigation determined.

The Fire Department's and the city's top-level managements' responses and actions regarding the Deutsche Bank building fire, both before and after the fire: What are your thoughts?

My opinion is that the building was standing in the way of an enormous amount of development. It was also that development played a role that would impact the Silverstein Properties if it wasn't brought down on schedule. There were several years of trying to get the building down. There was a lot of community resistance because the people in the area believed strongly that the building was so heavily contaminated. Because of this and the financial pressures from Port Authority, I think that quickly demolishing the tower was a very high priority for this administration. They urgently wanted to get this building down so they could move ahead with development. They wanted to move ahead with getting downtown back on track. They wanted to show that with all the failures through all of the previous administrations that this particular administration was going to succeed where others had not.

I think that the Fire Department top management felt that they had to take the fall. It was clear that we had not followed procedures. It was acknowledged that we hadn't done our inspections. It was clear that there was operational chaos during the fire and I think that they felt compelled; they would be forced by the mayor's office, by the mayor's appointees, by the LMDC. They felt that they were in the way of a very big set of forces that were beyond their control.

Afterward, at least during my work in Safety Command, there was some resistance on having the safety investigation address factors from the building. Generally, these Fatal Fire reports are a self-critique of the Fire Department's own operations and are meant to be used as a learning tool to prevent similar problems in future fires. Once we determined that the standpipe wasn't working because a large section was missing and that it had been deliberately removed, we looked at other aspects of the building conditions. The more we examined, the more apparent it was that the building conditions were a major factor in creating the deadly conditions. There were so many safety violations uncovered after the operation that management was willing, after some discussions, for our report to include this information and to state that these conditions directly led to the deaths of firefighter Beddia and firefighter Graffagnino. The upper-level commanders of the fire department included this in the final report. The final report that we issued emphasized a lot of the problems with the building. Not all of them, but it emphasized a lot of them. After the fire some members of the upper-level management were willing to take the chance of bringing the truth forward and resting on that, and I believe some had political fears of being in the crosshairs of the administration.

Your thoughts on the actions of the LMDC, Avi Schick, Dan Doctoroff, Mayor Bloomberg, and Governor Spitzer?

My thoughts are a combination of what I saw at the site, what I read in the newspapers, and what I accept as factual and my own awareness of what factors were involved and are still involved in developing the World Trade Center site. When it regards Avi Schick, it's that he was completely unqualified to be running that agency [LMDC] with the size and complexity of anything compared with the World Trade Center—he was appointed as a political gift—and he was completely unqualified and he had an obligation to the governor that appointed him and that he can't be relied upon to be truthful or competent.

When it comes to Governor Spitzer, I think he was determined that he was the governor that saw this project through but he saw himself at arm's distance (his point person was Avi Schick) and Avi Schick was going to be the sacrifice, on his own terms, and that he would be the buffer between the governor and what was going on at the site.

The real problem to me was the intersection of four main parties—Mayor Bloomberg, Dan Doctoroff, Larry Silverstein, and the Port Authority. Based on the information I had read, I remembered a letter from the Department of Investigation to Dan Doctoroff's people advising them that the people who were principals of the John Galt Corporation had previous criminal charges against them. The impression I had is that because of the financial impacts of any delays on that site and because of the economic impact on the city of that site being stalled for any more time, because of the pressure from the families of the 9/11 victims, Bloomberg determined that Doctoroff would be his point man to get that building down to the ground so that they could proceed with all the projects that they could not do with that building still being up.

I think that when you look at Dan Doctoroff's history that he was supposed to get that sport stadium on the west side, and he was fought successfully, and he lost that. He was supposed to get the Olympics to NYC, and he was fought on that and lost that battle. We had a guy that was driven to success, he was close to the mayor, and he didn't have a financial stake, because he had enough money, but he had a performance issue. I think that he was determined at any cost to get that building to the ground, to succeed where his predecessors failed, to have the city be able to develop the site, move forward with the museum and the memorial, and not have Silverstein's people receive any more penalty money out of the Port Authority. He was willing to override the advice he received from DOI [Department of Investigation] and was willing to set up any mechanism to get that building down as quickly as possible.

All of those things intersected together, which created an attitude of willingness to ignore any kind of rules or procedures they thought were a nuisance or that would delay the contract or to have an opportunity for Bovis to go back and ask for more money after having received extra money already. If you put all of that together, it was a top-down effort to get that building down as quickly as possible. Those are my thoughts on that matter.

When you look back on all the events and people that impacted the Deutsche Bank fire, what are your final thoughts?

I think that the Deutsche Bank building fire was the worst incident of tragedy in my entire career, even beyond 9/11, because in the case of the Deutsche Bank building we have the failure of every agency to do its job. Plus we have the disregard for firefighters, the acceptance by the general public that this was inevitable. It wasn't inevitable; it was preventable at many, many steps, and all of those steps were deliberately sidestepped in the name of somebody's ambition and in the name of money.

It was the defining event in my 20 year career. It completely changed my view of my job. It completely changed my view of government. It completely changed my attitude about how to handle the risks on this job. I was determined from that point forward to teach everyone I could that we have to look out for ourselves. It is naive to rely on the other agencies. We assumed that agencies such as the Buildings Department, the mayor's office, Corp Counsel, the governor's office, [and] the Port Authority would take safety and construction supervision very seriously. All of these agencies have a lot of power and a lot of funding. But they deliberately worked around rules that they would have applied to any other demolition project, and these agencies would never have permitted other contractors to be exempt from the rules that the agencies ignored on this project. And that this institutional evasion of safety led, in my opinion, to the completely avoidable death of two human beings. I'm convinced that this will go on again in the name of money and in the name of self-centered ambition if we don't put a stop to it. It will be the defining incident in my career, and I will continue to fight that we get this out and that we get all of the layers open to the public and that we make them understand how the hubris of power killed two people.

Lieutenant Gary Iorio

While Gilbane was the general contractor, the FDNY was actively involved in the emergency planning for the Deutsche Bank building site with the Emergency-Management group. The Environmental Protection Agency stepped in and demanded major changes for toxic containment within the building. Gilbane left and Bovis took over the abatement/deconstruction. Why did the FDNY drop out of the picture?

I wouldn't know anything about administrative protocol specific to outside my district. Prior to the Deutsche Bank fire we treated building inspections as something we do to familiarize our firefighters with buildings and how our tactics apply. It never progressed to the level that was called for with the Deutsche Bank building fire incident. We brought our men out in between calls and routine maintenance at the firehouse to have the firefighters become familiar with the buildings in our area, in the event a fire happened. We did inspections for gross violations, obvious stuff such as while school was in progress and there was a padlock and chain on exit doors. Today the unions are pushing for building-inspection training. We had no formal classroom training on inspecting buildings. Now we are starting to get training. It took the Deutsche Bank building fire tragedy to get the city to upgrade our computers, training, and start a hotline that officers in the field can call for clarification.

In reality it is almost impossible for an in-service fire company to properly inspect most high-rise buildings. If the city is serious about building inspections, you can't do this as a part-time job. You need a fire officer, an electrician, a plumber, an alarm expert—you need a task force to do this with experts in all the required fields. If done properly, it would take days, not hours.

Why would the FDNY go into a building if no one was in it?

In any building fire in NYC, even a vacant building does not mean that no one is in the building. There may be homeless people, vagrants, workers, or security people. We fight the fire due to our written procedures, and as the chief in charge arrives, he would make the call to stay or leave. That type of building was not the type that was in danger of collapse.

This fire was different than any other fire in that when we go in to fight the fire, we go in a floor below the fire because fire travels up. This was the first time I ever heard of that the fire and smoke came down. Our tactics were completely wrong for this fire because of those fans. I was very mad at OSHA and EPA for their rules in the use of internal fans, which we knew nothing about. They are so bureaucratic and required fans to catch little particles of asbestos, and in doing so they created a death trap. It's a typical case of the government overdoing something. I also couldn't understand why the stairwells were sealed up. This was our only means of escape. I thought I was in the wrong place. With the smoke coming down on us our visibility was going quickly. It took us a while to figure out the fans were doing this.

Why weren't the firefighters pulled out if there was no water to fight the fire?

I don't know; only the chief would know that. Since that fire we are more knowledgeable and cognizant of how long firefighters are in the building without water. We wouldn't be worried about building collapse, because the beams would hold the building up. I believe that the command post didn't know that the smoke was being pushed down by fans. They were constantly working to get water, and the clock just kept ticking. I gave one of the first urgent calls to notify command of this reverse-smoke situation.

The sprinkler system never worked, and the standpipe was broken for 12-18 months, yet the FDNY, OSHA, and the EMA stayed in the dark. Why?

I really can't answer that, but I would suspect that politics came into play. Nobody really knew how to unravel the red tape of OSHA.

The building was contaminated, and the building was coming down anyway. I believe initially that the building was not supposed to come down. I think it became a political football. I believe that the fire department was told or been made to feel to stay away from it. This is not new, because there are federal buildings that we can't go into to inspect, and Police Plaza we can't inspect.

Was there a plan for how to fight fires in high-rise buildings, and if so, was it used at this fire?

We have high-rise procedure plans, and they were definitely being used. However, because of the fans pushing smoke and fire down, our procedures didn't work.

On the day of the tragic fire some observers said that accelerants were used along with large piles of debris, pointing to possible arson.

I don't know. I know that there was a lot of wood and plastic burning and dripping through the floors. My priority was to put out the fire and watch out for my men.

How do you feel about the actions of the LMDC, Avi Schick, Dan Doctoroff, Mayor Bloomberg, and Governor Spitzer?

I think they all played into this. This is my opinion, but I think that Deputy Mayor Dan Doctoroff pushed too hard to get the building down. The question should be, did he rush things too much and not investigate fully? Because initially they weren't supposed to bring the building down, and then there was a big push to get it down. When it was decided to bring it down, there was a lot of politics.

What part did you play in the Deutsche Bank building fire?

I was involved in the fire operations, but I had nothing to do with the procedures, building inspections, or things like that. I will bring you through my day at that fire:

The day of the fire was my day off, but I was called in to cover for Ladder 8 (normally my assignment is Ladder 20). Upon arrival, we went up in the construction elevator. There was some confusion as to what floor you're on, such as; does the lobby count as floor one or two? The floor numbers were marked in spray paint on each floor, which cast doubt. So we use the fire floor as a reference and then use terms like the floor above or the floor below the fire.

There were several alarms. Which one was your unit called in on?

I'm not sure if it was the second or the third ... maybe the second. We went right into the command center and then up into the construction elevator. I had bad feelings right away. I'm not familiar with the guys I'm working with since I'm only covering this house. The majority of these firefighters are young and unseasoned. One of the chiefs outside mentioned that there was plywood up there so you should bring a saw with you just in case. Good thing he said that because that saw saved our lives. I told the operator to put us one floor below the fire. We went up the stairs to attack the fire, but there were already firefighters there. They were trying to get through the plywood barriers on top of the stairwells. They were operating saws trying to cut through. I realized this was a dangerous situation, so I brought my guys down to the floor below (where we started).

My job now is to scout the area out, to review the floor plan, because it's probably going to be the same on the floor above. On my way up, as soon as we got off the elevator, we passed 24 Engine, and I hear either Bobby or Joey, because they had the hose line, on the radio call in, "We have no water. Check the isolation valves. Repeat, check the isolation valves, the isolation valves." This call probably saved a lot of lives because it told other firefighters there was no water in the standpipes, which means we can't fight the fire. But I knew right off there were problems. Isolation valves are something that I learned about late in my career, that in high-rise buildings isolation valves are used if you have a leak; you can shut off the floor until a plumber can make repairs, and the rest of the building is not affected. We learned about these in a training class after a fatal fire in Brooklyn. I said to myself that if they have no water and they're looking for isolation valves in this piece-of-shit building, we are in bad shape. This is not a quick-fix situation.

Later on I would pass 24 Engine a second time, and I heard them yelling to "Throw a line outside the building!" I said to myself, "Is it possible to create your own standpipe by linking hoses together, but would the water pressure be sufficient to reach this high up in the building?" I wasn't sure that it could be done. As I'm walking around the floor—and it is a huge area—I saw over in a corner something burning. So I walked over 20 or so feet and saw a lot of electrical cables burning up in the ceiling area and some sheets of plastic burning, but it wasn't a lot, and I knew the main fire was above us. I thought this was weird because the fire was above us. My background or expertise is that of tenement buildings; I'm not a high-rise guy, so I'm still learning about high-rise buildings. Then I see over another 20 - 30 feet something orange that's glowing. The area between the drop ceiling and the floor above is called the plenum, where all the wires and pipes are run. The floor I'm on is crystal clear; there was not an ounce of smoke on it. As I get closer to the area that was orange, it's now red, and as I get closer, I see that the area in the drop ceiling, which had maybe three missing ceiling tiles, has a full-blown fire roaring in the ceiling plenum area.

We know as firefighters that the floor below the fire is safe because fires burn up. Smoke goes up, and the air lets the fire burn up. Also, this is a cement floor, so the fire is not going to burn through it. I can't believe this, but I realized that the fire was actually burning downwards. I have seen where drop ceilings have a fire in them and in seconds the fire races through the ceiling and then it comes crashing down. I then realize that the firefighters have no water and the fire is coming down on them. I head back, and I pass the burning plastic sheets, and I called out to Acting Battalion Chief Neil Cronin. As I yell out, there was a big noise when the electrical cables burned out, which created a big spark, and that got everybody's attention. I yell that we have a roaring fire in the plenum and they have no water above us, we have to get everybody down to the next-lower level. I envisioned the ceiling just crashing down on us. Within minutes the entire floor was covered in this dense, black smoke from the layers of plastic sheets burning above us. The plastic must have found holes in the floor and started dripping down to our floor and started more fires on our floor. The fireproof floor was pierced, which allowed for the fire to come down. We had to put our face pieces on. My face mask must have gotten caught on something and was ripped, so I had to keep it on by my hand. In a way I'm glad because I had a taste of that dense, black smoke, and I knew that if our masks came off we were all doomed.

We couldn't go down any further, because the stairwell that we were in didn't go down. I initially thought I was in the wrong place because the stairs going down to the next floor didn't exist. Later I learned they had been sealed up. Now we are getting very worried. Maybe I'm in the wrong stairwell. I tell my guys to stay with me and that our mission is to find a way to get to the floor below. In minutes the smoke became so dense we couldn't see anything. Our position was becoming untenable. I had thoughts of dying right there. I said, "This is impossible! This is the World Trade Center all over again, but this happened already! It can't happen again!" Now we are no longer looking to fight the fire; we are only looking for a way out. I realize that we need to get to the north side of the building, because that is where the elevator is. There are all kinds of equipment and hoses for the asbestos abatement on the floor. When we got off the construction elevator, you were in an open-air area, and as you went in, there was plywood all around you. Eventually we made our way to this wall. I knew it was the right-side wall, but we are 14 stories up. We move around the wall until we come to more of these large funnel hoses. We rip them out of the way, and we see daylight. All I could do was stick my arm out the funnel hole. We feel around and find the plywood, so we start the saw up and start cutting through the plywood. Other firefighters hear us on the other side, and they start helping to break through the plywood to rescue us.

We are all scared and exhausted at this point. I make sure I have all the guys in my company. I realize there is no water. I gave one of the first urgent calls at 1620 hours [4:20 p.m.] "We are in trouble, Ladder 8 up on the 15th floor." I was on 14 and 15 at different times. I believe when I gave the urgent we had worked our way to 14.

"Ladder 8 to command post, Urgent. We're gonna need a Fast-Pak. We need some air up here. We're running low on air. We're all taking a beating on 15 … It's starting to get bad up here on 15 (In reality I was on the 14th floor.) We're gonna force our way. We gotta breach through some of this, ah … plywood to get the hell outta here. It's getting bad. We're losing visibility. We're gonna need Fast-Paks, extra air bottles, and fresh troops." [A Fast-Pak is a portable air-bottle unit that hooks directly into your face mask. It holds approximately 20 minutes of air.]

This way at least command knows there is trouble up here. Then all the maydays started coming over. I realize at that point that we have to go back in. We're exhausted and almost out of air in our air tanks. One of the senior guys from Ladder 8 goes with me. We find a fireman who is pulling out another firefighter (detailed Brooklyn fireman), so we help him out. We see more firefighters coming in.

At that time Chief Galvin (City-wide Command Chief) took command and handled the radio chatter to prioritize urgent and maydays; everyone else shut up. He stated that needed supplies were on the way. I felt relieved when I heard him take command.

At this point Lieutenant Iorio started to review the FDNY Investigation Report, which was a tactical report of what happened at the Deutsche Bank building fire.

A saying came to mind that was said by the old chiefs at the Fire Academy, that a well-placed hose line saves more lives than any other means. All good firemen want to be the first one up the ladder to save a life, but the hose line saves more lives. Joey and Bobby knew this and held their assigned position as things went from bad to worse. They fought to the end to get that line in place. We will all be forever grateful to them. It was always said that you could get out if you followed the hose line out, but with that acrid smoke … one whiff was all it took, and it was over.

Firefighter Jay Bangash

In your own words, what was that day like?

I was at 5 truck that morning. I was the in-house watch. It was a beautiful day. I was updating the house watch journal. Bobby Beddia poked his head in saying he was in on overtime, so I put him in the book. We had a manpower shortage call. Ladder 6 in Chinatown had no one to drive their rear/tiller, and since we were also a tiller truck, they needed one of our guys. They had a crew of engine men all detailed in. They would swap us one of their engine details for one of our members who could drive the tiller. We couldn't find anybody to go to 6 truck so I went. We had different people filling different positions in the truck and the engine. I didn't realize that Joey was working that day for the engine, or I would have asked him to go to 6 truck. I heard Jimmy Lanigan ask Joey if he wanted to switch back to the truck that day. He declined, because he wanted to work with Bobby Beddia.

At 6 truck we did drills in the morning, but we were a mixed crew of guys from different companies. The chauffer and I were the only regular tiller truck members riding that morning. That afternoon we got the call for the Deutsche Bank building, as the first truck on the second-alarm response. We went across town and down West Street. Traffic was light, and we were flying, so we made good time. We saw smoke as we drove towards the building; it looked big, but it was much worse when we got to the building. We proceeded past the hotel and came around the block to where the command post was. The command post was just north of the Deutsche Bank building, where the trailers were, next to Liberty Street. We were able to get close to the building. 24 Engine was already assigned to the fire and was there, but Ladder 5 was not present, as they had yet to be assigned. I saw Ken Fulcher, who was the chauffer for Engine 24 that day; he was working the fire hydrant on West Street, and he was in an energized state.

There was a ton of chatter on the radio describing problems that firefighters were having—blocked stairs, water issues, etc. I kept running back to the truck to get more tools to combat these issues (partners saws, sawzall, hand tools, RIT pack, etc.) because I thought we were going directly into the Deutsche Bank building and we may need these things based on all the transmissions, but we didn't go in right away. When we first got there, we were called up to go in, and we loaded up near the hoist elevator and waited, but then we were told to stand down, so we didn't go in. I don't know why. Perhaps someone at command saw we were all from different companies and we had a lot of engine guys on the crew. I don't know. I heard a lot of radio transmissions— multiple alarms, more fire trucks coming to the scene. 5 truck arrives and was next to us so we filled them in as to what we heard. I know there were water problems. We heard a radio transmission that the floors were sealed, another transmission from somebody that stated, "We're never getting through these floors." There were repeated calls of water problems; I thought that someone should check the basement. There was a large, wide truck ramp that went down towards the basement. I was going to try and run down to check, but we were set to be deployed into the building, so I couldn't go off to check … At that point we are playing catch-up in trying to ascertain what is going on and on what floor. The better educated you are about everything that is going on in the building, the safer and more effective you're going to be. So we are taking in lots of information, lots of transmissions, and everything is going on simultaneously.

What was your job function that day?

I was the tiller man, which is the outside vent person who steers the ladder on the back of the truck.

I have never seen a fire like that in my life. I was only on the job a little over two years at that point, so I didn't have much experience, but I remember looking at that building, and I saw that it was just breathing smoke. Kicking that dark, gray smoke out and then sucking it back in fast. It reminded me of a fire-breathing dragon. I have never seen anything like that. Just by looking at that building you knew it was going to be a different type of day. At least I felt that way.

As time went on, the situation constantly got worse. Within the first five minutes of our arrival we knew there were water issues, because it was constantly repeated by different chauffeurs on different engines. I remember a radio broadcast that, it might have been Kenny Fulcher on 24 Engine, stating, "My rig is jumping off the ground." It was bouncing due to the water pressure he was giving to push the water from his engine into the Siamese connector that goes into the building standpipe. I said to myself that this is not a question of power to pump the water up 17 stories. You knew something was very wrong. That stuck in my head to this day.

These guys were pumping a ton of water from their rig almost to the point of the truck overheating. This is not the problem, so I don't know what is going on now. I'm not on the command channel, so I have no idea what the chiefs are doing or saying. I don't know if they have checked the basement, because in hindsight they would have seen that the basement is, by now, flooded. It would have been flooded because of the pipe that was cut, which we found out later. I heard afterward that there were many feet of water in the basement. I was always told to check the basement, especially in Manhattan, because there could be a standpipe valve open. I have been in high-rise-building fires where that were the case; water wasn't getting up to the floor it was needed, and we would find an open valve. We would close it, and the water would flow to where it was needed. As a policy we check all the valves to see if any are open.

More and more fire companies are arriving. As I'm waiting, I see Engine 24 all suited up with fire hoods on, all going into the elevator hoist. I remember thinking, *Why are they going in? There are all these water problems. They're going in alone, and they don't have tools or a truck company with them. Maybe they are going up to replace the companies that are already up there? Maybe the guys up there are running out of air or need relief?* I don't know exactly why they were going up. Maybe it was to relieve guys who were exhausted.

After Engine 24 was up there, I remember seeing an Engine 4 firefighter by the hoist on an upper floor. I heard that they hooked up with another engine company and they were coupling all their hoses together. They were linking them all together, and another firefighter from Engine 4 was standing on top of the exterior hoist elevator, and he was unraveling lengths of hose from one of the upper floors. They were creating their own standpipe with their lengths of hose. I saw the guys on the ground bringing out the manifold. The manifold basically allows our department to get water to a difficult location, fully pressurized, from our pumpers.

At the manifold, we control up to eight outlets and can send water, or cut off water, to any one outlet. It's only used in large operations. They were able to get water from an engine on West Street, which was hooked up to a hydrant for supply, and send pressurized water through the long, yellow tubing and into the manifold, which was at the foot of the building. From the manifold, we can send water to any one of the eight outlets, one of which was hooked up to the self-made standpipe the members of 24 and 4 created with their roll-ups. This was how they eventually were able to get water into the building. I am relaying to you what I saw, but there were so many things going on at the same time. All I can say to describe what was happening was chaos. It was a mess. In every fire there is organized chaos where everyone is hurrying to do their job. It is chaotic, but you just follow your protocols, and you get through it. You're dealing with hundreds of guys, and the Deutsche Bank building fire was like that, except that you're dealing with a much-larger fire, with a lot more men involved, which makes it that much more chaotic.

I remember that they couldn't get through the stairs. There was no interior elevator, so we had to use the external hoist elevator to get up to the fire floors, because the stairways were sealed. There was no other way. I remember a contractor yelling, "Make sure there is no water in that hoist, in the well at the bottom of the hoist, or it will shut down." I remember relaying that to my boss as a potential problem, because if that hoist breaks, then we are really screwed.

The fire continued to get worse, lots of maydays on the radios, maybe as many as 30 maydays. I remember seeing guys breaking the windows and jump out from the window area onto the scaffolding, which was away from the building. There were lots of guys jumping onto the scaffolding in order to get out of that building.

I never heard Bobby Beddia's mayday, but I did hear Joey's mayday. His vibra-alert was going off, which meant that he was running out of air, which worried me a bit. He said he was on the 14th floor near the stairway. He was very calm and clear. I still didn't know what was happening on each floor, but I knew there were lots of guys on every floor. There were FAST [a special team of firefighters that search and rescue firefighters in trouble] trucks in each sector. I saw firefighter Darren LeBow from 5 truck. Darren ran to the command post to let them know about Joey's mayday. He then heard Bobby's mayday, so he ran back to the command post and relayed to them about Bobby's mayday. With all the maydays going on, command might have missed his mayday or just never heard it, as there were so many. Some guys in Ladder 5 heard both maydays; some heard just one.

Then 5 truck gets the call to go in. It seemed like such a long time, but it was probably only a few minutes. The men were all primed and ready to go, to try and help ... energized but anxious ... Anyway, off-duty firefighters from our house were coming in to help. Guys came into work early, and they came in from home, on their day off, when they saw the fire on television or heard it on the radio. They grabbed spare SCBAs [air tanks] from the firehouse, but they had no radios. They asked me if they should go in, and I told them no. With no radio or even a record of them being there, I thought it was too dangerous.

I remember that when all the maydays were going off, I looked around and saw Lieutenant Garcia sitting outside the building all covered in black soot. He was just blankly staring straight ahead towards the direction of the building. I remember walking over to him and asked him a couple of questions, but he never answered me. I started yelling at him, in front of his face, to get his attention, but he never acknowledged I was there. He had this glassy look, but he didn't hear me or see me, and I was right in front of his face. He was looking right through me. He was covered in dark soot, and he smelled all burnt, and he was just staring. He was catatonic.

I spoke with firefighter Jimmy Lanigan, who was in Ladder 5 that day and sent to the 12th floor to break through the wood and plastic that sealed the staircases to open the floors. There were blocked staircases on floors 11, 12, 13, and 14. They were trying to break through, but they said it was impossible. It was basically a floored-off staircase, where you climb up but you are still maybe six steps from the top of it, but your head is hitting it, so you have to crawl into this tight triangle area. Even when you are in this tight triangle area to start to cut around the wood or around the plywood edges, it was very difficult. The guys doing this were all experienced guys; they knew how to use tools. They couldn't get the saw into the wood. The tip of the saw ran off every time. Didn't matter if it was the sawzall or the roof saw, it couldn't find a way to bite into the wood. They were forced to use hand tools and brute force to keep hitting away at it. It turned out that it wasn't just wood, but it was a type of thick plastic that was sealed tight from above and over the staircase, in addition to the wood.

One of the construction guys came over to me when he heard the firefighters' transmissions that they couldn't get through the sealed staircases. He said there was an opening in the staircase covering, and he drew this tiny hatch cover on paper. The covered hatch was padlocked, but there was a key next to the lock and an X-Acto knife, to cut the plastic, with the keys on the side of every hatch. I told him, "How is anyone supposed to see this lock, knife, opening, or anything else in a location where there are no lights, its pitch black, along with thick, deadly smoke where one puff of it and you're delirious or unconscious? How the hell is that supposed to happen? This is your system? Are you shitting me?" Plus that "system" he had in place was only if you were above the blockage, not below it.

Someone told me that they eventually forced an opening, a small opening, coming up from the staircase, maybe 12-inches high. Jimmy Lanigan took his air tank off and was able to force his way through into this smoke-filled environment onto the floor. He then took his knife and tried to cut through this thick plastic that covered the plywood. He had to stick his head back below every few seconds to come back for air breaths where someone was holding his face piece and mask, and then he'd return to continue cutting. While he was cutting from the floor above, other firefighters were forcing the wood up from underneath. They were eventually able to open the staircase onto the floor.

I remember a chief call out on the radio that he found a member but that he needed help because he was too heavy. The chief was by himself. I saw Kenny Fulcher by the hoist when they brought Joey down and yelled for him to bring him towards me. I grabbed an EMS chief and asked him where the closest ALS [Advanced Life Support] bus was. I saw Frank McCutchen and Kenny Fulcher on the raised dock area carry Joey down on a board-type stretcher. Lieutenant Iorio from Ladder 20 came over to be with me on the western side of the loading dock. I was told by the EMS guys that the ALS buses were on West Street so we'd have to take him there.

The EMS guy brings a wheeled stretcher, and we placed him onto the stretcher. Lieutenant Iorio calls for other firefighters to help out. We had several guys running alongside the stretcher heading to West Street. There were plenty of obstacles along the way, like hoses and construction trailers, and we were running fast. I started doing compressions on Joey. An orange-speckled, gel-like substance came from Joey's mouth—it didn't look good. Lieutenant Iorio thought maybe it was a positive sign, but I think he was just telling himself that to stay positive. I thought I should jump onto the stretcher and continue to do compressions, but then I thought I might slow us down, and I didn't want that to happen.

I saw up ahead that there are trailers, and I knew it was going to be tight, and we are running at full sprint, and I don't think we will be able to get through the space between the trailers. The firefighter in front of me hit this trailer at full speed. He had to knock himself out. I jumped on top of the gurney to get through the space. I got scraped a bit but made it through. When we got through, I jumped off and ran beside him, and a group of other firefighters were right behind us. When we got to West Street, the ALS bus was on the other side of the highway. We wondered what the hell it was doing all the way over there.

We had to get over the highway Jersey barriers. We had to lift the stretcher up and close the wheeled legs and then open them again, I kept holding onto Joey to stop him from falling off the stretcher. We finally got him to the bus, and I was upset because the bus was young EMTs and not paramedics and it wasn't an ALS bus. Anyway, then we got the call that they found Bobby, and we had to rush him to the ALS bus. I ran back to the Deutsche Bank building, and Bobby was handed off to us. I was going to start doing compressions, but I was told by an EMS guy in a blue plastic hat that Bobby had a pulse so don't do compressions. Later someone told us that Bobby didn't have a pulse. We went back to the same area for the bus on West Street—again not paramedics. They got a police escort to the hospital.

We stayed at the fire scene for several hours. We went up to the 14th floor. The main body of fire was out by then, but I still think that was the hottest place I have ever been in my life. I had no idea about the negative-pressure environment. Engine firefighters were putting out small pockets of fires that are in and around debris piles. I remember that I couldn't get near the smoldering pile of orange. Every time I got near it, pieces of it would come up and burn me. It was hot.

What was the building like when you went into it?

It was still smoky, and you had to wear your mask, but it was starting to clear somewhat. Many of the glass windows were broken by this time. It was still hot, and there were pockets of small fires around. There was still water dripping down from the floors above; there was lots of burned construction debris. All the wood shanties were burned down. The floor was wide open by then since everything that was in it had burned away. It seemed that in the locations where fires still burned we couldn't tell what it was that was burning. Looking around, it seemed like the exterior of the building was burning.

I wondered how Joey and Bobby were doing. I didn't feel right not knowing what was going on. I found Joey's gear—his coat and tools up there on the 14th floor. I took his gear down along with all the other tools that we brought up there, the various saws and other things. We had to go through the decontamination procedure. I dropped the 6 truck equipment near the truck, and I carried Joey's gear and equipment to where 24 Engine was. I put his stuff inside the rig so he wouldn't lose it.

It was around nine at night by then, and I kept asking different guys, while I was getting decontaminated, what happened to Joey and Bobby, and all of them said that they didn't hear anything. I just thought that once they were at the hospital that they would be okay. I don't know why. Turns out guys just didn't want to tell me what was going on. The captain of 6 truck told me just before we were ready to drive back to the firehouse, "About your two friends ... it's not good news." When I returned to 6 truck house, I was told that I was wanted back at my regular firehouse, 24/5. I hopped on my bicycle and pedaled back, and when I got there, I looked for some of the guys who worked the fire, and I was told that they were at the hospital. I just wanted to crawl into a hole. I was told that by the time they got to the hospital Bobby and Joey were dead.

I remember Acting Battalion Chief Cronin being so clear that day at the fire. I was fascinated by him trying to maintain control in all that chaos. He stayed calm and in command in such a large fire. He had a sector that he was in charge of, and I was very impressed with him.

I was at another fire in a position I was detailed to. I was in the FAST [Firefighters Assist and Search Team] truck, and the fire was near Chambers Street. It was a four-story building, and the fire was on the third and fourth floors. The Chief-In-Charge came in from Brooklyn. He was running the fire, maybe covering for someone. Anyway, he ordered everyone out of the building. Squad 18 was there, and they said, "No, that's okay; we got this." Here is this squad of men, all gung ho to fight the fire. They think they had it and could put out the fire. They had no idea, being on the third floor that the fire was blazing out of control on the floor above them and on their own floor. The chief yelled at them to "get your asses out of that building immediately." Then immediately you heard, "10-4, Chief." They got right out. Command chiefs' perspective is quite different than that of a firefighter in the midst of a fire. They see things we don't, and we see things they don't.

Firefighter Kenneth Fulcher

In your own words, what was that day like?

That day started out on Friday night. I had come into work at 4:30 p.m. Joey was in the firehouse, and we started joking with each other. My wife dropped by the firehouse. Joey started talking with her, and we all had an enjoyable time. My wife then took our car and went home. We had a fire run around five in the morning. I saw Bobby Beddia come in and said hello. We had an emergency-service run, which went okay. It's now time for breakfast, and we were teasing Bobby Beddia for bringing in breakfast croissants.

I asked Bobby if he would chauffeur for that day, but he insisted on being the nozzle man. He said he was on overtime and senior man in the house so it was his choice as to the position he wanted. Joey started breaking my chops about taking the easy job as chauffeur when the senior man should be doing the driving. Jimmy Martin was there, and he laughed as we went back and forth with the kidding. For lunch we wound up having sandwiches, which bothered me because we had three goods cooks in the firehouse that day. Bobby was an excellent cook, Joey and I could cook, and we settled for sandwiches. I asked Joey if he could give me a ride home after work and take Jimmy Lanigan with us since we all lived in the same general area. He said, "Sure, no problem."

It was after 3:00 p.m. when we got the call for the Deutsche Bank building fire. I drove, but the traffic on Houston Street was very heavy due to roadwork and street barriers blocking the way. I had to drive against the traffic for three blocks to Varick Street and down to near Chambers and turned there to get onto the West Side drive. I pulled Engine 24 alongside the Marriott Vista hotel. I looked up, at the Deutsche Bank building, and saw the smoke pouring out of that building. It was the thickest, blackest smoke I ever saw in a fire. I had about 10-12 years as a firefighter then, so I had worked several large fires, including 9/11.

I saw a firefighter from Engine 7, and he recognized me as a chauffeur. He said that they were having problems with water. When we came up the block, we came into the southwest side of the building. We looked up and saw the screen shroud that hung from the building was on fire. I was ready to drag extra hose to supplement another chauffeur that was there before us. There was no fire hydrant or Siamese standpipe that we could see on that side of the building. This was confirmed by Squad 18.

We saw that a different fire had started across the street from the Deutsche Bank building. It was in the basement of a new building. I looked up again and saw the thick, black smoke that had debris falling from out of the smoke. I ran back and got my helmet because various items were falling all over.

Why was there no fire hydrant on that side of the building? Wasn't there suppose to be one there?

The fire hydrant was hidden, so we never saw it. Another hydrant was found further down the block. We established a hose line at the fire hydrant and went to put out the fire in the foundation of a new building. One of the firefighters said that there were large metal canisters, possibly propane gas, in the basement of that building. Now we rushed to extinguish that fire lest it ignited what was in the metal canisters and cause an explosion. We tried to establish radio contact with the command station, but there was a lot of radio chatter going on. I needed to contact the command to let them know that there was another fire going on at the southwest side of the building, across the street, and that building had metal gas tanks in it. I ran to the command center, which was where the World Trade Center buildings stood. I went up to command and asked for a chief to come and oversee this other fire. I was basically ignored, so I ran back and assisted in putting out the fire in the basement of the new building high-rise.

At this time the fire department was trying to get a super-pumper truck to the Deutsche Bank building because water wasn't getting up to the floors that the fires were on. The officers were conducting roll calls for the guys in the fire. There were guys coming down from the building. These were the original firefighters sent in to battle the fire. This was 10 Engine and other groups. I looked into their young faces, and they looked worried. I don't think they ever faced anything like this before. I told them to get to the other side of the building to the command center because they were looking for them. We couldn't tell if the fire department had people inventorying the firefighters who were coming and going into fight that fire, mainly because there were many people in acting positions covering for others. We didn't know if a board was set up to keep track of the companies that are there to work, companies already sent into work, and the companies on standby to go into work. We had engines, trucks, rescues, and squad companies. There were extra chiefs, so where would this chief be or that chief be? Now realize that this wasn't something I was supposed to do or be worried about, but generally in a fire this control board is something we take notice of, and it was odd that I didn't see it.

The super-pumper truck finally arrived from 9 Engine. This truck can pump large volumes of water for a longer distance, using multiple hose connections for wider hoses. The street hydrants were too far away, and the building standpipes just dumped water into the basement. The only other way to get water into the building was by linking up hoses and dropping it off the building to be hooked up to the super-pumper engine, and from the pumper they ran manifold yellow hoses over 200 feet to a working fire hydrant in order to get water up to them in the building.

I saw our boss, Lieutenant John Garcia, and I asked him, where were our guys? Lieutenant Garcia looked very dazed and confused and didn't answer me. I then saw Jay Bangash, who worked in our firehouse, 24/5, but he was detailed to 6 truck in the Chinatown firehouse, and I asked Jay if he saw our guys. He wasn't inside the building, so he didn't see them. I then asked for a roll call of the men from 24/5 firehouse. Neal Cronin was the acting battalion chief. Lieutenant Garcia was on the ground near me and Chief Galvin, but the Lieutenant couldn't speak for himself, because he was disoriented. I was the chauffeur. The nozzle man, which was Bobby Beddia, there was no answer, or a possible mayday came back over the radio. The backup man, which was Jimmy Martin, was heard on the radio, but he was lost in a stairwell.

The control man was Joey; again no answer or a possible mayday came over the radio, and we couldn't be sure.

Chief Galvin continued to call for roll calls with 10 Engine. I interrupted him and said that they were down from the building already and at the command station. It might have been seconds, but it seemed like minutes, and minutes seemed like an eternity. Chief Galvin wanted to continue with roll calls but was interrupted by Rescue 3 issuing maydays. Rescue 3 needed to get out; they were out of air. The chief cut them off, stating they needed to find missing men and for Rescue 3 to find their way out to the hoist or scaffolding.

The next radio call was when they found Joey. I ran over to the elevator, and I couldn't understand why a civilian was running the elevator. A firefighter always ran the elevator during the fire, but later they said it was a special elevator. Anyway, Frank McCutchen was with the men that brought Joey down. I was there with Jay Bangash, and we carried Joey a couple of hundred yards across West Street road barriers to where the ambulances were. We were performing CPR on Joey the entire way to the ambulance.

I left with Joey in the ambulance. The ambulance people were from Staten Island, and maybe that's why it took longer than it should have to arrive at the hospital, at least in my mind. I continued to perform CPR until we arrived at Beekman Downtown Hospital.

Why were the ambulances on the opposite side of the highway as opposed to being near the fire trucks, close to the building?

I think that was probably the closest they could get. Also they weren't from Manhattan, so they might not have known the area and how to get closer to the building.

Why weren't fire or police department EMS crews there?

Probably because whatever they had there was taking other people to hospitals. They were probably overworked, it being the summer, and many senior personnel were on vacation.

When I got to the hospital, I left Joey with the three EMS people to find help. They finally got Joey into the emergency room, followed shortly after by Bobby Beddia. Lieutenant John Garcia was on another bed in the emergency room. He was suffering from smoke inhalation and carbon monoxide poisoning. This explained why Lieutenant Garcia was disoriented. He could have died that day.

The doctors started working on Joey. I left to call my wife and told her that Joey and Bobby were hurt. I returned and saw that Eric Staiano was with Bobby. I went out of the emergency room and walked down the hallway, where I saw Joey's wife, Linda. Linda wanted to go into the emergency room to help since she was a registered nurse. I had to hold her back because the doctors and nurses were doing all they could for those guys, and I didn't want her to see him with all those tubes and the hospital staff working on the three of them.

When the doctors came out and told us that they had expired, there were only a couple of us firefighters still there. I told the nurses to clean them up real good because Joey's wife and mother were there to see him. Meredith, Bobby's girlfriend, went in to see him. They worked on Joey for maybe an hour and 15 minutes and Bobby for maybe 50 minutes. The hospital released Joey and Bobby to be sent to the medical examiner because of the New York City requirement that any city employee who died in the line of duty, an autopsy was required. Tony Salerno or Steve Altini rode with Bobby, and I went with Joey. A lot of our firefighters came in from their days off and from vacation when they heard about the fire and our brothers being injured. We had a contingent of our brothers from 24/5 firehouse go to the medical examiner out of respect and to honor our fallen brothers. The medical examiner had me identify the bodies of Joey and Bobby.

When we got back to our firehouse, 24/5, there were many supporters there. Retired firefighters, 9/11 widows, neighborhood people, Deputy Chief Richard Fuerch, and Chief Jonas were there to support us. We got everyone together, and we had a meeting to discuss what had to be done in the next few days. We had the mass and the wake. We wouldn't have Joey waked on his birthday; that wouldn't be right. The counseling unit was there also.

I found out later that Governor Spitzer went into that building after the fire with a contingent of his detail and several Orthodox Jews. They stayed for 20 minutes.

Firefighter Francis McCutchen

In your own words, how did that day progress for you?

It was a warm, sunny day when Chief Spadafora visited the firehouse with his girlfriend and her grandchildren. The chief lived in the area, so it was no surprise when he came to visit the firehouse. We were hanging out at the house watch while Joey and Bobby were with the grandkids showing the fire trucks and equipment. That's what Joey and Bobby did. They always took the time to show friends, tourists, and anyone the fire trucks or just talk fire stuff. I think of that afternoon often. It just shows how fragile we really are, because just hours later both Joey and Bobby were gone. I miss Bobby and Joey, and they will always be in my thoughts and prayers.

We received a call around 3:30 p.m., and Engine 24, Ladder 5, and Battalion 2 responded. Captain Neal Cronin of Engine 24 was the acting Battalion Chief. We heard the call that we were going to the Deutsche Bank building. I immediately thought, *Aren't they taking that building down?* As we were going down West Street, we noticed there was a tremendous amount of smoke coming from the upper floors of that building. I wasn't too concerned, because the standpipe system should be intact, so we should have no problem getting water to fight the fire. Also, the building was open; there should be good ventilation. Little did I know that it was just the opposite. My thoughts at the time were, *Okay, a good fire. Let's get to work and do what we do!* Unfortunately, though, it was going to be a fire with many obstacles. This would include standpipe sections illegally removed on different floors. That information was never passed on to the FDNY.

My job was to drive the battalion chief. I was the Battalion 2 aide, and my function was to stay with the battalion chief and to assist him at the fire. Acting Chief Cronin was already dressed, but I had my bunker gear off because it's difficult to drive with it on. Acting Battalion Chief Neal Cronin told me he was going up inside the building and that I should meet him there. I suited up with my gear and took my Scott mask, radio, and tools. I then stepped into the outside elevator that would take us up to the fire floor. I'm in the elevator with Joey and Bobby and five other firefighters. We all have our bunker gear on with fire protective hoods, Scott masks, and tools. We nod and wink to each other; we're confident. When we got to the floor, other companies were already there. You could see heavy smoke 20–30 feet inside the building. When I stepped inside the building, it was like a wall of black smoke.

I decided to go look for Acting Battalion Chief Neal Cronin, so I went with the guys, and we are going up the stairs, and it is pitch black; you can't see anything. I hear on the radio and the guys are saying, "They can't get through" and "Go down, go down." We started going back down the stairs, but there were no railings, only plastic sheets. The stairs weren't flat; there were pieces of wood on them like a lip. I wound up falling down a flight of stairs and injuring my knee. It was so dark; it was like I was in a darkroom. I put my hand out to try to feel where I was going. After a while, I don't hear voices anymore.

Where were you when this was going on? In the stairwell? And on what floor?

I was on the 14th floor because that was what the elevator operator said. I took out and activated my large flashlight. After unsuccessfully trying to reach the upper floors, I'm back down on the 14th floor. I start moving around until I come upon the standpipe. I turned the standpipe on to see if there was water in it. It was dry. I thought maybe they were using another standpipe or maybe they were trying to get water into the standpipe. I decided to continue to search for Acting Battalion Chief Cronin. I finally get to the other side of the building, and it is still smoky there. The visibility is much better, and I can actually see firemen. It was a good feeling to see them.

I hear the sound of fire crackling, so I looked up to the 15th floor, and I see the scaffolding mesh netting on fire above us. I left this area to continue my search for Acting Battalion Chief Neil Cronin. I'm now trying to find my way back towards where the elevator area was, but with so much smoke it's easy to become disoriented. A firefighter sees the glow from my flashlight and calls me over. I asked him if he knew where the elevator was, and he said he did and takes me over to the elevator. Now I am with a different group of firefighters from different companies, and I can hear them talking that they can't go up or down the stairwells. Everything is locked up. It was like a trapped maze inside the building. I saw Captain Bob Scott from 7 Engine, and he said that he thinks that fans were running. I didn't understand what he was talking about at the time. This is the first time I experienced anything about a negative pressure system to keep the asbestos inside the building. I found out later that the foot-and-a-half-wide, silver, round, plastic piping was used for trapping contaminants.

At the time, did you know about the fans or a negative pressure system?

No, I didn't. It wasn't until after the fire when we were talking about the fire amongst ourselves that we found out about the system to contain the asbestos. This was why the building was coming down slowly, because they had to contain the asbestos from being released into the atmosphere.

Do you remember when you were called in to fight the fire? Was it the first, second, or third alarm?

We responded on the second alarm. The Deutsche Bank building was in Battalion 1 district, and they were on the first alarm; Division 1 would be responding, and their Deputy Chief would take charge of the fire. Now I am at the elevator area, and I am hearing all this confusion from the men. They were saying, "There is no water to fight the fire. We can't get water." Now they decide to run a hose line down the side of the building to try and get water in from the outside. I again meet up with Joey and Bobby. There must have been 15 guys there connecting hoses together, linking them up and putting them on the elevator hoist, to get water up into the building. They finally get the line up, and we are all happy. Ten to 15 minutes go by. I finally see Acting Battalion Chief Cronin. He is on the scaffolding on the north side of the building, not far from the elevator. I asked him, "What are you doing on the scaffolding?" He said it was the only way to get to different floors in the building. He then orders me to go down to the ground. I said okay, and as I start walking towards the elevator to take me down, I met Battalion Chief Pritchard. He asked me if I could stay with him. So I said, "Sure, I can stay with you." So he gets on the radio, and I'm standing near him. We are on the 14th floor near the elevator area. I'm helping guys with their gear, handing out water, changing guys' face masks, basically doing whatever I can do. At this time the guys are really beat up from fighting the fire and the heavy smoke.

A few minutes later I see Lieutenant Garcia walking by. He was with a few firemen I didn't recognize. With so many firefighters coming and going this was no surprise. He headed to the elevator. I couldn't call out to him, because I needed to remain silent while Chief Pritchard was on the radio. After a few minutes went by, I turned around, and everybody was gone. I'm standing there by myself. My radio is dead at this time. Chief Pritchard may have received an urgent call or a mayday call, so he took off or maybe went down to the ground floor. I decide to take the elevator down to see what was going on. When I get to the ground, I hear a couple of firefighters talking that there are a couple of guys from 24 and 5 companies missing. I said to myself, "I hope this isn't true."

At this time I realize that I left my flashlight upstairs, so I get on the elevator and go back up to the 14th floor. As soon as I got to the floor, I see three or four guys carrying a fireman towards the elevator. My thoughts are *This ain't good.* At the time I didn't know it was Joey. He was unconscious, so when they put him in the elevator, we started doing CPR on him. I couldn't recognize who it was because he had a fire-protective hood on.

He started vomiting, so I wiped his face and continued doing CPR. We finally get to the ground floor, and we put him on a stretcher. The paramedics start working on him and took him away. After a few minutes the elevator came down again with another firefighter, and he was also unconscious. We picked him up and put him on the stretcher. I didn't know who the fireman was, so I picked up the bunker gear next to the stretcher, and I see the name "Beddia." I'm now in shock and scared for my friend's life, and I'm thinking, *What the hell happened?* I see Kenny Fulcher, and I asked him, "Who was the first guy they brought down?" It was either him or someone else that said it was Joey, your son. At this time it was hard to take it all in. I went directly to Beekman Hospital, and as I went into the emergency room, I saw maybe eight doctors and nurses on both of them. I was overwhelmed at this point. I couldn't believe what I was seeing.

I turned around and saw Jimmy Martin, who was working in Engine 24 that day. I asked him, "What happened?" He told me that they were in the building for a while and Lieutenant Garcia went looking for the fire. Lieutenant Garcia got lost and issued an urgent call that he was lost and running out of air. At this point Bobby Beddia decides to go looking for Lieutenant Garcia, and Bobby gets lost. I asked Jimmy what happened with Joey. Jimmy stated that Joe had run out of air and he tried to buddy system [share the working air mask]. Then Joey collapsed, and Jimmy went looking for help. This is what I was told.

How many years have you been a firefighter?

I had 18 years on the job.

Several conflicting statements were reported about how the fire was started. Do you believe that the Deutsche Bank building fire was started by a lit cigarette? Others said accelerants caused the fire to spread so quickly.

A lot of smoke and fire in a short time makes you question the fire. No one should be smoking in the first place. It could be all of the above. It is possible that an accelerant may have accidently fell over in or near the fire area to cause it to spread. Or there was arson committed. However, this is my opinion: for a cigarette to have caused a fire like that, it would have had to be burning for some time. They are supposed to have fire watches and fireguards throughout the building. They would have smelled the smoke almost immediately. They are supposed to have fire extinguishers every 1,500 square feet on each floor. I'm not an expert or a fire marshal; those guys are the experts. I certainly believe that there was more to it than a lit cigarette.

When going through the floor, did you notice piles of debris?

I didn't see piles of debris, but I saw piles of sheetrock, wood, and stuff on pallets around the peripheral areas. There was a lot of black smoke, so I couldn't see everything. I did not see piles of garbage on the 14th floor area.

It's been said that the plywood, plastics, and other materials used by the construction people were not fire resistant. Any idea why?

Yes, it is cheaper to buy regular plywood and other materials than it would be to purchase fire-retardant items.

Can you think of anything else that comes to mind?

So many regulations were broken; it was obvious that no one checked this building at any time. The Fire Department should have been in that building on a regular basis. We need to ask the question, "Why?"

There were multiple agencies that were supposed to have been in that building every day, and yet no one saw or did anything. Where was the Building Department? Where was OSHA? Where were Site Safety LLC and the fireguards? OSHA showed up afterward to give out fines for violations. This building was being worked on for years. If it was a private building, they would have been crawling all over it. They showed up after the fire is out, and we have two dead firefighters and 105 more injured.

I'm sure many people must be asking themselves today, why didn't they inspect that building? Why did they turn the other way? I'm just telling you what I saw, what I heard, my beliefs and feelings. I know that after this fire, there have been many improvements to building and fire safety, but unfortunately at a terrible cost!

~ 3 ~

The Call

I sensed—no, I knew—something was very wrong. My entire being screamed at me in alarm. I knew I was in the midst of something tragic, but I couldn't comprehend what it was.

It's funny how you remember certain things down to the minutest detail and other memories just become a blur. I remember the last time I saw my son was at his home, which was two blocks from my house. Brooklyn families enjoy living close to each other to share both good times and bad.

The mood was festive because Joe had recently been notified that he'd passed the lieutenant's test for the FDNY. He had mixed emotions about it because he would have to leave the firehouse he loved. He had many good friends there and had developed close relationships with the men both on and off the job. I think the tragedy of losing so many firefighters, eleven from his firehouse alone from the 9/11 disaster, made the men bond even closer.

Joe also thought about his future as a firefighter, and with his family growing he needed to make more money and prepare for a brighter future. We spoke about this and also that his 34th birthday was coming in a few days. He teased his wife, Linda, when she asked what he wanted for his birthday. He said, "I want *you* to cook something." He enjoyed cooking, and Linda enjoyed his cooking, so it worked out well. We all planned on being at his house that Sunday to celebrate. My wife made a batch of chocolate brownies, which he always enjoyed.

Saturday, August 18, 2007

I was getting ready to leave my home to attend the 5:30 p.m. mass at St. Bernadette's RC Church. I had just returned from a three-day business trip to Raleigh, North Carolina, the evening before, and I was packing to attend a four-day telecommunications conference in San Francisco, which started on Monday. I normally work the noon mass at St. Ephrem's Church, where I am an usher. Since I planned to leave the next day, I decided to attend the 5:30 p.m. mass at an adjoining parish. My mother-in-law went with me. It was a beautiful day, sunny and dry, temperature in the high 70s. Before I left for church, I went into the living room to shut off the TV. I stopped to listen to a newscaster reporting a major fire at the former Deutsche Bank building in Lower Manhattan. Riveted to the TV, I watched the burning building, which was enveloped in a blanket of flames. Fire engines blared, and cameras homed in on the out-of-control fire.

Before I turned off the TV, I heard the newscaster say that the building was empty because it was Saturday. I assumed the FDNY would let the fire burn itself out. I was always concerned when I heard or saw fires, since my only son was a firefighter. I'd been even more sensitive since 9/11. We had lost many neighbors, and my son had lost many fellow firefighters, including several that had been in his wedding party.

When I got to the church, I took a seat with my mother-in-law. The mass had started when I received a call from my wife. I had my phone on vibrate should I need to answer it in an emergency. Instinct told me something was wrong. My stomach tightened; my heartbeat quickened. My wife knew I was in church and would never call unless it was urgent. As soon as I heard her voice, I knew she was upset. She said that Linda, our daughter-in-law, had received a call from the fire department that our son, Joey, had been injured in a fire. Linda had dropped our grandchildren, four-year-old Mia and nine-and-a-half-month-old Joseph, at their neighbors Fiona and Jimmy's house, so she could go to the hospital. Linda was too nervous to go alone, so Jimmy, another firefighter, and my wife, Rosemarie, went along with her. A fire department vehicle was on the way to Linda's house to pick them up.

I quickly explained to my mother-in-law that we had to leave mass. When I returned home in less than five minutes, I saw my wife and Linda in the rear seats of a fire department sedan. Linda turned her head to look at me through the rear window. She was frightened; her face radiated fear.

My gut was right. Something was very wrong. I was scared. I dropped my mother-in-law off; I followed the government sedan in my car.

Following the sedan wasn't easy. The Brooklyn–Queens Expressway was jammed with vehicles, more than usual. When I drove out of the Brooklyn–Battery Tunnel, I lost them near the FDR Drive. I asked a cop directing traffic on Whitehall and Water Streets how to get to Beekman Downtown Hospital.

As I approached the hospital, Jimmy, my son's neighbor, flagged me down. I asked him how my son was, and he said that they wouldn't tell him anything. They wanted to see me, my wife, and Linda immediately. By now, my stomach was in knots. I must have been priming myself for the worst. A million questions ran through my mind. Why the urgency? How seriously was he hurt? Were bones broken? Was he burned?

I'll never forget walking into the hospital, going from bright sunlight into a dark corridor. My eyes had to adjust to the sudden change in light. As I walked quickly, I noticed several people heading the same way. I saw Salvatore Cassano, the FDNY Chief; enter with a group of officers. Why was the brass there?

I stopped the first doctor I saw and asked about my son. I noticed a few hospital bed gurneys with curtains pulled around them, closing them off from view. I asked the doctor if they were working on Joe. What were they doing for him? I wanted to see him. The doctor said it wasn't possible right now. What was that supposed to mean?

I was ushered into a room where my wife and Linda were waiting. Linda was crying quietly, and my wife, Rosemarie, looked very pale. I looked around the room and noticed a couple of doctors and several FDNY officers, which included Rev. Msgr. John Delendick, FDNY chaplain. At that moment everything within my vision slowed dramatically. I sensed—no, I *knew*—something was very wrong. My entire being screamed at me in alarm. I knew I was in the midst of something tragic, but I couldn't comprehend what it was.

The doctors were speaking, but their words seemed to come in slow motion, and their movements had slowed to a crawl. I looked at the scene unfolding in front of me as if through a funnel. As I turned my head, I saw snapshots of people and heard snippets of conversations. Linda was shaking uncontrollably, and Rosemarie was sobbing. The doctor said, "We did all we could. Lack of oxygen caused cardiac arrest …" The chaplain said, "He wasn't burned. He never felt any pain."

I was numb; nothing was registering. This was a bad dream—worse, a nightmare. I was shaking my head hoping I would wake up.

A nurse came into the room and spoke in whispers with the doctor who had provided us with the information. We were told that we could see our son.

We were taken to the area I'd seen earlier that had the curtained-off gurneys. Linda went first. She broke down and cried hysterically as she hugged Joey's body. After Linda was escorted away by hospital personnel, Rosemarie went up to Joey, and she laid her hands on his head and chest and cried uncontrollably. She was speaking to him through her sobs. When she was escorted away by hospital and fire department people, I went to my son.

He looked as if he were sleeping. I touched his forehead, and it felt cool. I saw the stubble of a beard on his handsome face. I opened his eye and saw redness around the pupil, a sign that he'd fought and strained hard against the inevitable. In the military I had witnessed others that had summoned every ounce of strength in their struggle to live. I closed his eye and kissed his forehead and said good-bye to my son. I asked him to come back for me when it was my time to go. All the while, Joey's cell phone rang continuously.

Linda and Rosemarie cried as we were escorted to a black, unmarked fire department sedan. I faintly remember the driver explaining that, before driving us home, he was going to take a detour to lose any reporters that may be following us. As we drove away from the hospital, a large crowd of reporters was being held back by a police line across the street.

As we drove away, I don't know if I received a call or made a call to my director at work. Still numb, I don't remember what he was saying. I told him I couldn't go on the business trip. I vaguely remember him asking me why, and I answered, "Because my son was just killed in the Deutsche Bank building fire."

After speaking those words, reality struck me. My son was dead. I sobbed; I couldn't stop.

The next few days were a blur. As minutes and hours consumed days, I had no concept of time. I'm very grateful that the FDNY was kind, compassionate, and generous. They handled everything.

Thursday, August 23, was the day of the funeral mass and burial. That evening a group of firefighters, my son's friends, and a few family members found ourselves at the Salty Dog Restaurant and Bar. My wife and daughter-in-law stayed at my home.

Joey worked as a bartender at the Salty on his off hours. His close friends, the Fadel brothers, were the owners. They provided a private room for our friends and family to meet and share our grief.

I sat at a round table with several of Joey's friends who worked there; my oldest daughter's in-laws, Bill and Fran Breen; Father Caleb Buchanan from my parish church of St. Ephrem's; and my son-in-law Tommy, my youngest daughter's husband. I made a feeble attempt to participate in the conversation, but I couldn't concentrate on what was being said. I was consumed by my own feelings, which ranged from all-consuming grief to outrage.

I drank beer hoping to get drunk. No matter how much I drank I couldn't get drunk. My pain couldn't be numbed. After a while I gave up, and fire department friends took me home.

That night, I lay in bed staring at the ceiling of my bedroom, unable to sleep. I tried to make sense of everything that had happened.

I had lost many family members. I'd lost my dad to bladder cancer, an insidious disease that took a healthy man and just ate away at him until there was nothing left but a skeleton. My mother had intestinal cancer. Doctors successfully removed the cancerous cells, but she never got off the respirator. She developed pneumonia, which hampered her breathing, and eventually her overtaxed heart gave out. My baby brother died at 50 after choking on food. Friends of mine died as I was growing up. I fought in the Vietnam War with the First Marine Division and saw many people, on both sides, killed.

But I witnessed death as a separated but concerned observer. People die for many reasons—war, tragic accidents, terminal illness, old age, and other reasons. But it's very different when your child is killed. Age or circumstance doesn't matter. The scars are permanent. The deep, cold sorrow never goes away.

The wake was held at the Andrew Torregrossa & Sons Funeral Home, on 13th Avenue, two blocks from our home. Again the FDNY stepped in and managed everything. Visitors came from everywhere. I saw people at that wake that I hadn't seen in more than 40 years. They stood on line together and renewed their friendships. Family members that had been fighting with each other for decades patched up their differences and became close again. I witnessed a lot of healing for others.

When I spoke with the funeral director afterward, he said that this was the largest reception he had ever seen. Politicians and movie stars that had been waked there had not drawn the number of visitors my son received. The daily visitor line stretched beyond three blocks. The police had to close a section of 13th Avenue because of the large crowds of people.

Did all these people come because my son's death was televised or because he was well known and liked by everyone? Or did they see the tragic loss of a brave firefighter, loving father and husband, brother, son, and friend? Possibly all of the above. The funeral mass at St. Ephrem's was a one-of-a-kind ceremony. Our church's Director of Music & Liturgy, Thomas Marchesiello, created a compact disc for us with eight songs created especially for this sorrowful event. St. Ephrem's has a large church building that can hold 1,100 people. On this day the church overflowed; every square foot was occupied, including the choir loft. Those who couldn't enter waited outside. Ushers assisted fire department officers in finding seats and managed the crowd during the sacrament of Communion, along with making sure everyone entered and exited the building in an orderly fashion. The FDNY set up a loudspeaker system so the multitude of people outside could hear the service. Politicians came. Governor Elliott Spitzer and Mayor Michael Bloomberg paid their respects.

When family members were asked if they wanted to say something, I declined because I was too distraught, as was Linda. I was surprised when my wife got up and went to the pulpit. She spoke in a clear voice about our son, his family, and our grandchildren. She spoke of his good friends and extended family. At the end of her talk, she said, "My son always wanted a brother. Because of the New York City Fire Department, he has 10,000 brothers."

When we stepped outside the church, I couldn't believe the throngs of people standing shoulder to shoulder, a dozen or more deep. The enormous crowd spilled across the avenue into McKinley Park. Lines of firefighters, five rows deep, stretched for several blocks along Fort Hamilton Parkway. They came not only from all parts of the United States but from all over the world. I met firefighters from Canada, Great Britain, and Italy.

Most of the visiting firefighters were given sleeping quarters in firehouses throughout New York City, which is a common practice among the firefighter community. A few years ago, a veteran firefighter asked me if I knew why firehouses were called houses. I said I didn't know. He told me it was because firefighters are family and families live in houses. Truer words were never spoken.

The Funeral

The casket was placed on a fire truck that slowly wound its way to Brooklyn's Greenwood Cemetery. We had to stop once when the casket appeared to be loosening from the fire truck. A person from the fire department's funeral detail stopped the procession so he could secure the coffin to the fire truck. I thought of Joey then and how, with his weird sense of humor, he would have laughed if his casket rolled off the truck and slid down the street.

Linda had picked a modern wall-vault chamber that allowed for a picture of the deceased in front. The interning of the casket was quiet and solemn. Inside the mausoleum all that was heard was muffled sobs. I was the last to leave.

For several days after the funeral I couldn't do anything. All I could think of was how I could have prevented my son from being killed. In the dark depression following a tragedy of this magnitude, there is little else to think about. A parent is supposed to die before his or her children because it is the natural order. For my wife, daughter-in-law, and my daughters, life was turned inside out.

I took a week off from work. I can't remember much of what happened during that horrible week. But I remember neighbors and a couple of the local firehouses bringing us food. The food was far more than a gesture of heartfelt kindness; it was also a symbolic gesture that life goes on.

Outside our home there was a police presence to protect our property while we were out and to keep reporters away. None of us wanted to deal with anything at that point.

My thoughts kept returning to my guilt. What could I have done to prevent this tragedy? Why had it happened? I needed to know all the details. No matter how long it took, I wasn't going to stop until I had answers.

I returned to work at the General Services Administration (GSA), a purchasing agency for other federal-government agencies. GSA is also the largest federal-government landlord, because it buys and leases space for other government agencies. I worked in Federal Technology Services, which is responsible for the engineering, purchasing, and installation of voice, data, and video systems.

When I returned to work, I met with the Assistant Regional Administrator, Patrick Donovan, who offered sympathy and condolences. He said that if there was anything he could do to help, all I had to do was ask.

One Year Later

My family was summoned to a meeting at FDNY headquarters when the final investigative report of the fire and what had transpired was concluded. The report contained information on what had gone wrong and the exact condition of the building. I attended the meeting with my wife and daughter-in-law. At the conclusion of the briefing I asked FDNY Commissioner Nicholas Scoppetta and FDNY Chief Salvatore Cassano, "Why didn't you know the interior conditions of that building? Was it because it was a state-owned building that was off-limits to the FDNY?"

There was no reaction whatsoever. They just stared at me and said nothing. I took their reaction as a sign that they were not going to answer any questions I asked. It also made me more determined to learn the truth.

I devoured everything published or broadcast about the Deutsche Bank building post-9/11. The more I read, the angrier I became. Emotional gut reactions were substantiated by facts. My family—and the public—had been lied to by the people we'd elected to protect us and safeguard our rights. Elected officials had used their power to manipulate and deceive us.

~ 4 ~

What Went Wrong?

Misleading and inaccurate information was created to push the blame and guilt on others so that decision makers at the highest levels of city and state agencies—with the cooperation of New York City's DA's office—would not be blamed.

It's abundantly clear that the Deutsche Bank building fire wasn't an anomaly, freak accident, or a communication breakdown. Lifesaving rules and protocols were sidestepped by city, state, and federal agencies. Contractors and top decision makers were complicit in the cover-up and in the distortion of facts. The result of their malfeasance was a preventable disaster that caused the deaths of three firefighters and injuries to more than 100.

What was initially thought to be a routine fire rapidly escalated into a blazing inferno, a seven-alarm fire that resulted in the deployment of 224 firefighters and that took over seven hours to control.

The minute-by-minute details of the Deutsche Bank building fire were brought to light by the *Fire Department Safety and Inspection Services Command Investigative Report (Case Number SB 75/07, Fatal Injury to Firefighter Joseph Graffagnino, Ladder Company 5, and Firefighter Robert Beddia, Engine Company 24)*. The details of this official report were corroborated by the National Institute for Occupational Safety and Health (NIOSH), an institute within the Centers for Disease Control and Prevention (CDC). NIOSH is a federal agency responsible for conducting research and making recommendations for the prevention of work-related injuries and illness.

NIOSH created the Firefighter Fatality Investigation and Prevention Program to examine deaths of firefighters in the line of duty so that fire departments, firefighters, fire service organizations, safety experts, and researchers could learn from incidents such as the Deutsche Bank building fire and make recommendations to prevent similar occurrences.

The 176-page FDNY Fatal Investigative report was more detailed than the NIOSH report. There were also variations between the two reports because of different viewpoints of the respective agencies' investigators during and after the fire. The DA's report also differed from the FDNY and NIOSH reports and from a report by the New York City Department of Investigation (DOI), which investigates questionable administrative issues. More confusing still were significant and incriminating discrepancies in eyewitness firefighters' taped interviews of the event.

The DA never mentioned the existence of the EPA fans in his statement or in the charges against those he indicted. The DA also contradicted the medical examiner's cause of death. The internal fans brought the fire and smoke lower into the building and were responsible for killing two firefighters and injuring more than a 100, according to FDNY officers and New York City's medical examiner.

The owner of the building, the Lower Manhattan Development Corporation (LMDC), had a signed contract with New York City that they would abide by all the city's building and fire codes and New York State's building and fire regulations. If there was a discrepancy between codes, they were to use the stricter code. However, they failed to abide by any safety codes or regulations, and they never adhered to the building and fire-safety contracts they signed. And yet the DA never mentioned the building owner's responsibilities.

It's more than apparent that misleading and inaccurate information was created to push the blame and guilt on others so that decision makers at the highest levels of city and state agencies—with the cooperation of New York City's DA's office—would not be blamed. Federal agencies that were involved in harmful decisions on a day-to-day basis for more than two years were not mentioned. From the information gathered, most of which was public record, both state and federal prosecutors took a hands-off approach to pursuing in-depth investigations. The DA's office controlled the case, deciding how to investigate and who to prosecute and, conversely, who not to prosecute.

Part II

Players and Agencies

~ 5 ~

Lower Manhattan Development Corporation (LMDC)

An organization with a less-than-stellar history of reckless, life-threatening decisions.

The Lower Manhattan Development Corporation was formed in November 2001 by Governor George Pataki and Mayor Rudolph Giuliani to plan the reconstruction of Lower Manhattan after the September 11, 2001, terrorist attacks and to distribute nearly $10 billion in federal funds to rebuild Downtown Manhattan. When Pataki was elected governor of New York, the state was in control of projects using the joint NYC/NYSD corporations of Empire State Development Corporation, Lower Manhattan Development Corporation, and Lower Manhattan Construction Command Center. When Spitzer became governor, the power shifted to the city's control. Bloomberg took advantage of that power by hiring people and companies that were loyal to him.

A joint state–city corporation governed by a board of directors, the LMDC is a subsidiary of the Empire State Development Corporation, a state authority mandated to implement various New York State projects that are not subject to legislature approval or any oversight. The LMDC's original board consisted of 11 members, seven appointed by the governor and four by the mayor. When Republican Michael Bloomberg was elected mayor in 2002, Pataki allowed a change in directors to eight appointees each, so the current board consists of 16-members, half appointed by the governor and the other half by the mayor.

In 2004 the state of New York bought the damaged and contaminated 41-story Deutsche Bank building, at 130 Liberty Street, for $90 million.

An agreement was reached that the insurers of the building, AXA and Allianz, would be responsible for 75 percent of the demolition costs exceeding $50 million and that the LMDC would be the landlord of the building. Governor Pataki announced that the building would be demolished in a year.

The same year the building was purchased, the LMDC signed a contract to decontaminate and demolish the Deutsche Bank building for $45 million dollars with the Gilbane Building Company. Problems surfaced when the EPA created elaborate and expensive procedures for the removal of contaminants, including asbestos, from the building. Gilbane Building Company pulled out of the contract after the EPA rejected its demolition plan.

In 2005, the LMDC contracted with Bovis Lend Lease to be the general contractor to demolish the Deutsche Bank building for approximately $81 million. Needless to say, the selection of Bovis, especially at a considerably higher price tag, was questioned. No answers were provided. The EPA signed off on the dismantling plan in September 2005.

Why didn't Bloomberg and Deputy Mayor Doctoroff question the LMDC's less-than-stellar history of poor, reckless, life-threatening decisions? With many reputable New York construction companies, why did the LMDC choose Safeway Environmental Corporation, Regional Scaffolding and Hoisting Company, and the John Galt Corporation, all of which were tied to Bovis and convicted criminals?

The LMDC Board Minutes of January 13, 2005, mentioned the rebirth of business in Lower Manhattan, largely triggered by the announcement that JP Morgan Chase would be relocating 1,415 employees into 447,000 square feet of office space. The LMDC chairman announced that the JP Morgan Chase move was a signal that Lower Manhattan was back on its feet with a well-deserved new look. LMDC President Kevin Rampe said that this was the "beginning of a trend that will continue."

When Eliot Spitzer became governor on January 1, 2007, he appointed his former deputy attorney general, Avi Schick, president of the Empire State Development Corporation. Schick was the New York State Attorney General's lead prosecutor when Spitzer was New

York State's Attorney General. Schick was later appointed Chairman of the LMDC.

Deconstruction of Deutsche Bank building Halted Because of Complications

The Deutsche Bank building deconstruction came to a halt in December 2006–January 2007 when Bovis Lend Lease and the John Galt Corporation went to the LMDC stating that the project was much more complicated than originally estimated. The general contractor and subcontractor wanted an additional $30 million. The costly problems were attributed to strict environmental regulations.

Emergency Meeting Called

Because of this unexpected job interruption, Bloomberg called an emergency meeting at Gracie Mansion for January 29, 2007, to resolve the money and work issues with Bovis and Galt. Because of its importance, the impromptu private meeting was reported by the news media. Reportedly, Doctoroff, Spitzer, and Schick, along with executives from Bovis and Galt, attended the meeting.

It's reasonable to conclude that the LMDC Board Minutes of February 14, 2007 (see appendix A), approved the increased funding and other issues negotiated in the January meeting at Gracie Mansion. An important excerpt from those minutes was that LMDC Director Malloy requested verification that he was correct in his interpretation that this action would allow for the job to be finished without disruption or delays and further that any money issues would be resolved after the job had been completed. Chairman Rampe stated that that was correct.

In essence, it's obvious that the emergency Gracie Mansion meeting was called to give Bovis and Galt the green light to decontaminate and deconstruct 130 Liberty Street as fast as possible to comply with the deadline decreed by JP Morgan Chase. Delays in taking down the building would result in penalties and loss of financial incentives.

By the time the meeting ended, an additional $30–$40 million dollars was added to the contract. The state's senior politicians decided to advance the money and litigate with the LMDC in the hopes that some of the money would be recouped.

According to the media coverage of the meeting, the city's leadership made it abundantly clear that Bovis and Galt would be financially penalized if they failed to meet a year-end deadline to bring JP Morgan Chase Bank to the site a deal that was rumored to have been negotiated by Dan Doctoroff. Additionally, financial incentives would be offered if the building was brought down prior to the year-end time frame. The commitment was finalized just months before the fire.

It was also rumored that money wasn't the only issue at that meeting. Since speed of execution was a top priority, it was understood that safety regulators would be kept at bay in order to bring the building down within the agreed time frame. It's been speculated that both the mayor and the governor were instructed to keep city, state, and federal regulators out of the contractor's way.

It was reported that a day before the fatal fire, Schick and president of the LMDC David Emil stood on the 26th floor slab of the Deutsche Bank building. Schick said that in three years there would be a banker on this spot. Schick and Emil were determined to complete the removal of the Deutsche Bank building to pave the way for JP Morgan Chase investment-banking headquarters. He mentioned that the banking company was betting that the LMDC would have the existing building disassembled on time. Emil stated that the Deutsche Bank building removal would be completed in early 2008. The agreement was that Bovis would have an added incentive ($6 million) bonus if they completed the project by December 31, 2007.

After the Deutsche Bank building fire, the New York City Council held a hearing to determine responsibility for the fire and if the LMDC had done everything in its power to prevent the fire. City Council Member Alan Gerson chaired the hearing and became frustrated that all the witnesses, contractors, and city agencies he interviewed gave the same excuses—that [the project] was a large team with many players that had many meetings and many stakeholders.

Councilman Gerson concluded that apparently no one was in charge of the project. Emil declined to comment on whether the LMDC had done everything possible to prevent the fire. No one knew anything about what had happened prior to the fire, but many cited the vast improvements moving forward in building and fire safety.

Gerson questioned state officials as to why they continued to use Bovis Lend Lease after the fire that killed two firefighters. He cited that just days before the fire, URS Associates, a safety consultant to the LMDC, had warned that Bovis could no longer be trusted to ensure building safety and had said that the Deutsche Bank building was an accident waiting to happen. Yet Bovis remained in charge of the project. He asked Emil what had changed with Bovis to give him confidence in them. Emil refused to comment.

Despite all the controversy, funding continued to pour in, unabated, into the project. LMDC officials continued to state that additional funds were required to keep the project moving. Not one city, state, or federal official questioned if taxpayers' money was being wasted or why funds continued to be funneled into the project without a challenge.

A change of viewpoint happened in February 2010 when the LMDC board approved an additional $102 million for the Deutsche Bank building project and then discovered Bovis was suing them for $80 million. LMDC officials screamed that Bovis was violating their agreement not to sue until the building was completely demolished and howled that Bovis had already been paid $61 million over the contract cost (and they'd just approved $102 million more for the project; what was that money for?). Reportedly, the LMDC filed a countersuit against Bovis for $100 million.

Project costs had escalated from $80 million to $300 million. Bovis claimed the reason costs had catapulted was that the LMDC had ordered them to perform additional work that was not part of their contract. What changed? There was the original Gilbane contract of 2004 and the proposed contract, which was the LMDC plan (September 2005) that had Safeway and Regional Scaffolding listed as the contractors. The goal of both contracts was to abate and then demolish the building. Both contracts with Gilbane and Safeway were canceled.

When the contract was assigned to Bovis and Galt (February 2006), their implementation plan, dated September 19, 2006, stated that the procedures of the project were to conform to NYC DOB, FDNY, NYS Department of State (DOS), DOL, and OSHA requirements. The DOL sections state that the contractors were to comply with all federal, state, and local codes and regulations. Permits and notifications required for the project included EPA, DOL, and DEP permits for asbestos and a DOB work permit for building demolition (not building alteration). The contract also mentioned that utilities were to be disconnected and capped prior to deconstruction, with the exception of temporary water, sewer, and electric to be maintained by the general contractor along with the water risers (standpipe/sprinkler systems) and drains. Any deviations or changes were to be submitted to the LMDC for approval. It wasn't until February 2007 that the project was changed to simultaneously abate and demolish the building.

With the unprecedented simultaneous abatement and demolishing of a city skyscraper, the scope of work changed and meant additional resources (manpower and equipment) would be required. This additional work came with a cost increase. However, after the fire the scope of work reverted back to the original plan (abate and then demolish). This project change would require fewer resources and equipment. Fewer resources should have meant a cost reduction, not an increase.

In addition to the scope-of-work change, after the fire the FDNY and DA's office discovered that the material that had been used was substandard. The plywood, plastics, and other items were not fire retardant, and they should have been. Untreated wood and plastics are less expensive than fire-retardant equipment. Not only would the use of substandard material justify a price decrease, but the contractors should have been fined by the contracting officers for buying and installing unauthorized material. The implication is that the contract between the LMDC, Bovis, and Galt was violated and that funds from the city's taxpayers and the federal agencies that paid for these cost increases had been misappropriated.

Did the LMDC, along with the mayor's and governor's offices, Bovis, and Galt, defraud New York taxpayers and the federal government? A federal-government audit of the contracts and funding for the 130 Liberty Street project should have been ordered.

Over the objections of the City Department of Investigations and continuous complaints from Community Board 1, the contractor and subcontractor were hired without competition. How could a $220 million cost escalation—an astronomical change never challenged by anyone—be justified?

The 130 Liberty Street building was finally demolished on March 3, 2011.

It's interesting to note that, after the fire, when the public demanded that Bovis be removed from the project, Schick and Deputy Mayor Casswell Holloway defended Bovis. This was in the wake of the LMDC's claims that Bovis had not performed the work in a safe manner and had coerced additional funds that they weren't entitled to via threats, complaints, and delays of the project's progress. The following obvious questions have never been answered:

- Why did the LMDC unanimously vote to grant Bovis every cost increase, without question?
- Why did it cost $300 million to complete this project, almost seven times the original cost of the Gilbane contract ($45 million) and $220 million more than the original Bovis contract ($81 million, nearly double the amount of the original Gilbane contract)?
- Why did the building take six years to come down when it was supposed to be down in one year?
- Why weren't both Bovis and Galt removed from the project?
- Why was Bovis given the project without competition by the LMDC?
- Why did Bovis hire Galt after the DOI repeatedly told them not to for various valid reasons?
- Why did the LMDC have Regional Scaffolding create the John Galt Corporation (a reincarnation of Safeway, LMDC's original choice) and then have Bovis hire them after other reincarnations of Safeway were found to be unqualified and lacking in experience and to have organized crime affiliations?
- Why was there no oversight for the LMDC regarding their competence and financial and business decisions?
- How could a corporation comprised of political appointees (most of whom are lawyers or corporate executives) manage and control construction and deconstruction in Manhattan, control

billions of dollars, have absolutely no experience in construction or deconstruction, audit themselves, and have not one federal or independent agency to oversee or audit them? What happened to organizational transparency?

Josh Silverstein, creator of the blog *Joshing Politics*, in his February 21, 2008, blog "2.2 Million Excuses and Counting," questioned the LMDC's payment of legal fees to attorneys defending them. Silverstein could also have included New York City's payment of attorney fees for city employees that the DA's office wanted to question regarding the Deutsche Bank building fire. Reportedly, the LMDC spent approximately $900,000 in 2008, with an additional $2 million increase in March 2011. The city's legal fees were about $6.5 million. Tack on the victims' family's lawsuits of approximately $16 million, of which Bovis paid the majority. Who is picking up this tab of nearly $26 million? The LMDC stated that it would try to recover those costs via insurance (the insurers of the building, AXA and Allianz, would be responsible for 75 percent of the demolition costs exceeding $50 million) and NYS recovery costs from Bovis. Silverstein doubted that the insurance companies or Bovis would wind up with the bill. He believed that taxpayers would ultimately pay the bill. Were these costs another reason for the escalation of expenses to demolish the Deutsche Bank building?

To this day, the LMDC's existence is still questioned. Some observers question whether it should have existed in the first place. The LMDC has few supporters, and the prospect of closing it down garners overwhelming support.

In the summer of 2006, the *New York Times* ran a prophetic headline: "LMDC Is No Longer Needed – Yet It Stays Forever!" The chairman of the LMDC at that time said that, with the exception of the legal purpose of doling out grants, the LMDC's mission would come to an end within a few months. Even Doctoroff, who was a driving force on the city's behalf, said it was correct to transfer the responsibilities to another agency.

The loudest critic of the LMDC was Julie Menin, one of its board members and the chairwoman of Community Board 1 in Lower

Manhattan. Menin repeatedly argued that the LMDC should never have been involved in the Deutsche Bank project, because it had no experience in environmental issues. She also asked the LMDC for a cost-benefit analysis of itself and its dismantling of the 130 Liberty Street building. It's doubtful she ever received it. Menin cited the project's agonizingly slow progress, which was attributed to LMDC leadership issues, waffling decisions, and lack of communication with the residents and businesses in the area.

As for the bureaucratic screw-ups, out-of-control costs, and the death of two firefighters in the fire of August 2007, she laid the blame squarely on the LMDC when she said that it did not have the background or the expertise to handle such a gigantic project. At an LMDC board meeting, she stood alone and objected to the budget because it did not include a firm resolution to shut the LMDC down. Critics of the LMDC attribute construction delays to the LMDC's mismanagement and mishandling of federal funds.

Community Board 1 had approved resolutions that the LMDC should not have hired Galt because of the contractor's lack of experience and alleged links to organized crime. Menin's successor, Catherine McVay Hughes, was equally outspoken about the LMDC, but, like Menin's protests, Hughes's were almost completely ignored.

A group called the Reconstruction Watch, which promoted fair and effective use of the city's development resources, published a report in August 2004 stating that the LMDC favors big business, real estate interests, and the economic interests of LMDC board members' friends. Small businesses and middle and low-income residents fare the worst when grants are doled out. The corporation lacks openness, diversity, transparency, and accountability to low to middle-income taxpayers. The LMDC has commissioned several studies in order to boost funding allocations on how needs are prioritized. The results of those studies have not been made public, which leads to questions about the LMDC's funding practices.

David Dyssegaard Kallick of the Fiscal Policy Institute said, "The LMDC is not serving any useful purpose. Disbanding the LMDC is a step in the direction of transparency, democracy and the checks and balances of the normal political process."

The LMDC has always been tardy in responding to requests. An example is when a safety and health professional accused the LMDC of lying. Dave Newman, industrial hygienist for the New York Committee for Occupational Safety and Health, requested a copy of the fire-safety agreement between the city and the LMDC by exercising the Freedom of Information Act. Six months late, the LMDC's counsel responded that the document doesn't exist. Newman then produced a letter from Schick and Deputy Mayor Edward Skylar, dated September 11, 2007, to the EPA about the LMDC's building and fire-safety commitment. The LMDC did not return calls seeking their comments.

For several years, Bloomberg said that the LMDC should be closed and the remaining funds should be transferred to a city agency so that they could be appropriately dispersed. And Governor Paterson stated that he is frustrated over the LMDC's over-budget projects, ineptitude, and preventable construction accidents. He said he wanted to slash their staff to five people to oversee the remaining $3 billion in federal funds slated to help rebuild the area. According to a *New York Post* story, The LMDC failed to spend $540 million of that money and has another $250 million set aside as "undecided," with no plans as to how the funds would be dispersed.

Community Board 1 committee member Bill Love argued that bureaucracies such as the LMDC tend to perpetuate themselves longer than necessary. The community board voted unanimously to urge the LMDC to release its remaining grant money and transfer any additional legal and compliance tasks to other state and city agencies. This transfer deadline was to be no later than the 10th anniversary of 9/11.

While decision makers and concerned taxpayers wanted to close down the LMDC, unexplainably, it's still in existence. If the mayor and his top decision makers wanted it gone, why were they pushing to have the LMDC build the NY Performing Arts Center? Why wasn't the public outraged when Bloomberg and his loyal lemmings flip-flopped their allegiance? For years, Bovis enjoyed unprecedented perks, not to mention sidestepping an equitable and democratic bidding process. But when the tables turned and Bovis was caught with its pants down by blatantly bilking city coffers, decision makers wiggled out of the mess—a feat requiring shameless audacity.

Once again, New York City's relationship with Bovis is alive and well, backed and supported by the LMDC. A March 2, 2015, *New York Post* editorial said, "We refer to the 'temporary' agency that refuses to die: the Lower Manhattan Development Corp ... More than 13 years later, it lives on in all its governmental glory—defying repeated calls from pols (and this newspaper) to phase it out, trim the bureaucracy and save New Yorkers money."

A March 25, 2015, story in the *Capital* said, "The Lower Manhattan Development Corporation announced a tentative agreement with Lend Lease, the construction company that was dismantling the Deutsche Bank building ... The settlement will free up $50 million for the LMDC—$40 million from Lend Lease and more than $10 million in claims that Bovis is forgiving, and for which LMDC had held money in reserve. David Emil, LMDC president, said the organization is still overseeing several projects. A new executive was recently brought on to oversee the distribution of the Lend Lease Settlement money. Today, the corporation has a $2.5 million budget and the equivalent of about a dozen full-time staff." The LMDC has funded many projects on the Lower East Side, including the renovation of the East River waterfront. One of its last grants was awarded to Pier 42 at Montgomery Street. The agency allocated $14 million for the first phase of a new park that's being planned.

The functional stepchild of the Lower Manhattan Development Corporation was the Lower Manhattan Construction Command Center (LMCCC), created in 2004 to control funds that manage and coordinate construction projects south of Canal Street. With a $20 billion budget, it funded independent studies, conducted stakeholder meetings, evaluated environmental impacts, and monitored quality of life. While the LMCCC reported to the LMDC, it was reportedly a positive force for residents of Lower Manhattan. The LMCCC was disbanded in 2014.

~ 6 ~

City Hall and Bovis

Bovis Lend Lease was criticized for grossly inflating construction costs and for a number of major safety incidents, which included the death of a worker at the Bloomberg building.

By the end of 2010, Bovis was one of the largest real estate investors in the world. Formerly Lehrer McGovern Inc., Bovis changed its name to Bovis Lend Lease LMB Inc. in February 2000. It is owned by Australian-based Lend Lease Corporation, which has offices in 40 countries, 18 in the United States. In 2008, Bovis was ranked New York City's top contractor, with revenues exceeding $2.3 billion. During Bloomberg's 12-year reign, Bovis held the favored position, winning many of the city's major construction projects. Doctoroff, operating with Bloomberg's carte blanche approval, selected the projects. Doctoroff was the head of the city's Economic Development Corporation when it selected Bovis to work on several projects, along with granting Bovis renewed construction projects that previously had been awarded through a bidding process.

The Bloomberg administration wanted complete control over choosing people and companies to work with on construction and real estate projects. Reportedly, Bloomberg and Doctoroff had a very close working relationship with Bovis.

Bovis enjoyed a virtual monopoly over many of New York City's big-bucks construction projects, including the $15 million construction of the city's new wedding chapel, design of the mayor's townhouse, a $20 million security and streetscape improvement for Wall Street, a $2 million cleanup project of Brooklyn's contaminated Gowanus Canal, the city's sanitation buildings, FDNY projects, $600 million

Citi Field projects, the September 11 Memorial (for which Bloomberg was chairperson), Bloomberg LP headquarters, and the Bronx Hall of Justice, to name a few. Bovis was awarded these projects even though the company had been criticized for grossly inflating construction costs and for a number of major safety incidents, which included the death of a worker at the Bloomberg building. Bovis was also sued for not complying with best-practice standards.

The LMDC hired Bovis as the general contractor for the Deutsche Bank Building project in 2005 and reportedly without competition. Former council member Alan Gerson, the chairperson of the committee that monitored the LMDC and whose geographic area the Deutsche Bank building was in, believed that Bovis received preferential treatment from New York City, which was most evident in the Deutsche Bank building contracts. The Deutsche Bank building project proved to be Bloomberg and Doctoroff's biggest nightmare.

In April 2012, following a two-year federal investigation, Bovis admitted to inflating bills on city construction projects for a decade. It agreed to pay $61.6 million in fines for overpriced invoices at Citi Field, Grand Central Terminal, the American Museum of Natural History, and other large projects. James Abadie, a top Bovis executive, pleaded guilty when charged with fraud conspiracy.

~7~

Bovis Lend Lease and the John Galt Corporation

Galt doesn't seem to have done much of anything. Many of its top executives were tied to city and federal criminal investigations.

Talk about a marriage made in hell. Again and again Bovis and John Galt went to the altar, using different names on a number of separate occasions, in their attempts for a city- and state-approved contract until they just said *fugetaboutit* and eloped anyway. Let's trace this illicit love affair from its earliest beginnings.

In July 2005, the LMDC approved Safeway Environmental Corporation for the scaffolding on the Deutsche Bank building. Bovis had separate contracts for demolition and abatement cleaning of the Deutsche Bank building. Bovis wanted to use Safeway as a subcontractor on its contracts with the LMDC. In January 2006, problems arose when the DOI notified the LMCCC (the quasi-city/state corporation under the LMDC) that a Bovis-Safeway project on 100th Street and Broadway had a partial building collapse that had injured 10 people. The incident triggered a criminal investigation by the DA's office and the DOI. After the prior mishaps, the DOI, sanctioned by an LMDC agreement, was responsible for investigating proposed companies before they were awarded contracts by the LMDC. The LMDC notified Bovis that it wouldn't approve the Bovis-Safeway partnership.

Early in 2006, the LMDC requested that the DOI check another company. But this time, the DOI should perform only a quick background check, nothing in-depth and nothing on any relationships between the new company and Safeway on the John Galt Corporation. The DOI had asked the LMDC for a Memorandum of Understanding that would be used to financially reimburse the DOI for the time and resources spent on all the various company investigations. The LMDC ignored the DOI. The DOI pushed for a meeting with the LMDC to find out why it was so determined to hire Safeway employees, following a long list of shady, unqualified companies with a litany of screw-up, shoddy dealings, and executives with criminal ties. Again, the DOI was ignored.

In April 2006, the DOI notified the LMCCC that Galt was another Safeway company. In a separate meeting, Ronald P. Calvosa, director of fraud prevention for the LMCCC, told the DOI that the LMDC had already approved Galt to be the subcontractor to Bovis months earlier. This infuriated the DOI because it insinuated that the DOI had approved when the DOI knew nothing about it. Understandably, the sidestepped DOI was very upset and pointed out that there were serious problems having Safeway-affiliated companies work for a general contractor authorized by the LMCCC, whose main priority was to coordinate construction projects and to reject unqualified companies.

The DOI accused the LMCCC of deliberately withholding information that would prove that Galt was unqualified. When asked why they didn't hire one of the four DOI-suggested companies that had acceptable credentials and were picked from a list of approved companies by NYC Design and Construction, the Mayor's Office of Contract Services, and the NYS Dormitory Authority, Calvosa said that those companies were too expensive. He was reminded that New York City hires the lowest-priced responsible bidder because unqualified companies cost more in time, mistakes, and problems. Calvosa admitted that Galt had practically no experience with environmental issues or demolition. Calvosa further said that Steir Anderson, the Deutsche Bank building monitor, never sent any questions to the DOI but that Steir Anderson was checking Galt's bonding.

City and state executives who did know about the hiring of Safeway personnel include Martha Stark, the NYC Commissioner of Finance who served on the Deutsche Bank building committee for the LMDC, and Charles Maikish, Executive Director of the LMCCC. Both Stark and Maikish were copied on the February 16, 2006, confidential memo. This proves that the city and the LMDC knew what they were doing.

Out of all the city agencies that were involved in the Deutsche Bank building fiasco, the only one that did an outstanding job, under extreme duress and frustration, was New York City's Department of Investigation. They thwarted Bovis and the LMDC's plans every time they wanted to use Safeway Environmental Corporation, in its many disguised forms. When the DOI discovered a secret memo dated February 16, 2006, from the LMDC that allowed Bovis to hire Safeway people and equipment with the LMDC's permission and authorized the hiring of Safeway executives, the DOI felt betrayed. The LMDC had secretly drafted an unethical agreement, ignoring the DOI's advice and warnings.

Gilbane had a contract for $45 million but balked at the severe EPA restrictions. The project was awarded to Bovis for $80 million to separately demolish and abate the asbestos and other toxins with the same methodology imposed by the EPA and the DOL. Both Bovis and Galt agreed to this. What changed to justify the marked increase in price? Was the job more difficult? Did it require more work? Why didn't the LMDC fire Bovis and Galt and hire qualified and approved contractors? Why was nothing challenged or questioned? Why were convicted criminals with little experience hired? Why was so much money added to the contract?

As time went on, the project took even more bizarre turns.

Doctoroff had two aides that worked with him on the LMDC Deutsche Bank building project. In February 2006, he admitted he'd signed the Bovis-Galt contract over the DOI's continuous objections. Bloomberg sided with Doctoroff when he said that only one contractor was prepared to demolish that building. Robert Roach, chief of staff to the DOI commissioner, contradicted this statement, saying there were several qualified contractors willing and able to demolish the Deutsche Bank building.

As part of the deal, believed to be engineered by Doctoroff to placate the DOI so he could use Safeway people and equipment, the LMDC, the LMCCC, and Bovis would have an independent company, Steir Anderson, as the Deutsche Bank building monitor. Steir Anderson was selected by the LMDC to verify that Bovis and their subcontractors would abide by the legal agreements and to notify the LMDC, which in effect notifies the city and the state administrations, if there are any improprieties. In this way the LMDC could stop any contractual violations before they became illegal. Steir Anderson was never heard from. Safeway was banned from the Deutsche Bank building site. Doctoroff also inserted into the agreement that two of Safeway's executives, Mitchell Alvo and Donald Adler, would cooperate with DOI investigators. It's curious that less than two months later the DOI sent a letter to Alvo, president of Safeway, that he was in default of their agreement to have contracts with the NYC Sanitation Department and that Alvo and Adler refused to submit to interviews with investigators, which again violated their agreement.

The contracts between the LMDC, Bovis, and Galt had several binding sections that went ignored, with no repercussions from any agency, building monitor, or law enforcement group. (See appendix B.)

In 2007 the building was listed as an alteration by the LMDC and not as a demolition. Yet in 2005—with Gilbane and later with Safeway and with Bovis in early 2006—it was listed as a demolition. City code states that the owner did not have to notify the DOB and FDNY for an alteration, but if it was listed as a deconstruction, the owner would have to notify the DOB, FDNY, and EPA, among others. Did the LMDC deliberately list it in this manner to maintain a low profile and to avoid any in-depth scrutiny? There was no mention in the DA's investigation as to why the DOB issued alteration permits instead of demolition permits. DOB's LiMandri was aware of the types of permits issued. The mayor's spokesmen stated that "the issuance of alteration permits had no bearing on the level" of DOB oversight. That was true since the DOB reported to Doctoroff.

Subcontractor Problems

The plot thickened when DOI officials questioned the hiring of Bovis's subcontractors. The subcontractors had little experience, and their officers were reportedly tied to organized crime. The DOI discovered that every time Bovis wanted a new subcontractor, it was basically the old company with a new name and the same people.

When Safeway was rejected by the LMDC, Bovis requested that North American Demolition Company, headed by Philip B. Schwab, replace Safeway. A DOI investigation found that North American executives also had ties to convicted criminals, along with lapsed insurance policies and no professional credibility among national demolition organizations.

Even with a shoddy reputation, which rendered them unsuitable as subcontractors, North American's executives pressured the LMDC to authorize a deal that allowed the discredited company to buy Safeway's equipment and perform the work with Safeway's employees and executives. The contractors would be paid from the funds of the Deutsche Bank building project. If North American had been approved, Safeway would have been back in the picture performing work under a different name.

Another proposed company was Donjon Marine Company, a marine salvage company with little experience in building demolitions, abatements, or environmental issues. Donjon was to provide the same services as North American, hiring and using Safeway's equipment and people for the Deutsche Bank building project. Donjon was also rejected because of its lack of qualifications.

Bovis proposed other companies, all of which had minimal experience with building demolition or abatement. However, with every company proposed, Bovis planned to use Safeway's equipment, workers, and executives.

Reportedly, the DOI questioned Bovis about bringing on companies that were tied to Safeway, but it's doubtful that any Bovis executive was held accountable.

In early 2006, Regional Scaffolding and Hoisting Company, hired by the LMDC, proposed yet another Safeway reincarnation, the John Galt Corporation, a shell company with ties to Safeway Environmental. Also of concern, Galt's executives were former Safeway executives, several of whom were tied to city and federal criminal investigations.

In mid-2010, Regional Scaffolding was hired for a project in Lower Manhattan. At the time, Regional was being questioned by the DA for financial wrongdoing. Regional's attorney stated that Regional had responded to the LMDC's request to help create the John Galt

Corporation. Regional's legal counsel stated that the company was treated unfairly, yet admitted that the company was another Safeway reincarnation, orchestrated by executives of the LMDC.

The Mayor's Office of Contract Services, which tracks and monitors vendors and contractors that do business with the city, put Regional on the list of questionable companies that it cautions against doing business with. And the School Construction Authority's inspector general, responsible for determining which companies can bid and work on school building and repair projects, disqualified Regional from performing any kind of school work. A July 21, 2011, *New York Post* story said, "Regional Scaffolding bigs get 5 years probation and fined $1.9M in tax fraud." Yet they were issued a permit to install a construction elevator at 4 World Trade Center. Most baffling was that city, state, dual city-state agencies, and Port Authority decision makers totally ignored all these warnings, as did construction and real estate companies.

The news media stated that the offices of Regional Scaffolding and Hoisting Company, which also double as the address of the John Galt Corporation, can be traced to the Bronx. Galt, a conglomeration of companies that shares officers with Regional Scaffolding along with an address, appears to be a ghost company. Two of its executives were formerly on Safeway's payroll. Since it was incorporated in 1983, Galt doesn't seem to have done much of anything. Public and private records give no indication of how many employees it has, what its volume of business is, or who its clients are. There are almost no accounts of any projects it has undertaken on any scale, apart from 130 Liberty Street. Court records are largely silent. Some leading construction executives in the city say they have never even heard of Galt.

Safeway had a list of nearly a dozen affiliated companies that shared addresses, work-related telephone numbers, and personnel. In the supposed safety requirement that became part of the Bovis-Galt contract (Separate Special Condition of Trade Contract), two companies were named that Bovis and Galt were not to have any business dealings with: Dynamic Equipment Corporation and the Big Apple Wrecking Corporation.

Galt was denied a contract to demolish the Bronx House of Detention and was later fired from the Deutsche Bank building, replaced by LVI

Environmental Services. The other affiliated companies continued doing business with New York City as if nothing had happened. Under Galt's president, Greg Blinn, Regional earned more than $17 million at the Deutsche Bank building site. Regional had contracts with the New York City Police Department and Citywide Administrative Services. Another company Blinn was president of, Eastern States Construction, had contracts with the city's Department of Transportation. A different company, Windham Construction, employed a Regional executive, Paul Mazzucca, as a project supervisor.

For Bovis and Galt to take down a 41-story skyscraper riddled with black mold, asbestos, human remains, and a plethora of toxins from the collapse of the Twin Towers, in a manner of simultaneous demolition and abatement never attempted in New York City history, is unfathomable. To successfully complete this complex, dangerous, and sensitive project, without releasing toxic carcinogen dust throughout the Lower Manhattan area, would have been very difficult, if not impossible. To do it safely, it would have meant closing Wall Street's trading exchanges, which would have had a disastrous effect on the global financial market. And to give this dangerous and sensitive project to incompetent companies chosen without competition—and with little or no experience in demolition and abatement—defies comprehension. Worse still, the LMDC and LMCCC buried incriminating financial and legal information.

Criminal Investigations

- Safeway Environmental Corporation's former owner Harold Greenberg was convicted of bid rigging, bribery, and wire fraud in 1988.
- From March 2004 until March 2005, Safeway paid Phil Schwab of North American Demolition and Alpine Scaffolding through a variety of corporations, such as Alpine Scaffolding and Irondequit Corporation. Instead of depositing the checks, Schwab cashed them at check-cashing companies in New Jersey known to have organized crime connections.

- In 2005, a supermarket wall collapsed at a Safeway project in Manhattan.
- In 2007, the Manhattan DA's office investigated Galt for hiring of no-show jobs at the Deutsche Bank building project. Bruce Greenberg, brother of Harold Greenberg, was investigated. Also investigated was Phillip Chasin, son of Safeway president Stephen Chasin.
- In 2009, Robert Chiarappa, former Safeway employee approved by the LMDC to work for the John Galt Corporation, was sentenced to two and a half years in prison for billing $1.2 million for supplies that were never delivered.
- Also in 2009, Milestone Environmental Services' senior asbestos supervisor Salvatore DePaola, who was also the foreman for John Galt on the Deutsche Bank project, was cited by New York State's Labor Department and the federal Environmental Protection Agency for environmental crimes that took place at New Paltz State University. DePaola faced additional criminal charges for project delays and cost overruns at the Ulster County Law Enforcement Center and for improper asbestos removal at the Rondout Valley High School.
- The Manhattan DA's office exposed a check-cashing scheme lasting from October 2006 to July 2008 that charged people triple regular check-cashing fees. Galt was mentioned as being one of the 389 construction-related companies involved with this $40 million maneuver. Two men were indicted on 122 counts of falsifying business records and 64 counts of not filing currency-transaction reports. One of the men had over $2 million socked away in a Swiss bank account. Four check-cashing companies were involved. Some of the checks were written by Regional Scaffolding and Hoisting to Galt.

Bovis and Their Subcontractors

From the beginning of the Deutsche Bank building project, Bovis pushed for Safeway to be its subcontractor. Despite objections from the DOI, Bovis failed to suggest another subcontractor. Even though Bovis lacked experience, had a terrible safety record, and had criminal ties, the LMDC approved them.

Here are facts about Bovis and its subcontractors, proving the DOI's concerns were legitimate:

- 1999: Bovis as general contractor (GC) had Rapid Demolition as their subcontractor (sub) on a NYC Department of Sanitation (DOS) garage project on West 57th Street and 11th Avenue to abate and then demolish the building. Phil Schwab, friend of Harold Greenberg, who gave him his job in demolition, was the demolition supervisor. Sam Runfalo was the site-safety manager. Phil Schwab and Sam Runfalo are both convicted felons. In fact, Schwab and Greenberg were both convicted of bribing an EPA investigator. The DOS garage project had a 30 foot-by-30 foot section of the roof collapse. The DOS then barred Schwab from the site, but videotapes of the project show Schwab there on numerous occasions. Bovis controlled site access, allowing him on site, and Bovis continued with demolition work after the DOB issued a stop-work order.
- 2002: Bovis was GC and Rapid Demolition was their sub on another DOS project when a wall collapsed after Schwab ordered the I beams severed, which caused the outside wall and scaffolding to collapse. Rapid Demolition then defaulted on the project, which caused Lumberman Mutual, who held the performance bond, to ask if Daniela, a company owned by Schwab and Runfalo, could complete the demolition.
- 2002: Bovis was GC and North American was their sub when a floor collapsed on a three-story garage. North American was controlled by Schwab and Runfalo.
- 2004–2005: Alpine Scaffolding, another company operated by Schwab and John Butz, president of North American, was involved in an illegal check-cashing scheme. Alpine and North American shared the same physical address, and North American and Daniela had the same telephone number.

- 2005: North American was cited for working without a permit and removing asbestos materials without permits from a Queens theater.
- 2005: Bovis was GC and Safeway was their sub on the demolition of a supermarket on 100th Street and Broadway. A partial collapse of the building injured 10 people and triggered a criminal investigation by the DA's office and DOI. As mentioned earlier, Safeway's founder, Greenberg, was a convicted felon. At the trial of John Gotti Jr., Gotti said that Greenberg gave hundreds of thousands of dollars annually to an organized crime syndicate.
- 2006: The DOI notified Safeway that it had violated a NYC Department of Sanitation contract by default since two executives, Alvo and Adler, refused to submit to interviews with DOI investigators.
- 2007: Bovis was GC and Galt was their sub at the Deutsche Bank building project.
- 2008: Bovis was GC and Difama Concrete was their sub at the Trump SoHo Hotel when a worker dropped 42 stories to his death. A second worker also fell and suffered a brain injury.
- 2008: Bovis was GC and Morrow Equipment Company was their sub in Miami when a partial crane collapse killed two workers and injured five.
- 2009: Bovis was GC at Lawrence Street, Brooklyn, when a worker fell three stories when the steel bars the crane was hoisting hit him.

In the fall of 2009, Bovis was reeling from all the safety violations and accidents on several of their work sites. In an effort to appease the public and neutralize the bad press, Bovis said that henceforth it would take necessary precautions to prevent careless accidents and on-site fires. Meanwhile, at the Deutsche Bank building, the demolition had stopped, and only the abatement continued until it was completed in September 2009. The methodology for continuing the demolition was approved by the LMDC in October 2009. Steven Sommer, the Bovis executive in charge of the Deutsche Bank building project, and First Deputy Commissioner of the DOB Fatma Amer addressed a meeting held by the LMDC. Sommer provided a detailed description of the new and safe methods and equipment that would be used to remove floors from the building. The broken standpipe now had pressure alarms in it. Amer proudly announced that the building would have seven DOB supervisors and 17 DOB inspectors on site. The floor being demolished and two additional floors below it were covered with fire-retardant plywood. And the building had new blue fire-retardant netting.

When Bovis bid on this project, they were approved by the LMDC, and the above safety plans were part of the contract. In their signed contract, both the LMDC and Bovis agreed to abide by stringent building and fire codes, which were in the original contract cost of $80 million.

Why the increased cost? Why were there DOB supervisors and inspectors, extra fire watches, FDNY personnel in the building, and more safety regulators when they were outlined and in place before the fire happened? Why should taxpayers pay additional money and time for what was originally promised?

Two months after Bovis executive Sommer and DOB executive Amer promised to institute safety regulations and procedures, there were a minimum of 12 safety violations in one month at the Deutsche Bank building work site. These mishaps included a melted spotlight due to faulty wiring and a dropped wrench that hit a worker, to name a few. Bovis and the LMDC agreed to review the entire project.

Within a couple of months, at another Bovis site, Columbia University on Broadway, a worker fell to his death in an open elevator shaft. Walter South, chair of the Landmarks and Preservation Committee of Community Board 9, said he had serious concerns about the death. He believed that there were many repeated safety violations. South said he doubted safety protocols were being strictly followed, because there had been an open window in an elevator shaft without a barrier. He believed it wasn't an accident but evidence of a pervasive culture that had no consideration for safety. The Bovis spokesperson stated that Bovis had learned a great deal from this incident and that they were making sure their projects were operating safely and in compliance with safety rules. Bovis stated that it wanted a positive outcome from this tragedy, so it pledged to institute reforms to enhance safety on all Bovis sites in New York City.

Even after hearing the redundant rhetoric, Dan Held, director of communications for Columbia University, stated that Bovis had won the GC contract as part of a competitive bidding process. The criteria for the contract were a strong commitment to environmental health and work-site safety, project-management experience, and a commitment to work with minority workers and women-owned and local businesses. Held said that the university was confident in Bovis's record. He added that Bovis had created a comprehensive safety plan for the Columbia project. Columbia University monitored Bovis to make sure it responded to investigations.

It's only conjecture, but it's reasonable to assume that Held was told by his superiors to defend the decision to use Bovis. Held's articulate defense of Bovis sounded like it was taken from a PR release. After a long string of accidents and deaths at major construction projects throughout the city, why else would he present such a glowing picture of a company with an inglorious past?

Still it was puzzling that Columbia University's top management failed to acknowledge all the safety problems, related deaths, fraud, and manslaughter investigations by the FBI, the US Attorney's Office for the Eastern District of New York, and the Manhattan DA's office. University decision makers had to know that a worker died at one of the university's construction sites and that Bovis was the GC.

- 2010: Bovis was GC and Breeze National was their sub at 3229 Broadway when Jozef Wilk, a Breeze employee, fell to his death from a third-floor scaffold into an open elevator shaft at a Columbia University building that was being demolished. According to a Bovis senior vice president, Breeze had a safety supervisor on site at the time of the collapse. Breeze's permit was issued to its vice president Toby Romano Jr., who had been convicted of bribing an EPA investigator. In addition, the Building Integrity Commission found that he had ties to the Luchese crime family.

- January/February 2012: Bovis was GC and Pinnacle was their sub on West 57th Street when a crane operator struck a load of rebar, which caused it to fall from the building. They were fined $5,000.
- March 22, 2012: Bovis was GC and Breeze National was their sub at the 604–606 West 131st Street Columbia University demolition project. A worker was killed, and two other workers were seriously injured at the site. This was the fourth lawsuit against Columbia that cited dangerous conditions, in the wake of 59 building code violations at this site. OSHA cited the subcontractor Breeze for failing to safeguard workers.
- May 2012: Bovis was GC when a crane operator lost control and broke windows on the 10th floor of a building.
- August 2012: Bovis was GC at a Hunter College construction site on East 79th Street and was fined $12,000 after a crane operator was seen operating in an unsafe manner. Bovis was warned that fuel was leaking from the crane.
- October 2012: Bovis was GC when a 150-foot crane collapsed when slammed by an 80 mile-per-hour wind.
- November 2012: Bovis was GC when a fire caused the crane boom to break at Sydney University in Australia.

Construction Safety Violations under the 2008 Non Prosecution Agreement

Since the signing of the 2008 Non Prosecution agreement with the Manhattan DA, Bovis has been slapped with more than 225 safety violations at its building sites. Thirty-four of those violations, nearly 25 percent, involve fire-safety hazards, including the following fire-safety violations:

- 11 violations for smoking at a construction site
- 3 violations related to standpipes being blocked or not accessible
- 4 violations for improper, unsafe storage of flammable propane gas, oxygen, and diesel fuel
- 2 violations for welding without certification

- 6 violations for excessive amounts of debris
- 1 for failure to provide a fire extinguisher
- 2 for use of explosive-powered tools without certification
- 1 for no fire-safety manager present on a construction site
- 1 open, unprotected elevator shaft
- 1 worker being electrocuted

Deutsche Bank building Violation Problems

There were many violations throughout the Deutsche Bank building demolition and abatement project. Most of the safety and building violations started around March 2007, a month after the LMDC agreed to employ Galt as Bovis's subcontractor. The grossly negligent activity of Galt's employees raises the obvious question of why the LMDC did not fire both Galt and Bovis. Aside from a couple of strongly worded memos, instead of firing them, the LMDC's city and state appointees to its board of directors praised them.

The most damning memos came from the LMDC's safety contractor URS, hired in September 2004 to monitor and provide oversight and recommendations to the LMDC mainly through the LMCCC. They notified Bovis directly about critical safety issues identified and e-mailed the LMCCC and copied the LMDC. In the May–June 2007 time frame, URS sent approximately 54 e-mails about safety issues that required Bovis's immediate response. URS had three safety people on site to monitor and report safety issues and provided most of the project documentation.

A safety issue, when reported to Bovis, might have required a contract modification if Bovis, the engineer of record as per the contract with the LMDC, believed the change or action went beyond the scope of their contract—an odd and rare revelation in the Bovis-LMDC relationship. Contract modifications are approved by the LMDC contract officer who is paying for the project and who is also responsible for the project. It is unheard of to have a GC decide on contract modifications or determine the scope of the contract. LMDC contracting officers should have been the ones to determine if the task was within scope or not. If this was the case, then URS notified LMDC of the change. The URS e-mail letter mentioned that when staffing was needed in December 2006, they responded immediately but that the funding from LMDC took seven months to process. URS also stated that LMDC supervisors were no longer on the site, so it could no longer report its concerns directly. It's interesting that the LMDC dragged its payment to URS but gave millions to Bovis and Galt within a week or two. What happened to the safety people and administrators from the LMDC? Why were they pulled from the project?

The next URS memo to the LMDC came on August 3, 2007, detailing both Bovis's and Galt's lack of response to safety issues. The frustrated tone of the letter detailed Bovis's failure to perform its contractual obligations. For several months, URS tried to persuade Bovis to remove garbage and debris. It was rumored that on a number of occasions Bovis begged Galt employees to do their work. The memo asked the LMDC to step in and hire an outside agency to perform the work Bovis had been hired to do and back bill Bovis or withhold payments to show that the LMDC meant business.

Meanwhile, several accidents occurred resulting in injuries, pointing out the fact that fire-watch safety issues were ignored. Multiple times expired permits had caused work delays. Accumulations of garbage and debris triggered small fires because Bovis failed to provide adequate manpower. Even though Bovis was still responsible for project management and building safety, it was once again living up to its reputation of blatantly disregarding contractual obligations and adherence to critical safety standards.

On January 29, 2010, the LMDC's Emil sent a letter to Bovis, approximately two and a half years after URS had requested the LMDC do so. The memo stated that the LMDC and LMCCC were very concerned about the number of safety accidents at the Deutsche Bank building site that could have been prevented if safety measures had been taken. They demanded no deviations from the approved implementation plan or permit drawings. Any employee that deviated from the plan must be removed immediately, and all fires must be reported to 911. The memo also asked for Bovis to make senior staff changes and to report back in two days with improved safety changes.

Following Bovis's abysmal track record, it's astonishing that the LMDC and LMCCC were still working with Bovis. After a series of accidents and safety issues in 2006, 2007, 2008, 2009, 2011, 2012, and 2013, the notion of giving Bovis another chance to redeem itself is beyond ludicrous.

Prior to the August 18, 2007, fire, over a two-month period, there were eight fires that went unreported to the FDNY. There were inadequate fireguards and often not enough fire extinguishers available. Worse still, during the August 18 fire, the site-safety manager and contractor's emergency coordinator were not in the building—a violation of the Emergency Action Plan. Following the August 18 fire, there were a total of 27 stop-work orders applied by either the DOB or the FDNY between March 2009 and May 2010. In January 2010, Bovis and its subcontractor were hit with more than a dozen safety violations.

Safety inspectors knew that there was a complete disregard for safety rules and procedures. Review of internal documents provides indisputable proof that many fires were started and that all warnings were ignored. The contractor and subcontractor were warned a dozen times to add more fireguards. As safety inspectors from Site Safety LLC, a contractor hired by URS, and FDNY inspectors walked the 6th floor, nine days after the tragic fire, they found many cigarette butts and a Weber charcoal grill. City, state, and federal safety inspectors regularly inspected the site, yet none did anything to stop the practices that led to the blaze.

One inspector reported that while making his rounds he found gasoline cans, metal compression tanks used to hold gas, and other fire-related safety hazards in the plywood shanties. He instructed Bovis and Galt supervisors to have them removed immediately. The following week, a Bovis supervisor told him to stay out of all shanties.

One of the safety inspectors said that the fire was not accidental. Hardly 15 minutes after the fire was noticed; the flames were already huge. The safety inspector believed that an accelerant had been used, because the thick steel frame beams had been bent in the area where the fire had started and the plywood shanty had been reduced to charcoal powder. It takes an enormous amount of heat to produce those results.

Just prior to the fire there were large piles of debris and flammable substances on the 17th and 18th floors.

Some of the firefighters that battled the blaze felt that the fire was fueled by accelerants. Rumors persisted that Galt's or Bovis's people had deliberately started the fire because there was supposedly no more money to fund the project and they wanted to get fired from the job. They never expected the FDNY to send firefighters into the building, because the shift was over and no one was supposed to be in the building and also because the building was still toxic due to asbestos and other contaminants. They expected that the FDNY would battle the fire from outside the building. In support of that theory is the fact that there were 9 to 10 fires in the Deutsche Bank building on July 31, 2007. There was only one fire-watch person and no safety people present. That fire-watch employee put out all the fires with fire extinguishers. The FDNY wasn't called.

After a second cutting of the standpipe was found, various groups called for the firing of Bovis. Caswell Holloway, acting for Deputy Mayor Skylar, stated that Bovis would not be fired but never said why. Brad Gair, deputy commissioner of the Office of Emergency Management, said that Bovis's safety reports were all fraudulent. He was there for several weeks after the fire broke out. Bovis ignored him.

Galt reportedly filed a lawsuit against Bovis for wrongful termination. A safety manager stated that responsibility for safety issues could not be contracted or delegated to another party. Responsibility rested with the landlord (LMDC) and the general contractor (Bovis). The day after the tragic fire, the FDNY ordered Bovis and Galt to remove all accelerants from the building. There were dozens of acetylene-torch metal canisters, scores of propane gas tanks, and many gasoline cans.

OSHA and EPA stated that the stairwells needed to be covered in plastic and wood. They must have known that this was a fire violation because it made it impossible to leave the floor quickly. The FDNY was not consulted.

The stairwells were being demolished throughout the building, and the staircase opening was to be an erect opening (a door), not via an open area on the ground. This was a DOB violation, yet even though it was on almost every floor, no one from the DOB complained or did anything about it.

Whistle-Blowers

Helen Rocos

A pressing issue at the Deutsche Bank building site was the ongoing search for remains of victims from the 9/11 terrorist attack and collapse of the World Trade Center buildings. Close to 800 bone fragments were found on the building's roof. Helen Rocos, a certified asbestos handler with hazmat (hazardous material) training, was hired by Galt to search for human remains in April 2006. Rocos was ordered to remove her asbestos mask and to continue working without it. When she asked Galt and Bovis supervisors why she had to work without a mask, they said because she was scaring the other workers.

Rocos and other hazmat workers were told that asbestos had been removed from the roof. Rocos didn't believe this. Other workers believed what they were told and wore regular clothing and didn't take precautionary measures. They stopped occasionally to eat without washing their hands or faces and then continued working. Rocos watched them comb through dirt and debris for bones unprotected. In April 2006, the EPA stopped the search because asbestos was found in the dirt. Rocos quit her job with Galt.

Renee Sewell

Renee Sewell, a former Bovis employee who worked in New York and New Jersey, filed a class-action lawsuit because she and other employees had worked overtime but hadn't been compensated for it. The lawsuit sought unpaid wages, attorney's fees, associated costs, interest, and damages. Sewell's attorney said that she was happy with her settlement.

Marshall Greenberg

Marshall Greenberg notified his supervisors at Galt and Bovis about safety violations in the Deutsche Bank building. He took photographs of fellow workers smoking, drinking, using drugs, and stealing and turned these photos over to his employers.

His observations were corroborated by coworkers, safety inspectors, and the integrity monitor. Instead of taking action, his employers harassed and ridiculed him. Greenberg was warned and later given a written reprimand for having conversations with safety and government regulators.

Greenberg filed a lawsuit against Bovis and Galt. When he reported to work in April 2008, the harassment continued. Intent on being heard, Greenberg refused to back off. He compiled a detailed list of safety violations and sent them to Bovis, who responded by placing him on paid administrative leave for several months starting in October 2008. Greenberg's paid leave ended in May 2009, and his union continued to deny him work, regardless of his seniority.

Rodrigo Barros

Rodrigo Barros was another asbestos worker hired by Galt. When he asked his supervisor for a replacement air cartridge for his asbestos mask respirator, he was fired. When he filed a lawsuit with the US Department of Labor, OSHA opened an investigation and agreed that the lawsuit had merit. Galt wasn't intimidated and refused to hire Barros back.

In January 2007, OSHA fined Galt $1,600 for asbestos workers not wearing proper respiratory masks. In October 2010, a federal judge ordered Mitch Alvo and Dorota Lebowska to pay Rodrigo Barros $55,000 in back pay.

Thanks to OSHA, Barros won his lawsuit and was compensated. But he never got his job back.

Despite Galt's long history of flagrant disregard for employee safety, the LMDC and the DA's office never lifted a hand to help these wronged workers. These workers knew they'd face repercussions from Galt, and still they had the courage to speak out against life-threatening violations. Like other construction workers, all they wanted was to work in a safe environment, but all their efforts were for naught.

Ultimately New York City's construction workers benefited from the push for work-site safety. Effective July 1, 2008, a city law prohibiting smoking at construction or demolition sites went into effect. The DOB and FDNY issued 932 violations for smoking on work sites and for not posting no-smoking signs. Fines ranged from $1,200 to $2,400 per violation. In less than a year, New York City supposedly made $1.8 million from smoking violations—if the companies paid the fines.

DEUTSCHE BANK BUILDING FIRE
TIME FRAME: 2005 - 2012

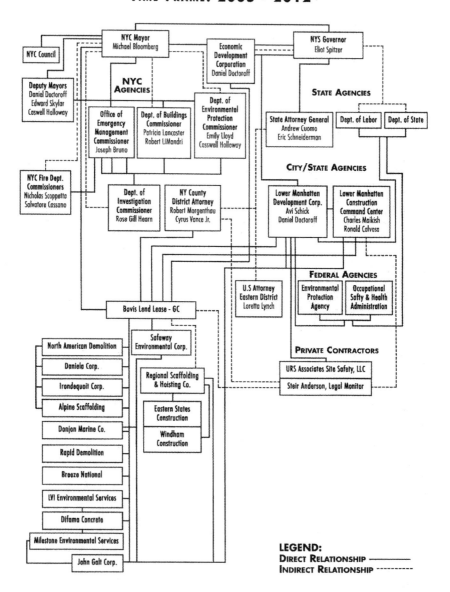

LEGEND:
DIRECT RELATIONSHIP ——————
INDIRECT RELATIONSHIP -------------

~ 8 ~

Department of Buildings (DOB)

The DOB was rife with corruption and unscrupulous, shoddy builders, architects, engineers, and developers.

The DOB is responsible for safeguarding the occupants of more than 975,000 buildings and properties by enforcing New York City's building and electrical codes, along with the city's labor laws and zoning requirements. In April 2002, Bloomberg appointed Patricia Lancaster commissioner of the city's Department of Buildings (DOB). Six years later, in April 2008, he accepted her resignation.

During Bloomberg's administration, the emphasis was on real estate and construction development. Perhaps this was due to the destruction of Lower Manhattan from the 9/11 terrorist attacks on the World Trade Center. In an aggressive effort to rebuild the city, the speed of development went unprecedented, but safety codes and requirements weren't rigidly enforced.

Reportedly, Lancaster took her job seriously and was too naive and honest to be a Bloomberg pawn. Fully aware of the long list of construction mishaps throughout the city, she was quoted saying that she would be afraid to walk under a building scaffold in New York City.

Following a crane collapse at a 43-story building, she went on record saying that the building permit should not have been issued since the area was zoned for no more than 30 stories. Year after year, building collapses, walls caving in, and crane accidents were commonplace. Repeatedly, people and workers were injured or killed in avoidable accidents.

The DOB's function is to safeguard, maintain, and rebuild the city's infrastructure, among other things. Despite the DOB's importance, New York City has neglected to support and properly fund this agency.

The DOB was rife with corruption and unscrupulous, shoddy builders, architects, engineers, and developers. With the city's unprecedented real estate and construction growth, one would expect the DOB to have the manpower and resources required to function properly. But stories of corruption, mismanagement, lack of inspections, and deficient policy/ code enforcements were rampant.

According to Jerry Russo, Bloomberg's press aide, and the DOB's Brian Keller, the updated 2008 DOB penalty assessment and enforcement policies were as follows:

For civil penalties under the construction codes, there were three categories:

1: $1,000–$25,000, major infraction
2: $10,000, infraction
3: $500, minor infraction

The penalty for working without a DOB permit on a one- or two-family home is a minimum of $500 for a residential dwelling, and a larger building has a minimum penalty of $5,000. Yet the agency failed to differentiate violations for residential and commercial buildings in terms of size and type. And once a violation was issued, there was no method of enforcement to ensure the fine was paid. Foreign governments and federal, state, or quasi-governmental agencies, such as the Port Authority and the LMDC, were exempt.

Despite the fact that the city made no effort to enforce payment, Bloomberg was adamant about having the federal and state government pay the city for DOB violation fines.

- Reportedly, Bloomberg wanted an impotent DOB so construction throughout the city could continue without interference. Meanwhile, the city's construction industry was rife with corruption. For example, a member of the DOB's Cranes and Derricks Advisory Council was hit with a 114-count indictment for bribing a crane inspector six times. He also bought copies of exams and intimidated a witness. Several other DOB inspectors were investigated on multiple charges

- A DOB inspector was arrested for filing a false crane-inspection report. The crane collapsed, killing seven people. During the ensuing investigation, a second DOB inspector was arrested for submitting a false report that he'd inspected a faulty crane.
- In 2006, two firefighters died in a Bronx 99 Cents Store. During the fire 10 firefighters fell through the floor because the engineer had illegally removed support beams in the basement and left weakened beams that couldn't support the firefighters' weight. It was learned that the engineer self-certified his work.
- In 2008, a bridge worker fell 35 feet while doing repair work on the Triborough Bridge. That same day, an office worker was injured. While these accidents were happening, DOB Commissioner Robert LiMandri was testifying on construction safety at a city council meeting.
- In 2010, a safety inspector certified to test for asbestos and lead in buildings and construction sites admitted that he'd never conducted the tests. For over 10 years he'd falsified reports at more than 200 building sites.
- In 2012, a crane accident on Manhattan's west side killed a construction worker.
- Mayor Giuliani changed DOB regulations to allow engineers to self-certify that their work was compliant with DOB codes and regulations. In the fall of 2007, the DOB started re-inspecting those buildings for which commercial engineers had submitted positive self-certifications. Out of the 155 locations inspected, 80 percent had problems. Over Bloomberg's three terms, engineers were still allowed to self-certify. It's more than apparent that engineer self-certification doesn't work, yet it appears that the city continues to use this practice.
- The city constantly used quick-fix solutions to resolve serious construction problems instead of taking long-term preventive measures.
- Building-violation penalties were seldom compatible with the gravity of the incidents, which were often incurred by uncaring and negligent construction companies. For example, if a worker died on a construction site due to unsafe practices, the penalty

would be $10,000. The worker's family would have to file lawsuits against the company involved that would take years to resolve. Another example: If an architect performed an unsafe excavation and performed only two of seven inspections and filed false paperwork, the people he caused pain and suffering must pay legal fees, emergency repairs, and engineering expenses initially of $50,000. And it could eventually cost them nearly $1 million to repair the multiple-dwelling building. The architect's fine would be less than $3,000.

- When New York City rezoned thousands of streets for real estate and construction development, the DOB's Doctoroff failed to hire and train building and crane inspectors. The deputy mayor's concern for New Yorkers' safety was blatantly obvious.

- In the wake of a long list of accidents largely due to hiring incompetent administrators and supervisors, Bloomberg added $20 million to the city's budget for IBM to develop computer software so that the DOB, FDNY, and EPA could share information on building and fire-safety violations and summonses. It is common practice to link data from varied corporate enterprises, so why not link data throughout city agencies? The shared-data project should have happened during his first term. Compared to former mayors, Bloomberg was the most computer literate.

- Since the Deutsche Bank building fire, the DOB did some housecleaning, updated its rules and regulations code book, and clarified procedures for violations for building penalties. There was a renewed hiring of administrative and building inspectors, and LiMandri replaced Lancaster as commissioner in January 2008. Doctoroff resigned as deputy mayor and from the LMDC board to work in the private sector for Bloomberg. The mayor moved the responsibility of the DOB to Deputy Mayor for Operations Ed Skylar, because he wanted the DOB to focus more on safety.

- In October 2007, the city increased the DOB's budget by $6 million and hired 48 employees. Yet with all these changes, the city's problems were far from over.

- By April 2008, 13 people had died in construction accidents, one more than in all of 2007.

- According to city statistics, showed that 29 laborers died between 2006–2007, and safety violations almost doubled at construction sites.
- In May 2008, the city added $5.3 million to the DOB budget and hired 63 safety inspectors.
- In 2002, there were 277 safety inspectors; in 2008, there were 461 inspectors, an increase of 66.4 percent.
- Construction-related accidents increased by 32 percent from 2011–2012 from 119 to 157.
- Construction-related injuries increased by 46 percent from 2011–2012 from 128 to 187.
- Federal Labor statistics show an increase in construction-related deaths from 28 in 2010 to 40 in 2011, an increase of 43 percent.
- The DOB cut construction inspections from a high of 244,000 in 2009 to 141,000 in 2012, a drop of 42 percent. There was also a decrease in construction- and safety-violation summonses of 6,600 in 2011–2012.

Insiders questioned why, when more safety inspectors had been hired four years before, there was a marked increase in accidents and deaths and also fewer inspections. There appears to be a direct correlation between the decrease in building and construction-safety inspections and the increase in accidents and fatalities, even though both Bloomberg and the DOB's new Commissioner LiMandri stated, more than once, that DOB employees are there to save lives.

Skylar developed the project that created Bloomberg's 33 safety recommendations. All recommendations were implemented by the City Council, and Bloomberg signed them into law. The major changes included a smoking ban at all construction sites; computerized data sharing between city agencies to enhance building, construction, and crane safety; and cross-training between agencies. The city enacted more-comprehensive plans and inspections for abatement and for demolition sites. DOB inspectors now had additional tools at their disposal, such as a standard inspection checklist, 30 hours of OSHA training, and a full week of on-the-job training with a Buildings

Enforcement Safety Team (BEST) inspector. Supervisors had monthly training and audit inspections with each DOB inspector.

With these changes, why were there more problems at construction-related sites?

With the resignation of Lancaster, Bloomberg inserted the DOB's second in command, LiMandri, as acting commissioner. Several months later the mayor wanted to promote his designee commissioner, but he had an obstacle to overcome: the DOB commissioner had to be a licensed engineer or architect, and LiMandri was neither.

The mayor overcame this detail by having the city council change the regulation. It is believed that the professional services of architects and engineers, as well as NYS Professional Engineers, sued the city to prevent the person responsible for all the public and private buildings in one of the world's largest and most complex city from being a mere administrative figurehead. However, with a wave of his pen, the mayor decreed that his appointee didn't need education or experience.

While LiMandri testified at his third city council meeting on construction safety, two construction-related accidents happened. At one of them, a laborer died. Because of the dramatic increase in construction accidents, the city's largest construction trade groups demanded that the DOB be removed and replaced with a public-benefit corporation similar to the School Construction Authority. Neither the city council nor the mayor could be swayed to change the status quo.

It was more than apparent that the mayor's biggest problem was placing incompetent people in leadership positions. When administrators were responsible for screw-ups, he didn't blame them. Instead an underling was blamed. Bloomberg was justifiably criticized for putting incompetent yes-people in charge of city agencies. The Bloomberg administration used smoke and mirrors to sidestep the blame and the responsibility for the accidents, injuries, and deaths that they caused.

DOB Problems at the Deutsche Bank building

The Manhattan DA's office released a report about the investigation of the Deutsche Bank building fire. The report cited city agencies for failing to do their respective jobs. DA Robert Morgenthau's comments on the DOB were as follows:

- DOB inspectors failed to adequately inspect and enforce the contractor's compliance. Despite being on site every day, DOB inspectors never once went to the basement area where the 42 foot gap in the standpipe existed. The DA's statement made mention of three separate breaches in the standpipe at different locations.
- DOB inspectors did nothing about the contractor's failure to maintain proper egress from the building. DOB inspectors knew, or should have known, that the building code required unobstructed egress and clear stairwells during demolition. In fact the stairways were blocked by unmarked containment barriers. The inspectors knew this but failed to recognize that it violated DOB code. More importantly, it created a severe safety hazard.
- Part of the failings can be attributed to the inexperience of the inspectors assigned to the Deutsche Bank building. Initially, the DOB sought to staff the project with inspectors from its BEST squad, which is comprised of inspectors who specialize in inspecting, among other things, deconstruction sites. This plan was altered, however, in the beginning of 2007 in favor of staffing the building with inexperienced inspectors who volunteered for the assignment. Neither team of inspectors traced the standpipe into the basement or otherwise discovered the 42-foot breach in the standpipe that happened in the fall of 2006.

DOB inspectors who volunteered for the assignment at the Deutsche Bank building had a minimum of five years' experience. They had to take and pass DOB classes on building safety and be certified before they could take on more-complex tasks. That level of experience would have provided them with greater technical knowledge, background, and insight than a building fire-watch person. I am a certified fire watch, and I had to pass an FDNY test comprised of basic, commonsense fire- and building-code violations. How was it possible that certified, professional building engineers knew less than a person with just basic common sense and no experience or professional training? It is incomprehensible that a certified DOB inspector, with five years of experience, can't recognize a standpipe or sprinkler system or other basic building code violations.

The DOI performed its own investigation into the administrative issues of the FDNY and DOB in relation to the Deutsche Bank building fire. The DOI pointed out that a DOB inspection-team task force had been created for the LMCCC to be stationed at the Deutsche Bank building. In February 2007, this task force moved into office space at 1 Liberty Plaza. The LMDC's offices are also at 1 Liberty Plaza, coincidently similar to the Safeway-Galt connection.

Results of the DOI investigation were as follows:

* March 2007: The DOB's LMCCC task force began inspections at 130 Liberty Street, effectively relieving the DOB's BEST inspectors from their periodic inspections of that building.
  June 25, 2007: DOB LMCCC inspector Aaron Williamson observed standpipe A capped on the 28th floor instead of the 31st floor and noted it had a plank of wood inserted through it.
* Unlike other locations, there was a full-time inspector stationed at 130 Liberty Street. The DOB hired four inspectors for the inspection team. Each inspector was required to have a minimum of five years' construction experience, but the inspectors had no experience with on-site safety or demolition projects. The BEST squad, whose function was inspecting site safety and demolition projects, periodically inspected the Deutsche Bank building. This BEST squad was required to contact the DOB LMCCC team for joint inspections for instructional purposes. However, this procedure was never followed. The DOB higher-level officials acknowledged that they never trained the DOB LMCCC team, nor did they tell the team what to inspect or what to look for.

* DOB executives informed the DOB LMCCC team that it was DOB policy that inspectors were not allowed to enter or inspect areas undergoing abatement or areas where there were stairwells or parts of the basement that were contaminated. Thus the inspectors stayed away from sections of the basement believed to be contaminated.

* Inspectors admitted that they never inspected the kick-out panels in the stairwells covered in thick plastic sheeting. They were also told not to go on abatement floors. The kick-out panels, covered in plywood (not fire-retardant plywood) and polyethylene sheeting (not fire-retardant plastic), were designed and approved by the city's Department of Environmental Protection and therefore not covered under their jurisdiction to inspect. The inspectors were only told to monitor the deconstruction process on the demolition floors. They further testified that they were never specifically told to check the standpipe, means of egress, or the site-safety log.

* Aaron Williamson reported the broken standpipe to supervisor Robert Iulo, who later testified that he could not remember that incident or any conversations with Williamson or a request for the standpipe to be tested. According to Williamson, Iulo never told Bovis to conduct a standpipe test, even though several people were aware of the break. The test would have validated the integrity of the standpipe from the street (Siamese connection) to the top most hose connection. Any breach—anywhere in the standpipe—would have been detected in such a test. This test was never performed.

* The DA's report found that Galt and individuals permitted to work with the company should never have been given this project in the first place. The manner by which they conducted this project and its lack of safety, which was part of a criminal investigation, was an underlying problem.

* When Williamson informed Iulo about the standpipe break on the 26th floor, he mentioned that he believed that the demolition of the building should be temporarily suspended while the standpipe was being repaired and then tested for other breaks.

Had the test been done, it would have revealed other breaks in the standpipe. This test might have led to additional testing of the second standpipe, which also had several breaks in it. Then possibly they would have tested the building's automatic and manual water pumps, and they would have discovered that they were also broken and useless.

✱ Instead, Iulo told his subordinate to continue working on the building and said that a cease-work order was not needed. He also told Williamson to omit the standpipe break from his report. The standpipe test was never performed. Williamson did what he was told and omitted the break from his official report. But Williamson prepared a second report that included the broken standpipe. He also took photos of the break in the standpipe. The paperwork covered him. When DOI and DA inspectors questioned him after the fire, he complied and produced the second report, with pictures.

✱ When Iulo was questioned by investigators, he denied seeing or hearing anything. New York City issued its own report that stated that none of the DOB inspectors assigned to the Deutsche Bank building had any experience with demolition projects and that they had no specific training for that particular building. One of the inspectors said that she didn't know what a standpipe was.

✱ Williamson said he instructed Jeff Melofchik, a Bovis supervisor, to repair a standpipe break immediately. Williamson returned a month later to find the standpipe still broken. He went to Melofchik and insisted that it be repaired immediately. This may have been a second break that Williamson found and not the one he'd reported to Iulo.

★ When the water was finally sent through the standpipes, a joint section broke off because of the water pressure. Yet in every weekly report Melofchik said that the standpipe was functional. Bovis had Williamson removed from the site and transferred to the Bronx because he was being difficult. The standpipe, by law, must be tested every time a floor is removed during deconstruction. The standpipe removal had to have started on the 40th floor, proving that the standpipes were never tested.

A DOB representative mentioned that the DOB inspectors for the Deutsche Bank building were still on that job and had not been replaced, since the fire. The inspectors never found the unsafe conditions, nor did they wear the protective gear necessary to find many of the building code violations. But now, post fire, they're required to have 30 hours of OSHA and 40 hours of site-safety training.

The FDNY Fatal Fire report said that a demolition permit was never filed and that the DOB never issued a demolition permit. Yet when Gilbane and later Safeway were scheduled to start the project, the task was clearly identified as an abatement and demolition of the building, and when Bovis and Galt took over in 2006, it was listed as a demolition project. But in 2007, the DOB issued alteration permits. Had a demolition permit been issued, the building would have required a working standpipe, sprinkler system, enclosed stairs, an unobstructed means of egress, and fireguards. Instead, the DOB issued alteration permits, generally one or two floors at a time. Alteration permits require building systems to be maintained and operational, excluding the floors covered by the alteration permit. An alteration permit requires functional standpipe and sprinkler systems, enclosed stairs, and an unobstructed means of egress.

By law, if a demolition permit had been issued, the building would have required inspections by city or state agency inspectors, instead of inspections by licensed professionals who, under an alteration permit, conduct such work for a landlord (LMDC). City officials tasked to improve oversight of demolition work concluded that the permits issued for the floor-to-floor dismantling of the building were adequate (even though they admitted that this was the most complicated deconstruction project ever attempted).

An example of a DOB-issued alteration permit can be found on the DOB website under 130 Liberty Street: job #110100587, "Remove Sprinklers in Building That Will Be Demolished." This was checked off as an alteration but not a substantial alteration. This official statement raises the question, how can a 40-story building's sprinkler system, even if damaged, be considered a minor alteration, especially when the title states that the building will be demolished?

A second example, in 2007, of an alteration but not a substantial alteration is job #104634148, "The Removal of Entire Floor." This type of listing went on for floor after floor after floor. This triggers the obvious question; Can the removal of an entire New York City block floor be considered a minor alteration?

LiMandri released a statement saying that DOB supervisors would be disciplined for failing to properly train inspectors at the Deutsche Bank building. The supervisors knew the inspectors were not properly trained but did nothing about it. The disciplinary action taken against these men was that they would no longer have supervisory roles in the Deutsche Bank building. The three DOB officers involved were Thomas Connors, executive director of construction site safety; Christopher Santulli, acting commissioner of emergency and safety operations; and Robert Iulo, supervisor. Iulo retired rather than take this disciplinary action. None of the officials were financially penalized; they continued to receive their $100,000-plus salaries, and their pensions were secure.

Two and a half years after the fire, the Deutsche Bank building had additional safety teams from a multitude of companies. Over a dozen DOB inspectors and engineers would visit the work site and interact with the six on-site, full-time DOB inspectors. During this period, safety violations and stop-work orders were issued.

A request for fairness and common sense came out of all these demands for job-safety scrutiny. The president of the Real Estate Board of New York said that the city needs to be clear on stop-work orders. When, why, and how long can the stop-work order be enacted? He stated that it often takes too long to get the crews back up to functional level after the stop-work order has been rescinded. This leaves people out of work, puts projects behind schedule, and escalates the costs associated with the project. There must be some sensible balance and negotiated agreements instead of arbitrary and subjective responses.

~ 9 ~

Environmental Protection Agency (EPA)

Safety experts and the FDNY pointed out that the EPA's restrictive directives prompted the contractors to find contaminant-cleaning shortcuts. Their strict adherence to the EPA's requirements resulted in the deaths of two firefighters.

Since September 11, 2001, the EPA was involved in the administrative decisions on air quality and the control of toxic carcinogens within Lower Manhattan. EPA decisions have been questionable and costly. The destruction of the World Trade Center buildings created an unsafe environment. Ash permeated the environment and made people sick. The ash deposits contained the pulverized remains of buildings, concrete, glass, metal, jet fuel, people, and thousands of other elements that traveled for miles into the surrounding areas.

Manhattan residents and employees questioned the safety of returning to their homes and work locations. The fires from the rubble of the Twin Towers burned for weeks. I worked for the US General Services Administration, a federal entity responsible for telephonic and data systems for most government agencies. We worked around the clock to try to restore telephone service for ourselves and other federal agencies. As we worked on the roof of the federal building on Broadway to install cell phone antennas, we had a "spotter" whose job was to watch for smoke coming off the destroyed buildings. If the wind shifted and the smoke headed our way, he would signal us to remain indoors until the wind shifted the smoke away from us.

First responders and rescuers searched for survivors buried in the rubble. They later searched for human remains so that they could notify families about loved ones who had perished. They had no "spotters." Those grieving, hardworking people from all walks of life relied on

147

what EPA professionals told them. Two days after the Twin Towers fell, Mayor Giuliani and EPA Federal Administrator Christine Whitman, the former governor of New Jersey, announced that the air quality was safe around Ground Zero. The first responders believed them. Many of them took this lie to their graves.

But the air quality wasn't safe. In 2006, EPA scientist Doctor Cate Jenkins, a senior chemist with more than 30 years of experience, said that the EPA knew that the air was dangerous around Ground Zero and falsified documents so that the public would believe the air was safe. She brought the documentation to the EPA's inspector general, Congress, and the FBI. In 1990 Jenkins had exposed EPA lies and falsification of records about the dioxins in Agent Orange, which the government used to deny veterans health benefits.

EPA Region 2's New York office attempted to stifle her, and the White House edited the EPA press release, deleting any warnings about 9/11. It was more than obvious that this wasn't an altruistic response but a politically motivated one to keep the stock market open and to give the impression that the environment was safe and that New York City's financial district was up and running as it always was.

At the end of 2010, the EPA fired Jenkins on trumped-up charges. She fought for her job by filing a grievance with the Merit System Review Board (MSPB). The board ruled that her job be reinstated, with back pay and interest. Instead of obeying the MSPB's ruling, the EPA kept Jenkins on paid administrative leave for more than a year and then refiled charges against her in 2013. On September 9, 2014, Public Employees for Environmental Responsibility (PEER) and Jenkins filed a lawsuit against the EPA for not changing the 1980 standard on alkaline, corrosive properties of dust from the destruction and demolition of large buildings.

With the help of PEER, the MSPB again ruled against the EPA. As of this writing, the EPA hasn't changed its policy and hasn't reinstated Jenkins despite several court rulings. Because of the EPA's negligence and blatant lies, more than 33,000 people suffered lung and respiratory problems and cancers from the toxic 9/11 air.

The US government continues to fight against paying health claims from 9/11-caused illnesses by limiting the time frames in which affected people can file claims under the Zadroga 9/11 Health and Compensation Act. Following the destruction of the World Trade Center, first responders working in the midst of corrosive dust suffered permanent damage to their respiratory systems and irreversible chemical burns. EPA critics pointed out that the agency promoted miscommunication on various levels.

In 2002, the EPA ordered General Electric to dredge the Hudson River in order to remove PCB contaminants. When costs reached $750 million, the project was stopped because it stirred the toxic chemicals back into the water. In 2015, New York State legislators asked General Electric to dredge the upper Hudson River again. This year they expect to complete 2.6 million cubic yards of PCB-contaminated sediment. Do they expect a different outcome from 2002?

In 2010, the EPA pressured the Department of Education (DOE) to test the air for PCB chemicals emanating from window caulking. It's possible that every school built between 1950 and 1977 may fail those tests. Then what? Many observers questioned the validity of the tests because the EPA couldn't confirm that exposure to PCBs, at the level of 50 parts per million, is dangerous.

There were other reasons for questioning the validity of air testing. A safety inspector with 10 years' experience admitted that he falsified test results. He was told to test for asbestos and lead contaminants in buildings and construction sites throughout New York City. In 2010, he admitted that he never performed the tests. Manhattan's US attorney questioned whether other inspectors had falsified test results.

There were unconfirmed reports that Doctoroff pressured the FDNY to approve temporary certificates of occupancy so that real estate salespeople could rent the lower floors of high-rise buildings while construction continued on upper floors. There were many fires in these partially constructed buildings. It was rumored that Doctoroff also pressured construction companies to complete projects quickly, which would, in turn, put quality and safety concerns on the back burner so that reconstruction deadlines could be met.

Present since the inception of the Deutsche Bank building project, the EPA was instrumental in implementing and enforcing stringent regulations. Because of their rules, Gilbane dropped out of the project when the EPA wouldn't approve their demolition plan. Following the EPA's erroneous assessment of the air quality downtown, the agency announced that it would contain and remove any asbestos or other contaminants in the Deutsche Bank building.

LMDC president Emil and chairman Schick walked through the 130 Liberty Street building the day before the horrific fire. They publicly announced that the EPA had approved the dismantling of the building after evaluating the contractor's plans for containing toxic chemicals so that they're not released outside the building. EPA officials from Washington and New York conducted weekly meetings with city and state officials. Governor Pataki kicked off the first few meetings, and Governor Spitzer led the rest.

During the first meeting, Schick said that a DOB inspector, along with inspectors from the EPA and the state labor department, would be at the Deutsche Bank building every day to check for environmental hazards. He also said that work could be stopped if any of the inspectors found any unexpected debris, the size of a dime, within an area the approximate size of an acre.

In February 2005, when the EPA rejected the Gilbane plan to demolish the Deutsche Bank building, the neighborhood and local politicians welcomed the EPA with open arms and prayed for the EPA's severe regulations. It was mentioned in the press that the LMDC had hoped to have the building dismantled in 2004 but that with the EPA's changes it would take longer. Some local community groups felt that the EPA did not go far enough in their asbestos- and toxic-containment efforts. Ironically, it was the EPA that demanded the internal fans, along with sealing the means of egress. If the windows, stairwells, and any area that might allow toxic particles to escape had to be sealed with wood, plastic, and glue on every floor, then why did the EPA allow holes to be created between floors, which allowed the smoke and fire to travel through the interior of the building?

The FDNY left the project when Gilbane's plan was rejected. The new plan from the LMDC and Bovis did not have FDNY input, but it had the DOB's. Why didn't anyone speak up about codes and regulation violations? With all that Bovis, the LMDC, and John Galt ignored, why did they carry out the EPA mandates that violated every safety-code regulation? To this day, the questions remain unanswered.

In 2008, when work had ceased because of the fire, the EPA was criticized for not approving the updated plans for abatement followed by deconstruction of the 130 Liberty Street building. The EPA countered by saying that the LMDC had taken five months to submit their plan and then had changed it two days later. When the EPA finally received the plan, there were protection changes included for the safety of first responders. These changes included wider staircases and relocated decontamination stations. The EPA's regional administrator rejected the LMDC's plan because the EPA wanted the same toxic-contaminant restrictions included. The EPA was determined to stick to their original plan.

Safety experts and the FDNY pointed out that the EPA's restrictive directives prompted the contractors to find contaminant-cleaning shortcuts. Their strict adherence to the EPA's requirements resulted in the deaths of two firefighters. In November 2008, OSHA fined Bovis for 19 safety violations, totaling $193,000. Galt was fined for 25 federal safety violations, totaling $271,000. With an additional 44 federal violations, the total fines amounted to almost $500,000. The violations and staggering penalties are astonishing considering that the EPA, state Labor Department, OSHA, DOB, and other regulatory inspectors were on the site every day since 2005.

~ 10 ~

Fire Department (FDNY)

*The FDNY had almost no knowledge of what was going on
in that building [Deutsche Bank building] regarding demolition
operations.*

—Deputy Chief

There was a rush to blame FDNY officers for not inspecting the
Deutsche Bank building. The accusations stemmed from the 15-day
rule, which states that every 15 days the FDNY will inspect buildings
in their area under construction and undergoing demolition. However,
FDNY field officers admitted that they never followed the 15-day rule,
unless they were officially ordered to do so, in writing.

During slow periods, some firehouses conducted building inspections
that concentrated on obvious violations visible to the inspection team. I
suspect that when city administrators realized they had no case for the
15-day rule, they didn't care and continued to press charges against the
selected officers.

There were several letters from FDNY chiefs that informed upper
management of potential problems with the 130 Liberty Street building.
On January 30, 2005, the first official notice was a memo from Battalion
Chief Robert F. Strakosch of hazmat operations to Robert J. Ingram,
chief in charge of hazmat operations. The Strakosch memo was his
review of the 130 Liberty Street Demo Emergency Action Plan (EAP)
created by Gilbane. The memo related his basic approval for the Gilbane
plan with some minor changes and stated that the Office of Emergency
Management (OEM) had also reviewed it. The OEM coordinates
actions between agencies and reports directly to the mayor. Part of
the OEM's function is to coordinate the operations of the NYPD and

FDNY. The Strakosch memo detailed the means of stairwell egress based on the numbers of workers on site. It also gave the contact number of the emergency coordinator and explained the methodology underlying attacking fires, along with decontamination plans and operations.

The memo also suggested that several different functional groups (e.g., hazmat, EMT, and local firehouses) should become familiar with the EAP and visit the site. The purpose of site visits for Division 1 units (which included firehouse 10/10 along with nearby firehouses) was to gain a working knowledge of the site (e.g., water access and means of egress) and to make sure the site's EAP was being adhered to.

The Strakosch memo concluded with the FDNY's recommendation that the FDNY should allow Gilbane to have the plan functional and have scheduled site visits to determine if it functioned to FDNY satisfaction. The Strakosch memo was written prior to the EPA's rejection of Gilbane's plan that lacked comprehensive procedures to contain the building's toxic contaminants. The Strakosch memo was sent through the FDNY chain of command on February 5, 2005, for a decision but was never put into action.

The FDNY was involved with plans to dismantle the Deutsche Bank building when Gilbane was part of the picture. This was the last time the FDNY was brought into strategy meetings involving the abatement of the Deutsche Bank building. When Bovis Lend Lease was awarded the contract, the FDNY was not consulted about the project.

On September 7, 2005, the LMDC created an Emergency Action Plan (EAP) that was approved by the EPA. Regional Scaffolding and Safeway Environmental were listed as the contractors on site. The plan outlined the abatement and deconstruction of the building as follows:

Phase I: Preparation phase
Phase II: Asbestos abatement and removal
Phase III: Structural deconstruction

This plan stated that the FDNY was involved in the planning and other aspects, such as emergency responses. The first mention of negative-pressure containment (the use of internal fans to keep asbestos and contaminants in the building) was Phase II. The FDNY said that it was never made aware of these fans. This poses the question, was the FDNY involved in the approval of the LMDC EAP or was it a copy-and-paste situation, with minor changes for EPA approval, from the Gilbane EAP? This plan was modified when Bovis was hired as the general contractor.

The Bovis, ATC & Galt Deconstruction Procedures Implementation Plan, dated September 19, 2006, references the LMDC plan and states adherence to all regulatory agencies' regulations, including DOB and FDNY rules and regulations. This latest plan was radically altered in February–March 2007 when Bovis and Galt enacted a simultaneous decontamination and deconstruction/demolition. When demolition was taking place on the upper floors, the lower floors were being decontaminated. The implementation of abatement and demolition simultaneously had never been done before. The frenetic rush to demolish the building created problems no one thought of.

Since the Deutsche Bank building had been purchased by a state entity (LMDC in 2004), why wasn't the NYS Office of Fire Prevention and Control (OFPC), a division of the NYS Department of Homeland Security and Emergency Services, called in, along with state and city agencies? The OFPC is responsible for state-owned buildings. The OFPC has performed over 35,000 safety inspections on approximately 15,000 state buildings in New York. This state agency was never mentioned by anyone involved in the EAP or the building-fire investigation.

In early 2005, FDNY Chiefs Siegel and Fuerch visited the site, which, at the time, was an empty office building with operational elevators. The visit was to gather information to create an action plan for minor fires and injuries that would be handled by the local firehouse or EMS ambulances. The responding firefighters would only respond to "clean areas" (areas that did not have contaminants). Site visits would be for the purpose of safety observations.

Around mid-2005, hazmat teams visited the site for surveillance and to recommend emergency action plans in the event that decontamination was necessary. Anyone who went into a contaminated area would have to wear a decontamination suit that covered their entire body and an asbestos-filter mask and then undergo a decontamination sequence when the visit was concluded.

Captain Bosco was in charge of Firehouse 10/10, directly across the street from the Deutsche Bank building. Neither Captain Bosco nor other members of his firehouse conducted inspections at the Deutsche Bank building. When asked why he didn't visit that building, he said because it was a toxic building.

Before Bosco arrived at firehouse 10/10, a letter from Battalion Chief William Siegel was posted that suggested weekly surveillances at the Deutsche Bank building. Reportedly, Bosco never went to inspect that building. In June 2007, Deputy Chief John Bley sent a memo to Bosco's firehouse saying to inspect buildings under construction every 15 days. Bosco still didn't inspect that building. Even though a pipe fell through the roof of his firehouse from the Deutsche Bank building in May 2007, he never conducted an inspection of the building. In August 2007, Bosco received a letter from Chief Norcross reminding him to take precautions and be aware of potential problems at that building. The evidence has shown that he still never inspected that building.

Why would an FDNY captain blatantly ignore multiple warnings about the Deutsche Bank building? Was it because he was never ordered by any of his superiors to inspect the building? In fact, the deputy chiefs who sent the June and August memos admitted that they had never enforced a 15-day-rule inspection in their entire careers. Other FDNY officers said the same thing.

All the field officers—lieutenants, captains, battalion chiefs, or deputy chiefs—had either heard about the 15-day rule but never enforced it or had never heard of the rule and never performed a 15-day-rule inspection in their 20 or 30-plus years with the FDNY. A different answer was played out at the Manhattan Borough Command where they were aware of the 15-day rule and expected that some type of monitoring system was in place for that type of building. At the executive level command, it was just the opposite of the field officers. They believed that building inspections were critical, a matter of grave importance, and they couldn't understand why they weren't being done. As for the pipe going through the roof, the commissioner and his executive-level staff went to the firehouse yet never asked if 15-day-rule inspections were being done. And they didn't order an inspection of the building.

It's important to point out the difference between the 15-day rule and FDNY building inspections. Special thanks to a deputy chief who explained the different procedures.

Prior to the Deutsche Bank fire, all units were scheduled to inspect buildings in their district during two three-hour periods a week (a total of six hours a week). Since the Deutsche Bank building fire, the number has been increased to three three-hour periods a week (a total of nine hours a week). During these inspection periods, firefighters would inspect buildings that were part of their annual goals. Since the Deutsche Bank building fire, they've created a new system for prioritizing these inspections. As part of this new program, every building in the unit's district is included and prioritized. The goal of these inspections was to inspect every building in the district over a five-year period, with high-priority buildings inspected annually. This building-inspection program was separate from the so-called 15-day rule, which only applied to buildings under construction or demolition. If it were complied with, the 15-day rule would include inspections in addition to the annual program. It was not clear whether these special inspections would have been done during the scheduled inspection period or at other opportunities when time was available. Also, it must be noted that fire companies were in service while performing building inspections. Thus, if a call came in while on inspection, they dropped everything and responded to the alarm. This was standard procedure.

The investigation mentioned the Strakosch memo of February 2005 that requested an operating procedure for fighting a fire in a toxic building, but the memo was ignored by the then Chief of Operations Salvatore Cassano. However, the Chief of the hazmat section stated that the standard operating procedure for fighting fires in high-rise buildings would be sufficient, with the probable inclusion of a decontamination process. The Strakosch memo gave the Gilbane Emergency Action Plan the green light. Once the plan was functional, they would determine if it was successful.

The Gilbane EAP was rejected, and Gilbane left the project. Battalion Chief Bill Siegel sent a notice in March 2005 stating that, due to the change in contractors, everything was on hold at the Deutsche Bank building. Thus, the Strakosch memo became a moot point.

In November 2005, Chief Bley sent Chief Sakowich a memo stating that the FDNY would attend advisory committee meetings with other agencies. The problem with this memo was that it referred to the LMDC Emergency Action Plan with Regional and Safeway as the contractors. This contract also never happened. It wasn't until February 2006 that a contract between the LMDC, Bovis, and Galt emerged. The DOI fought tooth and nail to prevent this contract, but the LMDC and the mayor's and governor's teams pushed it through anyway. The FDNY was never again invited back to any meetings regarding the Deutsche Bank building.

In April 2007, a lieutenant at firehouse 10/10 requested permission from Chief Sakowich to take firefighters into 130 Liberty Street in order to familiarize them with the building. He never received a reply.

A Deputy Chief cleared up several points of contention:

The 1ˢᵗ Division was not aware that demolition operations had commenced in 2005. The FDNY 1ˢᵗ Division was never provided with a demolition plan for review, nor was it given any information on what date that demolition or alteration was to take place or when it was to take place. To perform an inspection in a high-rise building, the procedure was that the division was sent a written request from headquarters to visit the building and make recommendations. We were not given any notification about the demolition of the Deutsche Bank building. Technically it was never a demolition since the only permits issued by DOB were for alterations.

The Fire Commissioner once commented that when demolition began, that signaled the requirement for the 15-day inspections. The problem with that was there was no actual signal. To my knowledge, the company, battalion, and division were never notified that demolition (alteration) operations were scheduled to commence or that they did commence. Even if the 15-day rule were commonly adhered to, how was the

Fire Department officers supposed to know when to start enforcing it without written notification?

In the *Fire Prevention Manual* in effect prior to the Deutsche Bank building fire, Chapter 5 is titled "Construction, Alteration, and Demolition Sites." It cites Chapter 11 of Title 3 (Fire Department) of the "Rules of the City of New York"—#11-01: Buildings in the Course of Construction and Buildings Undergoing Demolition. (Note: this section does not mention alterations.)

I never saw anything in writing that I should do a 15-day inspection other than this rule that was part of the "Rules of the City of New York" and a small section in the FDNY *Fire Prevention Manual*, which was deleted after the Deutsche Bank building fire.

It is my firm opinion that even if Engine 10 had done inspections of that building every 15 days as prescribed in the *Fire Prevention Manual*—(1) Surveillance Inspection, (2) Update building records, (3) Enforce Fire Department rules for demolition fires—the major factors that led to the tragedy would not have been found.

The spot inspection would be for information gathering rather than a comprehensive inspection. A comprehensive inspection of a building like 130 Liberty Street would not have been done by an in-service fire company. Certainly they would never have been given permission to don hazmat suits in order to do the inspection. Without access to the contaminated areas, they would never have seen the way the stairway system had been compromised. Regarding the standpipe system, an in-service fire company would not have the expertise to trace a complicated system, such as was installed in the Deutsche Bank building. It is extremely unlikely that they could have discovered that the system was out of service, if it indeed was. Based on newspaper stories, the cellar was contaminated with asbestos. That was apparently the reason that the pipe was cut. The NYS Office of Fire Prevention and Control takes two full days to inspect a high-rise building. A hazmat high-rise building would logically take longer.

In the Fatal-Fire Report it stated that companies would *conduct inspections of buildings under construction* when they received notifications of such from the Bureau of Fire Prevention. They even cited the notification form—A-102.

The *Fire Prevention Manual* (pre–Deutsche Bank building fire) Chapter 5 "special matters" regarding Construction and Demolition Operations included:

- 5.8.1: Companies discovering buildings under construction or demolition within their administrative districts shall inspect these sites every 15 days.
- 5.8.2: Notice of *demolition operations* about to commence shall be forwarded by Bureau of Fire Prevention on Form A-102 to Division and District Offices. Deputy Chiefs shall relay this information to the appropriate Battalion and Company for the purpose of
  - o Surveillance inspections during demolition period;
  - o Corrective maintenance of building records;
  - o Enforcing Fire Department rules for demolition fires.

The above quoted information is to reiterate that I cannot remember ever seeing a form A-102 and certainly never received one for 130 Liberty Street, the Deutsche Bank building. I was not aware that the Chief of Fire Prevention was ever asked why this section was not being complied with. In the Fatal Fire report, this issue was mentioned, but the ongoing investigation was cited as the reason for not knowing anything about it.

There is a difference between a rule and a policy. A rule to inspect buildings under construction/demolition every 15 days did exist, but there was no policy, procedure, or instruction requiring it to happen, because the policy in the Fire Department was that it didn't happen, and everyone knew it. It was a rule, but there was no policy to implement it, and that was the key difference. Evidence that there was no policy was the fact that the Division of Fire Prevention never sent the form A-102 to inform units of buildings under construction/demolition.

As for building inspections, the FDNY had a temporary inspection program authorized by Deputy Chief Richard Fuerch. In June 2007, firefighters on light duty would assist local firehouses in doing inspections for buildings under construction that they couldn't inspect every 15 days. The FDNY discontinued this program as well. Another FDNY inspection program, the Target Hazard Program, was more suited for problematic buildings. Under this system, a potentially dangerous building would be earmarked for mandatory inspections, a customized firefighting plan, and multiple unit drills. The unit was functional in 2007 but was discontinued by the FDNY before the Deutsche Bank building fire.

The FDNY Fatal Fire Report, produced one year after the fire, supported the Deputy Chief's comments when it stated, "At the time of the fire, there was no formal notification to the Fire Dept. when a building was undergoing demolition or construction."

Section 5.8.2 of the *Fire Prevention Manual* stated, "Notice of demolition operations about to commence shall be forwarded by the Bureau of Fire Prevention (NYS) on Form A-102 to Divisions and District Offices." It is not known why this section of the *Fire Prevention Manual* was not complied with.

At the time of the fire, there was no formal, written FDNY procedure for inspecting buildings undergoing asbestos abatement.

It should be noted that Chief of Operations Pat McNally created a specific firefighting plan for the Deutsche Bank building a week after the fire. McNally also issued new protocols for building inspections. Chief of the FDNY Cassano approved McNally's plan.

Each year and average of 100 firefighters die in the line of duty. To address this problem, the National Institute for Occupational Safety and Health (NIOSH), Centers for Disease Control and Prevention (CDC), has a program called the Firefighter Fatality Investigation and Prevention Program that conducts independent investigations of firefighter line-of-duty deaths. The Deutsche Bank building fire is report no. F2007-37.

The NIOSH report mirrors the FDNY Fatal Fire Report but provides more details about the internal fans. These fans not only kept the fire and toxins inside the building but actually forced the fire and smoke lower inside the building. The report cites the covered stairwells that prevented the firefighters from escape or rescue. Additionally it places the blame, liability, and accountability on the owner of the building (LMDC) for their obligations that were never performed, saying that the LMDC could not sign away responsibility to the general contractor and its subcontractors. An example of their recommended findings is that municipalities should establish a system for property owners to notify the fire department when fire-protection or fire-suppression systems are taken out of service (recommendation 16).

NFPA [National Fire Protection Association] 25: Standard for the Inspection, Testing and Maintenance of Water-Based Fire Protection Systems, per chapter 15, "Impairments," requires the building owner to establish a procedure for reporting impairments in sprinkler and standpipe systems to the local fire department. It is also the responsibility of the building owner to mark all the systems within the structure that are out of service.

This above recommendations triggers yet more questions:

- Why did the FDNY only briefly mention the fans and not mention that the fans were responsible for the smoke and fire dropping lower into the building?
- Why didn't the DA mention the internal fans in his report?

- Why didn't the DA hold the LMDC, the building's landlord, responsible for not performing their obligations of reporting and labeling building water systems that they knew no longer existed?

Observers contended that the seven FDNY officers blamed for not inspecting the 130 Liberty Street building were scapegoats. The charges against the men were for failing to ensure timely inspections before a fatal fire. Nine days after the fire, Bloomberg held a press conference where he stated that Fire Commissioner Scoppetta was reassigning three officers—Division 1 Commander Richard Fuerch, Battalion 1 Commander Battalion Chief Steve McDonald, and Company Commander Engine 10 Captain Peter Bosco. And then there was no official news until June 2009— 22 months later—when it was announced that seven officers would be disciplined because of the Deutsche Bank building fire. Initially the discipline against the seven officers was to be a command discipline. With command discipline, a letter of the charges is placed into your personnel folder, and then, if no further discipline arises, the letter is removed from your folder one year later. However, the discipline was changed at the last minute, without notice, into letters of reprimand, which would be a permanent part of the officers' records. To fight this blatant miscarriage of truth with a trial, the recipients could face dismissal and loss of pension.

The 15-day rule was used by the city administration and accepted by the DA as the only mechanism to place blame on the FDNY. This was far different from the simple scolding the DOB supervisors received. No one in the DOB was penalized, indicted, or blamed even though their responsibility and trained employees were constantly in that building.

Another aspect of the investigation raised eyebrows. When firefighters were called to testify before the grand jury, they were asked to appear before the general counsel for the city first (a request they refused), followed by an interview with the DA. This added level of scrutiny poses the question, if you're going to put FDNY personnel through rigorous scrutiny, shouldn't the same level of scrutiny be applied to DOB personnel?

Let's not forget that there were five inspectors and three DOB officers, and all of their responses sounded similar, as if they'd been coached by lawyers. If the general counsel of the City of New York and the city were paying for all the legal fees, why wouldn't the firefighters speak with the general counsel? As explained by a high-level officer, the firefighters refused to meet with the city's general counsel because they did not want to be "coached by the city's attorneys." Notice that the EPA, the LMDC, and state and city administrators were never mentioned and never penalized.

Both FDNY unions, the Uniformed Firefighters Association (UFA) and the Uniformed Fire Officers Association (UFOA) were outraged that the FDNY brass would file charges against those officers. They believed that the FDNY commissioner and the Bloomberg administration should have taken responsibility for not doing their jobs. Union leaders along with leaders of the Skyscraper Safety Campaign, headed by Sally Regenhard, and the 9/11 Parents & Families of Firefighters, headed by retired FDNY chief James Riches, all called for the Manhattan DA, the state attorney general, and the US attorney to pursue the investigation into the responsibility and actions/inactions of the LMDC and city, state, and federal officials, including commissioners involved with the Deutsche Bank building. All pleas were ignored.

As an echo to the security the political appointees enjoyed after giving testimony to the grand jury, FDNY Commissioner Scoppetta said that he would be surprised if anyone from the FDNY faced criminal charges. Confidential sources hinted that he was privy to the fact that "the fix was in" and that no one, in any city, state, or federal agency, would have to lose any sleep over criminal charges.

What should the FDNY have done to make fighting fires in high-rise buildings safer? From compiling and analyzing information and public records from myriad respected and expert sources, and as an ordinary citizen and not a firefighter or safety expert, I strongly believe that in addition, the following questions need to be answered to ensure firefighters safety.

- Real-time knowledge of every firefighter that enters and leaves a building

- Detailed awareness of when responders need to be rotated out and replaced with fresh responders
- When firefighters use their air tanks, how much air remains? Should the firefighter be replaced or given a replenished air tank?
- How can a lost firefighter be found and led to a safe area?
- How long have firefighters been in the building without water to fight the fire?
- How much heat and smoke are firefighters dealing with, and are they moving toward or away from the fire?
- Lipstick (micro) cameras that can transmit live video to the command truck
- Ear-insert, Bluetooth-type cell phones to be able to autodial the command truck if radio transmissions are not going through
- CADD drawings from the DOB available at the command truck to provide a schematic layout of the building interior for every building a firefighter enters
- Layer-type software programs that can overlap the CADD drawings to pinpoint every firefighter in and around the building—The software should be able to determine the firefighter's name, job function, engine/truck company, blood type, allergies, and other vital information. This information should be transmittable to a local hospital.

Most of the above suggestions are being considered, and some are in the process of evaluation with the hope of being implemented. The software technology I mention is called Radio Frequency Identification Technology (RFID). If RFID technology can be combined with Global Positioning System (GPS) technology, it will be a powerful tool that will make firefighters safer while battling large fires. Field testing is much more difficult than laboratory testing, and it takes longer to be evaluated. I hope and pray that this type of technology will be implemented in the near future.

Interview with Deputy Chief

The following are additional questions and answers from my interview with the Deputy Chief who wished to remain anonymous.

What is your viewpoint and opinion about the FDNY's management of the Deutsche Bank building before and after the fire?

From my point of view, our main concern at that time was that we had several minor fires and emergencies in a contaminated building, so we had to determine how we were going to deal with this. Do we wear Scott masks? What if we have to pull someone out, treat somebody? Do we need to be decontaminated, and if so, how are we going to do that? These were my concerns. Bill Siegel (Battalion Chief) had gone down there at my request, but contrary to what some people believe, to my knowledge he never went into the building. He spoke to a construction supervisor on the outside, got some information, and he sent me a memo. We exchanged e-mails with each other about the Deutsche Bank building. When the newspapers reported that I ignored his memos, that was blatantly false. I had an e-mail trail that they were not aware of. I was able to prove this at the grand jury, at the FDNY hearing, and other official interviews. They quickly dropped the idea that I ignored his memos. However, I was shocked that these memos were still prominently quoted in the district attorney's report, after I was told that those memos were no longer an issue. I can only wonder at why that happened.

Bill Siegel had been assigned to rescue companies during his career, and he had contacts in hazmat. He discussed the Deutsche Bank building issue with people in rescue and hazmat, and he got back to me via e-mail as to what our operations should be. Hazmat people suggested that if we follow our standard procedure (basic operations), we would be fine. Hazmat suggested that, in addition, a squad company should be routinely assigned on a basic response to assist in the decontamination of people as they came out. Also a Battalion Chief should respond on every call to supervise operations. This was implemented.

I don't know this firsthand, but I was told that, because of Bill Siegel's involvement, a hazmat crew went to the Deutsche Bank building and they did a survey. I was never notified of this, and I wasn't copied on their actions, but, after the fire, I learned that their visit generated reports through the SOC [Special Operations Command] chain of command, which included the Chief of Hazmat up to the

Chief of Operations (although, not to or through the 1st Division; the 1st Division was never informed of these visits), which was apparently the final termination point.

I have personally seen those documents. They were shown to me during the course of the postfire investigation. I only became aware of this after the fire. This was the involvement of hazmat, and I don't know what happened to their reports or their suggestions. Based on information I have come to learn, it was shortly after these events in 2005 that Bovis took over.

LMDC was in charge of the building from the time they purchased it from the Deutsche Bank Corporation in a legal deal that was supposed to result in its rapid demolition, and they originally had another construction company there; it might have been Gilbane, but I'm not sure. The last of three memos I received from Bill Siegel, in March of 2005, stated that due to the change in contractors everything was on hold at the Deutsche Bank. With the exception of being aware that a search for human remains had taken place at the Deutsche Bank building, that was the last I heard until May 2007, when a pipe fell off the building into the firehouse next to the Deutsche Bank building. During a period of time, about a year prior to the fire, human remains, presumably from 9/11, had been discovered in the building, and a meticulous search had been implemented. FDNY personnel were involved in that search. To my knowledge, that operation was coordinated out of the Manhattan Borough Command.

When you conducted a walk-through visit in 2005 of the empty Deutsche Bank building, did you wear a protective asbestos garment or a protective filter mask?

No, we did not wear filter masks. I was told that the areas we would visit were "clean," i.e., not contaminated with hazmat. I don't remember the specific layout—it was eight years ago—but as I recall, we entered the loading dock and took a freight elevator to an upper floor, where that particular elevator lobby was clean. I was told that in order to enter the contaminated area, you would have to go through a series of curtains. We did not enter that area. There was a decontamination room for anyone leaving the contaminated area. By the way, I would not have donned just a filter mask. If the air was contaminated enough to require a mask, my clothing could also have become contaminated. Decontamination would then have been required. If I had wanted to enter the contaminated area, I would have had to suit up in protective clothing, including a filter mask.

I was detailed to Ground Zero during the cleanup for the entire month of February 2002, and it was well known that no one from the FDNY was allowed in the Deutsche Bank building. I think some hazmat people went in. I don't know why they went in, but later we heard that there was a black-mold problem, in addition to the asbestos and other contaminants. Apparently, there was constant water leaking into that building, which helped the mold to form.

LMDC safety subcontractor company URS sent letters about safety violations to enforce safety measures. They were sent to Bovis, the LMCCC, and the LMDC to get their subcontractor John Galt to remove the large piles of debris on the floors of the Deutsche Bank building, without much success. The building's sprinkler system never worked.

I believe that is correct about the sprinkler system not working since 9/11. It's conceivable that the FDNY would allow the sprinkler system in an unheated building to remain out of service, as long as other measures, such as fire-watch personnel and additional extinguishers, were implemented. While safety measures, including debris removal and notification of FDNY for any fire, were very important, and apparently not complied with, the most grievous noncompliance was the scheme they used to isolate the floors being contaminated. In direct contradiction to the NYC building code, they removed the fireproof enclosures of the stairways, and they installed horizontal barricades which prevented the stairway from being used as means of egress and as a safe area from which egress could be made or a hose line could be stretched.

What knowledge did the FDNY have of the Deutsche Bank building prior to the fire?

I was not aware that demolition operations had started after 2005. I think that from 1st Division down the chain of command, FDNY had almost no knowledge of what was going on in that building, regarding demolition operations. As for the rest of the FDNY, I don't know. Division 1 had a response protocol in 2005, and that was described in Bill Siegel's memo. Regarding FDNY policy when they responded to a dispatch for that building, units would respond to the loading-dock area where the freight elevator was. As per the Standard Operating Procedures (SOP) in effect at that time, the first due ladder company would take the elevator to a floor below the reported emergency and walk up the stairs to evaluate the situation, and that was basically the initial operation. You must realize that when that response protocol was created [the Deutsche Bank building] was basically an empty office building, with operational interior elevators. In March 2005, I was notified by Chief Siegel that everything was on hold regarding any demolition plan. The contractors changed hands, and Division 1 was never directly notified of anything regarding demolition operations. Other than the search for human remains, I was not notified of what was going on from the borough level or at the battalion level. There were times when communications may have bypassed the division and went directly from the borough to the battalion level in terms of meetings.

Why weren't the firefighters pulled out if there was no water to fight the fire?

My first answer to that question is that as it became apparent that water was not going to be available in a timely manner and that conditions were deteriorating, firefighters were ordered to evacuate. Unfortunately, because of conditions in the building, that became a tremendous challenge.

Firefighters were initially told by construction personnel that the standpipe was operational. It is not unusual for firefighters to encounter situations where the primary source of water is not available. In those cases, alternatives are sought. That can mean anything from supplying the standpipe via a stairway outlet to opening or closing section valves or stretching a hand line up a stairway or up the outside of the building. Also, they would normally take refuge in a safe area, such as the fireproof stair or the floor or floors below the fire, awaiting water supply. Again, because of the unusual conditions encountered, this was not possible in some locations.

This building did not have a protective stairway on the floors where the fire started, and the fire and smoke spread; all [the firefighters] had were the outside elevator and exterior scaffold stairways. This was very unusual, and I believe that the first commanders on the scene were not aware that there were no interior means of egress from the fire floors and the floors below. Thus, normal operations for a vacant building or a building under construction or demolition is to retreat to a place of safety, such as a stairwell, if conditions deteriorate. To put it bluntly, from the very beginning the shit was hitting the fan. The information was coming into the commanders at a rapid rate. I believe they did try to pull firefighters out early when they realized they couldn't get water and especially when they began to receive mayday signals and the fire was rapidly getting out of control. Commanders probably thought the firefighters on the fire floors and floors below were in a safe-enough area that they could just back down the stairs. Like I said, this would have been [the case] in a normal situation. Once the fire commanders realized that this was not a normal situation, they had to come up with alternatives (and very quickly they did call for an evacuation of the fire floors).

I assume that you reviewed the Fatal Fire Report? A short time after they realized that they couldn't get water from the standpipe, they were trying to stretch a hose line down the side of the building, and I believe that Engine 24 eventually manned that line. Fire commanders were trying to deal with the fire and the situation getting out of control in real time. Decisions were based on many factors which they were aware of and which they eventually became aware of. They soon realized there was no water in the standpipe system, and there could have been a number of reasons for that. It could have been a broken pipe or a valve that had been closed. An FDNY Pumper could pump water and bypass the inoperable section of the standpipe. They wound up doing this, but the water only emptied into the basement, allegedly because of the 42 foot missing standpipe section in the cellar. The building engineers told the fire department that the standpipe was in service; hence the firefighters were ordered to look for section valves that might have been turned off, so they could get the water up to the floor that had the fire. I don't know if they were ever able to do this.

By the way, when water was initially supplied to the standpipe system, the pressure blew off a different section of the standpipe. This occurrence was detailed in a specific, well-documented article in the *New York Times* shortly after the fire. Had that section of the standpipe held together, I believe they might have gotten water into the standpipe system. That was the section of pipe that was found lying on the floor after the fire. It is my understanding that the pipe that had been previously cut was removed from the building months before the fire. My thoughts were that if you could get water into the four Siamese connections, then at least one of them would have gotten water into the standpipe riser. Check valves are installed in various locations in a standpipe system to prevent backflows to damaged or isolated parts of the system. FDNY commanders were dealing with misinformation and bad information that they didn't figure out until after the fire was extinguished.

Why didn't Captain Bosco perform building inspections? I'm referring to the building inspections that all seven of the FDNY officers were blamed for not performing the 15-day inspection. Newspapers reported that there were two memos stating that the Deutsche Bank building was a problem building. One memo was in June of that year, and the other was in August, 11 days before the fire. One of the memos was from the hazmat chief.

Hypothetically speaking, if he wanted to inspect that building, he would have gone to the construction manager and said the same thing as Bill Siegel said, "I want to do a surveillance inspection of this building." As described in the *Fire Prevention Manual*, which was in effect prior to August 18, 2007, the so-called 15-day inspections were described as "surveillance inspections." I am not aware of any definition of a "surveillance inspection," and so it is open to interpretation. However, the implication is that it would be an information-gathering spot inspection rather than a comprehensive inspection. For all I know, he might have done that. He would not have been allowed inside that building because it was a hazmat site.

Prior to the Deutsche Bank building fire, to my knowledge, the 15-day-inspection rule was not followed in the Fire Department. I have never done a so-called 15-day inspection at any building in my entire career. With some possible sporadic exceptions, prior to the Deutsche Bank fire, you will not find any division in the FDNY that implemented this rule. I can tell you categorically that when I was a Battalion Chief in Battalion 2, even when the present commissioner was the 1ˢᵗ Division commander, there was no program, policy, or instruction for implementing this rule.

Eventually these directives were consolidated into something called the 'Rules of the City of New York.' It was the kind of thing that you studied for prior to taking a test, but you also knew that it was something you probably would never do in your entire career. I can tell you honestly that there was never a chief to tell me to do the so-called 15-day inspection anywhere in my career.

Do you think that they came up with this 15-day rule because some lawyer had to come up with something to blame the officers for?

That would be my assumption.

Why did FDNY executives blame those seven officers?

If I had not visited the Deutsche Bank building command post that day, I would have found out that I had been relieved of my command in the 1ˢᵗ Division from my sister, who called me on my cell phone, shortly after noon, to tell me that she saw my face on NY-1 TV and they said that I had been demoted, which was incorrect. The FDNY staff didn't even have the courtesy to notify me that I was being relieved of my command before it was stated on television. I don't consider a serendipitous phone conversation on someone else's cell phone a notification. The same was true for Steve McDonald and Pete Bosco, who heard it on the radio while driving in his car. The way the FDNY handled that was nothing short of a disgrace.

I think they picked the three people in charge of the FDNY administrative units whose districts included the Deutsche Bank building, because it was logical to blame those officers. Then they waited to see what would happen. Over the next few months they came to realize that I didn't ignore the Chief Siegel memo, so they then used the 15-day rule. I thought the 15-day rule was going to be swept aside also because—as even the IG's report stated—the 15-day rule was one that was too often disregarded in the FDNY. In fact, there was no policy of complying with that rule.

The idea of disciplining seven officers wasn't brought up until 22 months after the investigation began. My perception is that they wanted me and Captain Bosco to accept a deal. Chief McDonald had already retired. I believe that the Fire Department wanted us to accept some sort of discipline, and then they could announce that to the public, and they could declare that the issue was resolved.

As it was portrayed to us, the discipline was supposed to be some form of informal discipline, and we weren't sure what this implied. My opinion as to why they brought the other five people in is that they wanted to put pressure on Bosco and me to accept their deal. The other five chiefs were assigned to either the 1st Division or the 1st Battalion on the date of the fire. Prior to June of 2009, there was no indication that the other five chiefs would be involved in any type of discipline. Initially Peter Bosco and I balked at the deal. We wanted to fight it. We felt that we had been wrongly accused and that they had nothing to charge us with. Also, we were advised that it was to be a command discipline. That is an informal discipline, where a letter describing what you are accused of would be put into your official personnel folder and after a year it would be removed. We weren't told that it was going to be a letter of reprimand, which is what it turned out to be. A letter of reprimand is a more severe discipline and becomes a permanent part of your official folder.

The fire department said that either all seven of us accept the informal discipline, or all seven will be given formal charges, with all the serious ramifications which that entailed. They expected the other five chiefs to quickly accept this action. The five were not in the newspapers, nor did they have to go through what Bosco and I did for

22 months. Also they would not be reassigned from their units. I guess they figured that a letter in their personnel folders probably wouldn't seem too bad.

Peter Bosco and I were adamant that we were not going to take it. We both told them that we did nothing wrong and they have nothing on us, so why should we accept any discipline? The deal, as presented to us, was either all seven accept the informal discipline, or we all get formal disciplinary charges. If even one of us refused the informal discipline, we would all get formal disciplinary charges. That is a serious matter, since we could each be subjected to a hearing, which is essentially a kangaroo court. Ultimately, no matter what the hearing officer recommended (guilty or innocent), the Fire Commissioner has the power, at his sole discretion, to terminate us, and we would lose our pensions. This is the hammer that they held over our heads.

Personally, I was willing to go through the trial. Even the attorney that was advising us admitted that there were many facts that the city didn't want brought out in a trial and that they might never hold a trial. The charges, however, would always be pending. We were advised and convinced that it would be foolish to take that route. We were advised that they would have undoubtedly preferred the charges against all seven of us. That would have initially resulted in very unfavorable media coverage for all seven of us. Also, they could have preferred charges (formal discipline) and then just sat on it indefinitely, which is most likely what they would have done, for the reasons just mentioned. We would all have been in limbo for the foreseeable future, possibly the rest of our careers, with no resolution.

By the way, the letter of reprimand did not even mention the so-called 15-day rule. I believe that BITS (the FDNY Bureau of Investigations and Trials) understood that the issue of the 15-day rule didn't hold water, so they simply reprimanded us; specifically for violating the following section of FDNY Regulations: "Section 6.4.5: Failure to properly enforce all Regulations and orders relating to the inspection of buildings and premises in his Division."

In a later paragraph, they even specified the dates, March 2007 to August 18, 2007. I guess demolition (alteration) operations must have begun in March of 2007, although I was never informed of this by anyone. What really makes that statement laughable is that most people in the FDNY knew that the 1st Division probably had one of the most comprehensive Fire Prevention programs in the FDNY.

You mentioned earlier that the search for human remains and other documentation that traveled between FDNY channels were coordinated out of the Manhattan Borough Command. This being the case, why wasn't the commander of the Manhattan Borough Command disciplined along with the other FDNY officers who had either direct or indirect knowledge of the Deutsche Bank building?

I don't know. But I can tell you that the Manhattan Borough Commander was a staff chief, and the Division Commander, Battalion Commander and Company Commander were all line officers. You can draw your own conclusion. I have drawn mine.

Let me mention the standpipe system. If you were going to inspect the standpipe system, it is very difficult to determine if it is in service within any high-rise building, and particularly the Deutsche Bank building. If you were to go into the cellar and try to follow the pipes as to where they go or where an isolation valve or check valve might be or if there is a section that's broken or even which way the water was supposed to flow, it would be very difficult. High-rise standpipe systems are complicated. It is conceivable that a section of pipe could be missing and that section of the system could be isolated, leaving the system in service.

As an example of how complicated the system could be, sometime in 2009, almost two years after the Deutsche Bank fire, a pressure-valve alarm in the Deutsche Bank building (required by the new regulations enacted after the Deutsche Bank building fire) went off, signaling that the pressure in the standpipe had dropped below what it should have been. The fire department units that responded searched the building, and it took them several hours to find that a section of the standpipe was removed from upper floors. If that alarm had not gone off, no one would have known that there was a breach in the standpipe system. There was no pressure alarm system prior to the fire. So to have an inspector look at the standpipe to determine a breach is almost impossible. Only a plumber, or other trained person, could really determine if that standpipe was in service by doing a pressure test. Based on one of the city's 33 recommendations they now require pressure gauges and alarms on standpipes in buildings under construction/demolition.

I understand that prior to the Deutsche Bank fire there was a person, an inspector from the Buildings Department, that wanted the standpipe tested, but when he brought it up to his bosses, he was transferred to the Bronx ... It was Aaron Williamson. I found out about this from reading about it in the *New York Times*. This indicates to me that there were people that didn't want anyone to get in the way of this building coming down.

Who approved the EPA plan that was an obvious violation of city/state rules and regulations?

I asked the same questions and never got an answer. Who approved that plan? Who allowed them to seal off those stairwells? Who allowed them to remove the fireproof stairwell enclosures? Someone must have approved it, and someone must have devised the plan. I don't know if this was ever submitted to DOB. These were clear violations of the NYC building code. To maintain interior means of egress, you must have fireproof enclosures. It is conceivable that a plan was submitted and approved and that, in some manner, these issues were addressed and approved by the Buildings Department. But I have no knowledge of that whatsoever. If the FDNY would have reviewed those plans, I believe they never would have been approved. I have no knowledge that the FDNY was consulted when these demolition/alteration plans were devised.

The internal fans were a major driving force in the fire and were instrumental in the injury of over 100 firefighters and the killing of two firefighters, yet nobody mentioned them. Is it possible that by bringing these facts to light, you would have to bring in EPA, DEP, OSHA, and the LMDC, the landlord of the building? Keeping these federal and state agencies out of the picture was obvious when the DA brought only three charges against those three individuals [Bovis and Galt supervisors] and a misdemeanor charge against John Galt Corporation. Why would the DA only bring those three charges when he could have indicted more people and have more charges brought against them? Why didn't the DA mention the fans? All the DA stated was that if the FDNY had water, they could have put the fire out right away.

First of all, I don't think the DA had the firefighting expertise to offer the opinion that "if the FDNY had water right away, they could have put that fire out right away." I believe that is a proposition that is open to debate. In fact, many of the statements made by the DA are open for debate. If you recall, a second alarm was transmitted right after arrival. A fire of that magnitude is not *put out right away* under any circumstances.

That fire spread very quickly. If you have a fire in a large, open area like that and, depending on the amount of combustible content, it would depend on how quickly they could have gotten water to fight that fire. Let's assume that the fire started from a cigarette in a wastepaper basket. Then the fire went from the basket to the wooden construction shack. Now if the FDNY gets up there before it reaches a flashover (a point in time when the fire envelops the entire space and the smoke banks down to near floor level), it is conceivable that they would have been able to extinguish that fire. However, no one in the building called the Fire Department, and no one called 911 right away. Someone on the outside street saw the smoke and then called 911. That fire had been burning for a while. It was of such a magnitude that first-arriving units almost immediately transmitted a second alarm. Had the FDNY been able to get there in a timely fashion and had they been able to hook up to a working standpipe, they might have been able to put out that fire. If they got there after the flashover and the smoke banked down to the floor, they might not have been able to put it out. They might have had to back out anyway.

If those fans had not been on, that fire would not have spread so far and fast. If they got to the fire area fast enough, it was possible that they might have been able to put out the fire with fire extinguishers. This is just my opinion. I heard from some individuals that by the time the FDNY reached the fire floor it was way out of control, and I'm not sure that one hose line would have been able to control it at that point. That floor had been pretty demolished before that fire started. I took a walk through the floor after the fire, and I saw the 17th floor, and it was mostly demolished by that time. This was a wide-open, huge floor, and it would have been very difficult to control it with a single hose line.

What was the response of FDNY's top-level management, and what actions did they take before and after the fire?

This is an area that has legal implications, and I'm not sure I want to get into that. Initially, after the fire—again, this is only my opinion—when the mayor's office got involved, all they were looking to do was damage control. All they wanted to do was cover their asses, from the mayor's office down to the upper levels of the Fire Department. During that process, they came upon some documents, which they made assumptions about.

Based on these presumptions, they then chose to put the focus on three FDNY officers who happened to be in charge of three of the administrative levels of command associated with the Deutsche Bank building. Prior to the fire, I have no direct knowledge. My assumptions are based on facts that came to light after the fire, and I would rather not express those opinions.

Your thoughts on the actions of the LMDC, Schick, Doctoroff, Bloomberg, and Spitzer?

I don't want to get too specific. As we all know, there were lots of building and fire codes that were not complied with. It is my opinion that someone at LMDC knew what was going on in that building. The very demolition plan that they implemented violated several building code regulations.

I believe that it served the interests of those that you mentioned to focus blame on certain members of the FDNY, so that no one would notice where the real focus should have been.

~ 11 ~

NYC District Attorney

Manhattan's DA never pursued criminal charges against Bovis for the 2007 fire. Bovis was given immunity from prosecution because of its agreement with the DA.

In the fall of 2007, New York County's DA, Robert Morgenthau, requested a meeting with our family attorney at his office at One Hogan Place in Lower Manhattan. My wife, daughter-in-law, and I, along with our attorney, were introduced to the lead investigator, Patrick Duggan, in charge of the Rackets Division. This section prosecutes criminal-enterprise cases.

Article 460 of New York State law also criminalizes "enterprise corruption." The enterprise-corruption statute is New York's version of the federal RICO Act and was added to the penal law by the Organized Crime Control Act of 1986 to combat the "diversified illegal conduct engaged in by organized crime," including the infiltration and corruption of legitimate enterprises.

Earlier I mentioned to the DA that I worked for the federal government and had 14 years' experience with the US Postal Inspection Service. I also said that I knew that the federal government had provided more than $300 million to clean up toxins from 9/11 and to find human remains at the Deutsche Bank building. I expressed my desire to go directly to the US Attorney's Southern District office and request a federal case be opened on the Deutsche Bank building fire.

Duggan assured us that his office was working in conjunction with the State's Attorney General and the US Attorney (we never met or spoke with any of these individuals throughout the course of this lengthy investigation). Duggan had a reputation for being an honest, dedicated, and thorough prosecutor. We believed that he would open an enterprise-corruption investigation because of the multiple groups involved (LMDC; LMCCC; city, state, and federal agencies; Bovis; and Galt) in the Deutsche Bank building fire. We assumed that the DA's office believed that there had been criminal intent, along with collusion from multiple sources that had led to the horrific fire.

At the end of the meeting we met with Dan Castleman and Morgenthau, who vowed to us that he would follow the money trail of this investigation, no matter where it led him. The money trail led to City Hall and Albany, and that's when the investigation took a surprise turn.

In the summer of 2008, various news media reported that the DA had a list of people to be questioned about the Deutsche Bank building fire. The list included a former deputy mayor, executives of the LMDC, construction contractors, officials with the DOB, and higher-echelon officers within the FDNY.

So what happened? We have no idea if the people targeted for interviews were questioned. If they were, we weren't told whether they were called to testify before a grand jury or whether they cut deals. At a second meeting, in December 2008, with the Manhattan DA, we met with Dan Castleman, Morgenthau's second in command. Castleman said that the possible crimes warranted indictment of a number of individuals, mostly subcontractors, on criminal charges. The LMDC, Bovis, and city agencies would not be indicted. The city was working on an agreement that would force Bovis to create a better safety team, have more trained safety people, pay for various safety issues, and be open to greater scrutiny from the city via the DOB, FDNY, and EPA.

When questioned by the media, Bloomberg admitted that the city, state, LMDC, contractors, and others did not do everything that they could have to prevent the deaths of those firefighters. He also said that his administration was negotiating with the DA's office.

What actions were taken by the city's highest elected officials?

Sovereign immunity was granted to all agencies involved in the Deutsche Bank building fire. State and federal agencies weren't mentioned. Sovereign immunity is a legal principal in which the prosecutor determines not to indict the public sector. Under sovereign immunity, the prosecutor has to prove that a city employee's (or employees') actions directly caused the firefighters' deaths.

The use of the sovereign-immunity principle raises many questions and issues. Here are a few issues, problems, and suggestions to consider:

- *Sovereign immunity isn't ironclad.* New Yorkers could argue against its use and attempt to have prosecutors return indictments against Bovis and city, state, and federal employees whose decisions directly led to the unsafe conditions at 130 Liberty Street. Sovereign immunity had never been used before by the DA. Sovereign immunity may work for an agency but would be more effective if used to seek charges against individuals in those city, state, and federal agencies, especially the board of the LMDC that deliberately approved contractors they were told not to hire. Hypothetically, the DA could use sovereign immunity every time a city-agency worker is indicted for a crime against the public.

- *Assuming sovereign immunity was correct in this instance, what does it have to do with immunity for Bovis?* Why would the DA state that economic conditions should forestall the pressing of criminal charges against Bovis, along with immunity for high government officials. If Bovis was convicted of a crime, the company could be permanently denied all government (city, state, and federal) contracts.

- *If it were determined that the DA failed to do his job, the governor would have the power to appoint a special prosecutor.*

- *The public should apply pressure to have the DA go back to the grand jury to address these wrongs:*

  1. The LMDC failed to oversee the safe and proper decontamination and demolition of the structure. Despite the LMDC's claim to have spent $20 million on "safety," safety was never even a consideration in the demolition. The LMDC never took steps to ensure that even the most basic fire- and building-safety measures were taken. The LMDC's lack of accountability and disdain for local fire- and building-code

regulations does not exempt them from responsibility for the deaths of two firefighters.

2. The NYS Department of Environmental Conservation and the EPA failed to enforce state and city building- and fire-code regulations. Their knowledge of the existence of highly combustible plywood, plastic, and glue to be used as containment barriers in a toxic building and their failure to dispose of these materials safely is criminal negligence. And the removal of existing fireproof stairwell walls—the only area firefighters could seek refuge and escape from the fire and smoke—was pure stupidity. When the Deutsche Bank building caught fire, these flimsy barriers not only failed to act as a fire retardant, they acted as kindling, an accelerant fueling the fire. Breaching these barriers allowed toxic material (including heavy metals) to be released from the building into the immediate neighborhood and surrounding areas. The internal fans, which created a negative-pressure system, had no cutoff switch. The system brought fire and smoke lower into the building, trapping, injuring, and killing firefighters.

3. Despite the fact that the Deutsche Bank building ranked among the most dangerous workplaces in the nation, OSHA failed to inspect and address and rectify its safety issues. Removal of exit stairwells; flagrant, unsafe smoking practices; and disabled fire-protection systems were just a few of the major safety problems that went uncorrected. There was a 16-month criminal investigation in which three low-echelon employees from Bovis and Galt were criminally charged by the NYC DA's office. After a 39-month grand jury criminal investigation, at taxpayers' expense, charges were brought against the men and the John Galt Corporation.

In a trial that was scheduled to last about four months, the judge granted lifetime immunity from jury duty for jurors willing to stay on the case. The original prosecution list of witnesses was close to 500 names, though the judge reduced it to 159 names. The defense attorneys called only one witness and rested their case.

The DA's office asked the Graffagnino family to attend the trial as supporters for the DA's case. I refused because I felt the DA was prosecuting the wrong people. I told the DA's team that in all my years of government service, I had never heard of a criminal case where only three people and one company were being prosecuted when so many city, state, and federal agencies had been involved. It's astonishing to think that in a complex case involving so many people, not to mention a general contractor and subcontractor, only three people were charged. In similar cases, there were hundreds of charges, and dozens of people were indicted.

Adding insult to injury, it was more than apparent that the case against these men was weak, because the people that should have been indicted from the LMCCC and LMDC, along with city, state, and federal agencies' decision makers, were not indicted.

I questioned the fact that the LMDC board and the City of New York spent millions in legal-representation fees for their employees. Why would millions of taxpayers' dollars be spent if sovereign immunity was applicable? Was it because no other individuals were charged with any criminal wrongdoing?

One on-the-scene observer who asked that his name not be mentioned said that the DA deliberately stretched out the grand jury investigation so that it coincided with the five-year statute of limitations regarding imposing criminal charges.

Why did the LMCCC, the LMDC, and city hall push so hard for Bovis and their suspected criminal subcontractors to bring down the Deutsche Bank building unless they had ulterior motives?

Bovis Walks—DA's Statement about the Deutsche Bank Building Fire

The DA's statement mentioned the plan the LMDC created in September 2005 to abate toxic contaminants and then deconstruct the 41-story high-rise building at 130 Liberty Street. On February 13, 2006, Bovis as the general contractor and Galt as a subcontractor had a contract that had been approved by the LMDC. By September 19, 2006, Bovis and Galt had issued their Implementation Plan. In February–March 2007, this plan was changed to be simultaneous toxic-contaminant abatement with building deconstruction. Per this plan, at the end of 2007, the Deutsche Bank building was to be nothing but an empty lot.

This plan to simultaneously deconstruct and abate a 41-story high-rise building had never been implemented before in New York City.

As part of the plan, Bovis and Galt agreed, among other things, to do the following:

1- To comply with all applicable laws and statutes.
2- To perform daily inspections to ensure that the work did not endanger the employees working there or the general public.
3- To maintain the building's standpipe so that it would be functioning and available at all times during the project.
4- To inform the FDNY of any change to the implementation plan. (The FDNY never received the Bovis/Galt plan.)
5- To coordinate their scope of work with the FDNY. (The FDNY never heard from Bovis or Galt.)
6- To prepare a fire plan that complied with all FDNY and NYC DOB codes.
7- To call 911 to report any fire in the building. (There were many fires prior to the August 18 fire, some with no fireguard present and no fire extinguishers in the area, and no one called 911 or the FDNY.)
8- To prohibit smoking in the work area.

Bovis and Galt were required to inspect, maintain, and protect the building's standpipe and to maintain unobstructed egress from the building. Bovis was required to hire a full-time site-safety manager to ensure compliance with its various safety obligations. (The LMDC hired a safety contractor for this purpose, but the LMDC and Bovis ignored this contractor.) Galt was supposed to hire a site-safety manager but never did.

A number of city agencies had regulatory responsibilities and obligations to enforce compliance by Bovis and Galt in order to oversee the safety of the project. Those agencies included the FDNY and the

DOB. Their responsibilities and obligations included the following duties:

- Inspecting the building's standpipe to ensure it was in good working order
- Inspecting the building's egress and enforcing compliance that egress was marked, visible, and free of obstructions at all times
- Performing inspections of the site every 15 days (this turned out to be untrue)
- Enforcing compliance that there would be no smoking
- Having city inspectors at the site every day

August 18, 2007: The Fire
Summary of the problems:

- Building contractors, on three occasions, inaccurately told several fire officials that the standpipe was in working order.
- Thick smoke and fire quickly descended downward. (The DA's report gave no mention of why or how.)
- Stairwells were blocked by wooden platforms wrapped in heavy plastic, as were the windows.
- Water to fight the fire finally reached the area 67 minutes after firefighters entered the building.
- Combustible equipment such as lumber, acetylene torches, and asbestos-abatement materials fueled the fire.
- The stairwell hatches were not constructed as described in the implementation plan, which led to confusion and great difficulty breaking through them.
- The isolation barriers were constructed within the stairwell and supported by two-foot-by-three-foot wood braces. These structures contained a hinged escape hatch that opened upward. The barriers were then covered with six-millimeter plastic sheeting and sealed with tape, glue, and foam. Those barriers were different from those described in the implementation plan.
- To expedite the cleaning process, in the fall of 2006, Galt supervisors decided to saw off the supports for the standpipe,

which caused a 42-foot section to break free and fall to the ground. Galt neither repaired nor reported it. This resulted in Galt officials preparing false paperwork that showed the standpipe in good working order.

The DA's office cited the following agencies for failing to perform their jobs:

FDNY

- The FDNY was cited for not following their own regulation on inspecting buildings according to their 15-Day Rule. This regulation required the FDNY to focus "particular attention" on 18 specified conditions, including standpipe systems. The standpipe requirements, taken in conjunction with DOB codes, mandate that a standpipe must be kept in a state of readiness at all time. (These points are rebuffed in chapter 10, "Fire Department (FDNY)," and in the interviews with FDNY personnel.)
- After the May 2007 incident where a pipe fell through the firehouse roof, the fire commissioner, accompanied by senior fire officials, went to the firehouse to inspect it but never asked if the Deutsche Bank building had been regularly inspected.
- The FDNY failed to develop a special firefighting plan for the Deutsche Bank building, despite numerous recommendations to do so since early December 2004. Another memo was issued in February 2005. (The implementation plans were scrapped due to the contractor-company changes.)

On three occasions between January and March 2005, a battalion chief, a hazmat chief, and a lieutenant from the local firehouse visited the building. They had interviews with the construction manager of the building and tours of the basement and first floors.

The battalion chief wrote memos summarizing each of the visits and made recommendations for a specialized firefighting plan for the Deutsche Bank building. The memos were ignored. (These points are rebuffed in chapter 10, "Fire Department (FDNY)," and in the interviews with FDNY personnel.)

- The FDNY's target-hazard program was discontinued. This program was established for large or complicated buildings that presented operational issues. If selected, the building would have been the site of multiple unit drills.

New York City Department of Buildings

- DOB inspectors failed to inspect and enforce the contractor's compliance with DOB regulations.
- Despite being on site every day, DOB inspectors never once went to the basement area where the 42-foot gap in the standpipe existed. The DA statement made mention of three separate breaches in the standpipe at different locations.
- DOB inspectors did nothing about the contractor's failure to maintain proper egress from the building. DOB inspectors knew, or should have known, that the building code required unobstructed egress and clear stairwells during demolition. In fact the stairways were blocked by unmarked containment barriers. They knew this but failed to recognize that it violated DOB code. More importantly, it created a severe safety hazard. Part of the DOB's failings can be attributed to the inexperience of the inspectors assigned to the Deutsche Bank building (each had to have a minimum of five years' experience). Initially, the DOB sought to staff the project with inspectors from its BEST Squad, which is comprised of inspectors who specialize in inspections of deconstruction sites, among other things. They abandoned this plan in favor of staffing the building with inexperienced inspectors who volunteered for the assignment. Neither team of inspectors traced the standpipe into the basement or discovered the 42-foot breach in the standpipe. (This plan for inspectors was altered around February/March 2007, about the same time Bovis/Galt started the deconstruction and simultaneous-abatement process.)

Environmental regulators

- The LMDC exempted itself from local fire and building safety regulations.(In every contract the LMDC signed, it stated that it would abide by any and all of the strictest fire- and building-safety regulations, but the LMDC, Bovis, and Galt opted to follow only the EPA's guidelines.)
- The state owned building became the exclusive domain of New York City's Department of Labor (DOL). (NYS has a Fire-Safety Bureau that performs building inspections exclusively for state buildings. Why didn't they inspect the Deutsche Bank building?) However, DEP inspectors voluntarily assisted the DOL by providing additional inspection staff and coordinating inspection activities. Federal EPA inspectors were also on site. (The federal EPA has jurisdiction over NY state agencies and thus should have enforced commonsense building- and fire-code safety regulations. Why didn't they? Also, federal OSHA inspectors were mentioned in other documents to have been on site. Why didn't they enforce regulations? After the fire, they handed out violation notices and fines totaling $464,500.)

The DA omitted from his statement that the LMCCC, the LMDC, Bovis, and Galt employed their own safety managers, and more importantly, they failed to achieve safety goals. Safety people from the EPA and OSHA, along with NYS's DOL, DEP, and DOB and the Office of Emergency Management's (OEM), were also on site. For years there were more safety managers and inspectors in the Deutsche Bank building every day than any other building, and their sole responsibility was to note, report, and, most importantly, correct building- and fire-safety violations. How is it possible that over a lengthy time period all these highly trained agency people saw nothing unusual or questionable? Not only is this inconceivable, but it also raises many questions, the most important of which is, were all these agencies' investigators actually there every day? If so, how long were they there, and what parts of the buildings did they see? And were they as qualified as their agencies led us to believe?

Considering the events in chronological order—pre-fire to the start of the fire and the FDNY's involvement—the credence of the official reports are suspect. Judging by daily newspapers' reporting, which pointed out glaring inconsistencies in the official reports from the respective agencies' spin masters, the truth never surfaced.

The public was duped. There must have been New Yorkers who questioned what they were told. If so, they weren't heard, or their protests fell on deaf ears. Only the city's daily newspapers—the *New York Times*, *Daily News*, and the *New York Post*—and weeklies, such as the *Village Voice*, and a few news magazines' investigative stories of the Deutsch Bank building travesty brought irrefutable facts to the surface, unequivocally proving that most of the government agencies, on the city, state, and federal levels, lied and that New York City's top decision makers, including the governor, mayor, and top aides, were complicit.

Using only public records as a running account of ongoing malfeasance, it's strikingly clear that all the events before, during, and after the Deutsche Bank building fire, which resulted in three deaths and more than a 100 injuries, were not the result of mistakes or tactical miscalculations by the FDNY but the result of decisions made by the city's top elected officials. The city's taxpayers were being taken to the proverbial cleaners. But the tragic and unforgivable part was that good men unnecessarily lost their lives and many more suffered long-term injuries because of elected or appointed officials' greed and lust for power.

The Agreements

- The city agreed to establish a dedicated inspection force whose only job would be to conduct inspections at buildings undergoing construction, demolition, and/or abatement. This unit, within the FDNY, would be called the Fire Prevention Construction Demolition and Abatement Inspection Team (CDA).
- Local fire companies would conduct familiarization building-site visits at each CDA site once every three months. Fire

companies would be required to certify that these drills had taken place.

- The FDNY would create several teams to assist CDA teams and other interagency coordination in performing quality assurance reviews, audit inspections, and labor-management committees. The city promised not to discontinue or diminish the personnel of the Fire Prevention CDA Prevention Team, the Fire Prevention Suppression Unit, and the Compliance Unit for four years.

- Bovis would not be prosecuted in exchange for taking remedial actions. Bovis agreed to the development of a comprehensive standpipe, smoking prevention, and first responder safety program at 130 Liberty Street and all other Bovis projects in New York.

- Bovis agreed to a program of management and staff changes to enhance its commitment to fire safety.

- Bovis agreed to the appointment of an independent monitor, approved by the DA, and agreed to submit semiannual reports of the monitor's findings to the DA. (Rumors from reliable sources state that these reports do not exist. News media asked DA Cyrus Vance about these reports, and he refused to discuss the reports or prove that they exist. In the spring of 2012, I requested that NYS Attorney General Eric Schneiderman look into the matter of these "secret" reports. This resulted in a telephone call from the Attorney General's office to the DA's office. The Attorney General's office asked if the reports existed. The person who answered the phone said that they did exist, and the conversation ended. No proof was asked for, and none was given. Also Bovis continued to be slapped with safety violations on their projects, continued to hire subcontractors with criminal ties, and continued to have deaths and injuries on their projects. If the independent monitor notified the DA's office, why wasn't anything done?)

- Bovis would establish a Fire-Safety Academy under the auspices of the Contractors' Association of Greater New York (CAGNY) or a similar group approved by the DA's office, in collaboration with the FDNY, for the training of construction industry personnel and for the research and development of fire-safety initiatives, with a funding from Bovis of $2 million.

- Bovis agreed to the establishment of a memorial fund in the amount of $10 million, consisting of $5 million for each of the families of the two deceased firefighters. The City of New York added $2 million to the memorial fund. This "donation" to a memorial fund effectively voided any possible civil action.
- The charges against the three defendants and the John Galt Corporation were two counts of manslaughter, two counts of criminally negligent homicide, and one count of reckless endangerment. As part of the non-prosecutorial agreement with Bovis, the major stipulation was if Bovis committed a criminal action, the non-prosecutorial agreement would be void, and Bovis would be charged with the original crimes in addition to the new charges.

I requested a face-to-face meeting with DA Cyrus Vance to demand a full and detailed disclosure and explanation of why the DA only indicted three people and did not go after the individuals who made the decisions within the various city and state agencies. My request was denied because all the prosecutors were busy.

The Trial

The investigation and grand jury lasted for 40 months (3 years and 4 months). The actual trial lasted only 2 ½ months. The charges against the three defendants—Mitch Alvo, John Galt's toxic-cleanup director; Salvatore DePaola, Galt's asbestos-cleanup foreman; and Jeffrey Melofchik, Bovis's site-safety manager—were manslaughter, criminally negligent homicide, and reckless endangerment. If convicted, they faced 25 years in prison. The John Galt Corporation was charged with reckless endangerment, a misdemeanor charge. If the corporation was convicted, it faced a $10,000 fine.

The DA based his charges on the broken and removed water-system standpipe. Because the firefighters did not have access to water, they could not put out the fire, and that's what killed them. Additional problems arose when the defense attorneys complained that the DA's office deliberately withheld information from the grand jury that could have affected the verdict to indict the contractors on criminal charges. The prosecutors never mentioned the internal fans or the sealed stairwells that the EPA, OSHA, and the NYS Department of Labor, along with other regulatory agencies, deemed necessary for keeping toxic contaminants inside the building.

Adding to the DA's questionable prosecution of the case, when Cyrus Vance Jr. replaced Morgenthau as Manhattan DA, there were many internal changes that seriously affected the Deutsche Bank building criminal case. Most of the DA's prosecutors abruptly quit their jobs just before the trial started. Robert Morgenthau retired; Dan Castleman left when Morgenthau refused to endorse him as his replacement; Patrick Dugan, chief of the investigation section and lead prosecutor, was reportedly forced out by Cyrus Vance Jr.; and junior prosecutor Cesar DeCastro also quit.

Why did this major shake-up take place just before the criminal trial? Was there rebellion in the ranks because some prosecutors wanted to do their jobs, refusing to accept an immoral, unethical, and possibly illegal deal for the LMDC and city and state appointees as well as disapproving of the Bovis/Galt deal with city and state officials, while others fought to take these deals? This must have prompted a major strategy change in the DA's prosecution style. Was this the reason for the personnel changes? Was Vance deliberately trying to build a weak case so the scapegoats would be acquitted? This way the city took the spotlight off the LMDC and city commissioners and the farce trial, so city and state political appointees could go about their business with no further intrusions.

The prosecutors called more than 70 witnesses, while the defense called only one person, a fire-safety engineer. The engineer demonstrated the effects that a negative air system (fans to keep contaminants in the building) had on visibility. With internal fans, the area filled with smoke in 4 minutes. Without the fans, the area was relatively clear after 14 minutes—the time firefighters started calling for help.

The defense attorneys argued that it wasn't the lack of water that killed the firefighters but smoke inhalation. The medical examiner's report listed smoke inhalation as the cause of death for both firefighters. The firefighters died because they were trapped in illegally sealed-off stairwells while groups of industrial fans pulled the fire and smoke toward them.

Also to blame were city, state, and federal regulators, namely OSHA, the EPA, the DOB, the FDNY, and a score of safety and site consultants hired by the construction companies. The LMDC was also at fault, because on several occasions it was told about the safety violations that were a regular occurrence on the site. The defense attorneys argued that their clients were lower-level scapegoats who had been charged only because the DA refused to charge the real culprits—the city, the LMDC, and Bovis. The city claimed sovereign immunity, and the DA could have gone after individuals. But he didn't.

Bovis bought its way out of a criminal indictment by spending millions, and the LMDC, with its board of directors appointed by the mayor and governor, wasn't even mentioned by the DA. The judge and jury found the defendants not guilty, except for the John Galt Corporation, which was found guilty of reckless endangerment. Requests to have DA Vance hold agency heads and high-level position holders responsible fell on deaf ears.

Criminal defense attorney Benjamin Brafman mentioned the discrepancy between the treatment of the defendants and the city. Why weren't the three people the DA wanted to prosecute given the option to pay a fine and walk away? Even if the inactions of others may have contributed to the firefighters' deaths, prosecutors are merely bound to prove that the defendants had a role, according to several lawyers. Could this be the reason prosecutors never mentioned the fans? It would have meant bringing in other agencies and raising questions about decisions made by LMDC directors.

Bovis's Second Trial

In 2009, Bovis vice president Brian Aryai, a former US Treasury officer, initiated an investigation into Bovis's inflated costs to pay construction foremen to keep projects on time. Aryai was a senior vice president in Bovis's New York office in charge of rooting out fraud. He reported his illegal discovery to Bovis's New York office in an attempt to stop the fraud. When he refused to back down, he was fired after being with the company only 10 months. At the time, it was unknown if he submitted his findings to New York's DA or the FBI.

At a later time, Aryai either visited or forwarded documents of his findings to Bovis's Australia headquarters. They were sent, along with supporting evidence, to FBI headquarters in Washington, DC. The FBI then sent the documents to New York City. The investigative agencies that participated were the US Attorney for the Eastern District of New York, the FBI, the Port Authority Inspector General, the NYC DOI, and the Manhattan DA's office.

The practice of overbilling was called "8 and 2," with construction foremen charging for extra hours that weren't worked and thus receiving an additional two hours of overtime pay in addition to their regular work hours. Allegedly, this was a common industry stipend for foremen. The president of the Building Trades Employees' Association said this commonplace practice was the cost of doing business. Prosecutors stated that the charges were kept secret from their customers' invoices, which was obviously illegal.

In January 2011, Mayor Bloomberg announced that Bovis had overcharged city, state, federal, and other government agencies on 100 projects between 1999 and 2009. The Deutsche Bank building was one of those projects.

Bovis would not admit to overcharges or to any liability. It walked again by paying a $5 million settlement to the city's general fund to pay for municipal operations. Bloomberg said that the settlement to the city reflected the city's commitment to stop waste and overbilling and to protect taxpayers and return the extra costs billed to the city. Neither Bovis nor the DOI would release the agreement or provide any details. Bovis said it didn't want the details of the agreement made public.

Yet again, an agreement was made to not admit to any wrongdoing. And taxpayers knew nothing about the shady deals made behind closed doors. In the end, they were duped. With the help of elected officials, the bad guys got the equivalent of a scolding. The fact that secret deals reeked of governmental cover-ups and corruption and that those political appointees and prosecutors took millions on settlements from companies they were supposedly prosecuting was irrelevant.

The powers that be—the US Attorney for the Eastern District of New York, the State Attorney General, the Manhattan DA, and New York City's mayor—remained silent and signed off on an agreement with Bovis. Rather than plead guilty, Bovis paid a fine, and it was business as usual.

Bloomberg, several government agencies, and dozens of political appointees took no responsibility for their actions. Their reputations remained untarnished.

Manhattan's DA never pursued criminal charges against Bovis for the 2007 fire. Bovis was given immunity from prosecution because of its agreement with the Manhattan DA's office. The agreement was formulated as a non-prosecutorial agreement. This means that Bovis agreed to pay monetary fees and to comply with the DA's terms. Pursuant to that agreement, if Bovis commits another crime, the DA can reinstitute the original criminal charges against them. In the past, these agreements have exclusively pertained to health care and the monetary misuses of financial corporations. This non-prosecution agreement is unique and like no other from the DA's office.

This 2008 agreement was made with the NY County DA's office as part of its safety reform practices. The basis of the agreement would be declared invalid if the company committed crimes within the future time frames of the settlement. This would leave the company and executives open to prosecution.

When a reporter asked Vance if Bovis had been complying with its non-prosecution agreement established after the Deutsche Bank building fire, he reacted in an unprofessional way. A DA spokesperson said he would not produce the semiannual reports, supposedly submitted by an independent monitor that Bovis had hired and paid for with the DA's blessing. Vance's office stated that the reports are not public and refused to comment.

Not public? The non-prosecutorial agreement was made public, as was the DA's statement of charges, failures by agencies, and other matters regarding this case. Why now are the semiannual reports not public? Why did the DA fail to do his job by repeatedly giving Bovis a get-out-of-jail-free card? I wondered if the entire non-prosecution agreement was a sham—something to tell the public. What if behind closed doors the DA's right to go back to prosecute Bovis for the crimes committed during the Deutsche Bank building fire was removed from the signed agreement? After all, the version of the non-prosecution agreement released to the public was not signed. It turns out that I was right ! The DA either had not inserted the good-behavior clause or removed all clauses which would allow the DA to reprosecute on the original charges. This was not an accidental omission, because those clauses would be the boilerplate of the agreement—the foundation, substance, purpose, and teeth of the contract. This clause could only have been removed or omitted at the very highest level of the Manhattan DA's office with pressure placed upon Morgenthau and then Vance to commit this unethical act. This suggests—no, screams—of an involvement obstructing a criminal investigation. When asked to comment, Morgenthau, as did Vance, clammed up.

In April 2012, US Attorney Loretta Lynch agreed not to prosecute Bovis in exchange for fines and restitution totaling $56.6 million. She used the exact, almost word-for-word phrasing that the Manhattan DA had used in its non-prosecutorial agreement with Bovis. The excuse was that too many workers would be out of work and that Bovis would be barred from any government contracts. Two Bovis officials pleaded guilty to one count each of conspiracy to commit wire and mail fraud. John Hyers Sr., general superintendent of field operations, should have been sentenced to at least 10 years in prison. And former head of the New York office James Abadie, who also pleaded guilty, should have faced up to a 20-year prison term. Both men received one-year probation and a fine.

Earlier I said that I felt the federal government should hire a special prosecutor to investigate both the billing fraud and the Deutsche Bank incident. "I don't think anyone in the city or New York State is capable of conducting an unbiased investigation." Spokespeople for the US Department of Justice and the US Attorney's Office declined to comment on my statement. This was not my opinion but my actual request for an independent investigation.

Lynch said that this was the largest construction-fraud settlement in New York City history. Yet she decided not to prosecute Bovis if it paid the fine and promised to be good. Lynch didn't want the company barred from government work. Wasn't it her job to arrest and prosecute alleged criminals, not to cut sweetheart deals? I contend that if this was another company without powerful political ties, there would have been several federal indictments, and no one would have gotten a get-out-of-jail-free card. Why was the non-prosecutorial agreement so secret? The public has a right to know what the deal was, especially since they paid for it in money and blood. Also they have a right to know if the same clauses, to prosecute Bovis for past crimes, were removed in the federal contract as they were in the DA's agreement. Why bother with independent monitors if no one ever sees any reports?

Regarding the non-prosecution agreements for both the DA's office and the US Attorney's Office, Bovis paid millions of dollars to escape criminal indictment and trial, but it was rumored that federal and state law enforcement and prosecutorial agencies shared in fines and penalties of convicted criminals and used them as bonuses for their agents. This raises the question of who shares in the penalty money.

~ 12 ~

State Attorney General

I received a phone call from the state attorney general's office stating that he had no jurisdiction over NYC's "elected by the people" DA and that they are separate units.

After the August 18, 2007, fire, council member Vincent Gentile, from the 43rd District, and Domenic Recchia Jr., from the 47th District, issued a press release in an attempt to demonstrate transparency and integrity following the Deutsche Bank building fire.

The councilmen requested that the attorney general (AG) take the lead and check any company selected to be a subcontractor at the 130 Liberty Street location. They hoped that a thorough search would lead to hiring a subcontractor that had experience demolishing contaminated New York City buildings and that employed experienced professionals who adhered to OSHA guidelines. They also requested that the AG institute a code of conduct to govern future deconstruction of the site. In an earlier letter to the AG, Gentile and Recchia called for a comprehensive investigation into those parties responsible for the loss of life at the site. As far as I am aware, there were no actions from the AG's office regarding either letter.

In the fall of 2007, I unofficially requested that the New York State Commission on Public Integrity (NYSCPI) investigate the mayor's and governor's roles in the LMDC's decision to hire Bovis. The purpose of the request was to discover the parties responsible for the decision to bring the building down as fast as possible. I was told that there would not be an investigation into the Deutsch Bank building fire.

I learned from a news story, "Troopergate" that many members of the NYSCPI had only recently started their jobs, newly appointed by Governor Eliot Spitzer. I also learned of rumors that Eliot Spitzer's administration was trying to influence the results of the Troopergate investigation. The NYSCPI has 13 members, seven of whom are appointed by the governor. The news media reported that the governor's appointees had either worked for him or contributed to his political campaigns directly or through their respective companies.

Albany's DA, David Soares, was reportedly pressured to rush a report that would exonerate the governor in an alleged scheme to discredit NY State Senate majority leader Joe Bruno for his use of state aircraft. Interestingly enough, when Soares released his findings, his decision was that there had been no criminal actions and that the governor's actions were justified. I don't believe that Soares said or did anything when the governor was forced to resign after it was discovered that he'd solicited out-of-state prostitutes while surrounded by state trooper bodyguards.

In the spring, 2009, I requested a meeting with Steven M. Cohen, counselor and chief of staff to NYS Attorney General Andrew Cuomo. The meeting was arranged by Martin Steadman, former investigative reporter for the *New York Herald Tribune* and press secretary to Governor Mario Cuomo. To support my family and friends position, FDNY Battalion Chief James Riches and our family attorney, John C. Meringolo, also attended the meeting.

We sat with Cohen for about a half hour and discussed the possibility of having the state attorney general open an investigation on the Deutsch Bank building fire. We provided our reasons and the rationale supporting it. Cohen was gracious and said he would look into it and get back to us. After we left, I asked Meringolo what he thought of the meeting. He said, "It was a complete waste of time," adding, "Steven Cohen didn't bring in an aide to take notes or to question what was requested and why it was requested, nor did he take out a pen and paper to take notes." We reasoned that Meringolo was right, because we never heard from Cohen or anyone on Cuomo's staff.

I later followed up with an official request for the New York AG to initiate a criminal investigation into the deaths of firefighters Robert Beddia and Joseph Graffagnino. (To review the letter, see Appendix C.) I never received a response from the AG's office.

When the DA's office refused to make public the documents supposedly submitted by Steir Anderson, the independent auditor that Bovis had hired under the guidance of the DA's office, I was insulted. Since the Deutsche Bank building fire, Bovis and its subcontractors have had many accidents stemming from failure to comply with any safety standards.

The evidence indicates that Bovis violated their non-prosecution agreement with the DA's office when it was indicted on their fraud case. I expected that the fraudulent details would be part of the documents Steir Anderson submitted on Bovis's behalf.

Taxpayers have a right to know the details supporting the contention that there was a breach of the above-mentioned agreement. In the spring of 2012, I sent a letter to NYS Attorney General Eric Schneiderman requesting that he find out why the DA refused to produce the compliance reports that Bovis's independent monitor sent to the DA's office. (To review the letter, see Appendix D.)

I received a phone call from the state's AG office approximately six weeks later stating that he had no jurisdiction over NYC's "elected by the people" DA and that they are separate units. As a courtesy, they asked the DA if Bovis was complying with the non-prosecutorial agreement as stipulated. The DA's office told the state AG's office that Bovis was complying with the independent monitoring company and meeting all the requirements of the non-prosecutorial agreement. To my knowledge, the state AG did not send out a letter or an e-mail with their findings.

I got the message. I wasn't getting anywhere because city and state officials had no intention of releasing any information that even hinted of wrongdoing. Answers to tough questions were answered with straight-faced, official bureaucratic correctness, sprinkled with doublespeak and political baloney. I could only conclude that I was persona non grata, blacklisted from accessing incriminating information either proving or hinting at criminal wrongdoing on every rung of the government hierarchy, starting with New York's mayor and the governor and going all the way to the lowest-ranking manager.

Stonewalled, I decided to try one last time to obtain an investigation by the state's inspector general or by a special prosecutor. I cited newly discovered evidence and new sources that I believed should be looked into. Naturally, this request had to be approved by the governor. (To review my letter to the governor, see Appendix E.) Not surprisingly, I never received a reply on this request either. It appeared that no state official wanted to work at getting to the truth.

Two years later, in July 2013, Cuomo created a 25-member commission to root out corruption within the state government. In December 2013, the commission completed a report that had many politicians worried. Even with this positive turn of events, Cuomo abruptly disbanded the commission, after only nine months in operation.

Reliable sources say that his office tried to steer investigations and block subpoenas about politicians misappropriating campaign funds and about ethics complaints related to the former legislative commission, the state Democratic Party, the Real Estate Board of New York, and the advertising company that promoted the governor's agenda, along with other groups that had ties to Cuomo. The major hindrance to the commission doing its job was Cuomo's appointed Executive Director, Regina Calcaterra. Calcaterra was paid an annual salary of $175,000 to be the governor's spokesperson and a barrier to anyone who tried to investigate corruption within the politicians' ranks. The US Attorney for the Southern District, Preet Bharara, asked the commission to turn over their files to determine if a further investigation was warranted.

I continue to pray for real justice to prevail. What a welcome relief that would be after all the lies and false promises from our elected officials.

Part III

The Game of Hide the Guilt

~ 13 ~

Outspoken Critics of the Investigation and Stonewalling by Decision Makers

The most outspoken critic of Mayor Bloomberg's screw-ups and incompetent handling of the Deutsche Bank building fire was Village Voice *reporter Wayne Barrett. His articles slammed the mayor and his appointees and their ties to Bovis.*

Martin J. Steadman performed an investigative study of the Deutsche Bank building fire. Steadman used to be an investigative reporter with the *New York Herald Tribune.* He went on to be press secretary to Governor Mario Cuomo and later became public relations director to the Uniformed Fire Officers Association, Local 854.

In May 2012, Steadman's study, "J'ACCUSE [I Accuse]: The Deutsche Bank Tragedy," was published. Steadman brought to light unknown facts, most of which had previously been buried by New York City's top decision makers. The actions of LMDC directors and city-agency heads were a calculated effort to move the blame from themselves onto others. He questioned the decisions and motives of the DA as they pertained to the Deutsche Bank building fire. (See Appendix F.)

The most outspoken critic of Mayor Bloomberg's screw-ups and incompetent handling of the Deutsche Bank building was *Village Voice* reporter Wayne Barrett. His articles slammed the mayor and his appointees and their ties to Bovis. The story widely believed to be Barrett's best, "Bloomberg's Biggest Scandal—the Deutsche Bank Fire—Should Be His Downfall. Why Isn't It?" was published by the *Village Voice* on July 22, 2009.

Barrett named the people and organizations he believed were responsible for creating the scenario that had caused the Deutsche Bank building fire. He provided details other reporters left out. Barrett blamed the ensuing cover-up following the fire squarely on the DOB commissioner and her deputy, FDNY commissioner and his second in command, the LMDC, the LMCCC's officers, and the mayor and governor and their appointees. Collectively, these people made the decisions that failed to oversee the 130 Liberty Street building's compliance with fire and building codes that subsequently killed firefighters Beddia and Graffagnino and injured more than a hundred more.

A blog in one of Manhattan's major newspapers addressed the similarities in the trials and acquittals of employees blamed for construction-accident deaths. A crane operator was blamed for a crane collapse that killed seven people. In the ensuing trial it was proved that the DOB crane inspector never inspected the crane, even though he signed an inspection report.

In the Deutsche Bank building trial, three people were tried for the deaths of two firefighters. In both cases, the attorney's defense was that city agencies and other politically appointed organizations were equally at fault. The defense argued that the city should have been on trial but that prosecutors were afraid to go after the city and state agencies because they were represented by major law firms. The NY DA could not prove these cases beyond a reasonable doubt, and the defendants were found not guilty.

The major problem in putting the city on trial is proving that its decision makers knew about the series of bad decisions that ultimately resulted in the tragic Deutsche Bank building fire. Defense attorneys argued that the city's representatives, be they DOB inspectors or firefighters, didn't inspect Deutsche Bank building when they should have. If an inspector didn't inspect a building or construction site and fatalities occurred, it would be a civil matter, because the city could argue that it did not actually know that the inspector falsified reports.

However, with the Deutsche Bank building fire, evidence could have been presented that the city and state were aware of the situation they'd created because both the mayor's and governor's direct reports made the decisions that created the death trap. The mayor and the governor attended meetings with the contractors and agreed to the change of plans for simultaneous abatement and deconstruction because of the short window of opportunity to demolish the building by year's end.

Just prior to the third anniversary of my son's death, the DA requested my family meet in their office. I represented my family, and the DA's office asked that we appear in court to publicly support the prosecution. As a family, we refused the offer, and I said, "Because we don't have any faith that the DA can prosecute it the way we feel it should be prosecuted." My son's widow, Linda Graffagnino, also felt that those indicted were scapegoats and that the people responsible for what had transpired weren't touched. She said that over the three years following the fire that took her husband, "The city has done nothing to move forward to bring the Deutsche Bank building down. We, as a family, are moving forward to change laws to stop tragedies like this from continuing."

Julie Menin, former chairperson of Community Board 1 and former LMDC board member, had been an outspoken critic of the LMDC. She directly blamed the LMDC for the fire and the deaths of both firefighters as well as for the ever-escalating costs of deconstruction because the LMDC allowed a subcontractor with associations to organized crime, the John Galt Corporation, to work this project. She stated that the LMDC did not have the background or expertise to take on such a task. Safety problems continued at the Deutsche Bank building site.

A blog published in a Manhattan newspaper criticized a reporter for approving of the actions taken by the LMDC, the LMCCC, and the LMDC's Chairman, Avi Schick. The blogger asked why the reporter never mentioned the missed deadlines, slow progress, empty assurances, and terribly managed project before and after the fire. He also cited the LMDC's and the LMCCC's refusal to move forward, blocking any progress and stalling the Port Authority from progressing with the World Trade Center rebuilding. He pointed out that the reporter never mentioned the extensive cost increases, with no one once questioning why the LMDC's ballooning administrative costs. Finally, he discussed how the reporter used fluff propaganda, smoke, and mirrors to hide the real news.

Community Board 1 in Lower Manhattan unanimously approved a resolution on September 18, 2007, exactly one month after that fatal fire that blamed government agencies, the contractors, and the LMDC for that fire. The resolution also cited safety concerns with the continued demolition of that building. The resolution mentioned the methodology needed to ensure the safety of people that lived and worked in the area. (See Appendix G.)

~ 14 ~

Media Control and Mayor Michael Bloomberg

Bloomberg's mayoral win in 2001 ushered in a powerful oligarchy with unchecked power.

Over the past three decades, the news media's power, reach, and impact have been rapidly eroding, largely due to the rapid growth of Internet news and commentary websites, dwindling newspaper readership, and consolidation of major national newspaper chains.

The Pew Research Center's *State of the News Media 2013* report said, "Estimates for newspaper newsroom cutbacks in 2012 put the industry down 30 percent since 2000 and below 40,000 full-time professional employees for the first time since 1978." The Pew report went on to say, "Across the three cable channels, coverage of live events and live reports during the day, which often require a crew and correspondents, fell 30 percent from 2007 to 2012, while interview segments, which tend to take fewer resources and can be scheduled in advance, were up 31 percent. *Time* magazine, the only major print news weekly left standing, cut roughly 5 percent of its staff in early 2013 as a part of broader company layoffs."

In the wake of these changes, the quality of TV news coverage has suffered, according to the Pew report. While sports, weather, and traffic account for approximately 40 percent of content on newscasts, "on CNN, the cable channel that has branded itself around deep reporting, produced story packages that were cut nearly in half from 2007 to 2012."

While an increasing number of newspapers' newsrooms no longer have the clout and independence they once relished, advertisers' power and influence over editorial content has catapulted. Where there was once an unwritten separation between news and advertising department's at most daily newspapers, large advertisers now have a say in what many newspapers publish. Because of these changes, deep-pocketed politicians who spend billions on media advertising can negatively impact the quality of news reporting and editorial content in general.

FCC: Impotent Industry Watchdog

Equally disturbing, the Federal Communications Commission (FCC) is incapable of monitoring and controlling the media industry the way it did in the past. The FCC is supposed to make sure that the media landscape remains competitive.

In the past, the FCC set limits and restrictions on how much a media company could own in order to encourage broadcasters to compete with each other to provide quality journalism. But that's no longer the case, because "powerful media companies have the FCC's ear," according to the Free Press. The result is that as powerful media companies have gobbled up more companies, journalistic principles, ethics, and standards have been compromised.

The vast media landscape, once made up of hundreds of independent newspapers and broadcasters, has shrunk so that hardly a dozen media conglomerates made up of both print and broadcast (network and cable) control what Americans read, hear, and watch. Big business's far-reaching tentacles have, in many cases, crushed the presses' cherished right to print or broadcast the uncensored truth. Reporting news in the various media outlets was once the domain of unbiased editors and reporters who were free of external pressures and who were impartial and neutral in reporting the news. Yet much of today's news is censored, controlled by multiple layers of authority. The news is often scrutinized, modified, and scrubbed clean of any information deemed unfit for the public to read, hear, or watch.

And newspapers continue to be acquired by well-heeled media companies. In 2011, the FCC approved a merger of Comcast and NBC Universal, creating the largest cable operator, controlling 40 percent of broadband-Internet subscribers.

As the FCC continues to lose its grip to enforce best-practice journalistic standards, most media companies have shown little interest in improving their products or in increasing their market reach.

In February 2014, Comcast announced that it planned to buy Time Warner Cable for $45.2 billion in stock. If these two largest cable companies in the United States were to combine, their total estimated number of customers would be 33 million. Many critics argued that less competition creates inflated costs and limits options for consumers. The only groups benefitting from these changes were company heads and lobbyists on their payrolls.

Powerful Pulpit for Michael Bloomberg

These historic changes proved to be a timely blessing for power-hungry billionaire, entrepreneur-turned-politician Michael Bloomberg, who was already a force in both the media and business worlds. In 2014 *Forbes* magazine estimated Bloomberg's wealth at $32 billion, ranking him among the "25 most transformative leaders, icons and rebels of the past quarter-century" and among the twenty richest people in the world. *Adweek* ranked Bloomberg a 35 rating in its "100 most influential, innovative and effective leaders controlling media, marketing and technology."

Bloomberg's mayoral win in 2001 ushered in a powerful oligarchy with unchecked power. Opposition to his decisions and choice of appointees was squashed before the public knew about it. Bloomberg had the right mix of qualifications to be a leader of Machiavellian proportions—wealth; dispassionate, myopic focus; the politician's magical charm to sway and convince skeptics; and a narcissistic thirst to control and squash opposition.

Unlike his predecessors, Bloomberg was a media visionary who had the foresight to create one of the first media empires to harness technology to bring real-time financial news and analysis to financial institutions throughout the world. He created and owns news service Bloomberg LP, a $9 billion financial-data and media company, encompassing TV, radio, a magazine (*Bloomberg Businessweek*), and digital outlets. It's no surprise that Bloomberg played power politics with astute cunning. He masterfully used the media as a weapon to squash dissenters so that his viewpoints prevailed.

In a Politico article, Bloomberg's Deputy Mayor Dan Doctoroff, former CEO of Bloomberg LP and good friend, referred to his former boss as "God." Said Doctoroff, "He [Bloomberg] created the universe. He issued the Ten Commandments and then he disappeared. And then he came back. You have to understand that when God comes back, things are going to be different. When God reappeared, people defer." A *New Yorker* profile of the three-term mayor said, "Bloomberg thinks of himself as a team player, as long as it's his team." Bloomberg spent $109 million on his campaign, compared to his opponent Bill Thompson's $9 million, and won by less than 5 percent of the vote. Many believe that he won because the Democrats believed the media blitz, decided it was a done deal, and gave up before the polls opened. In October 2012, Bloomberg announced that he planned to put $10 million into a super-PAC fund to influence elections across the country. This superfund could spend practically unlimited amounts of money on TV ads, mailings, phone calls, and other forms of advertising not directly coordinated with a campaign.

The Firing of Wayne Barrett, *Village Voice* Reporter

Adam Lisberg, formerly a *Daily News* city hall reporter, interviewed me one evening about the Deutsch Bank building fire and new city laws that would improve building and fire safety.

While discussing various topics, Lisberg stopped to check a text message on his cell phone. He showed me the message, which was about a story written by investigative reporter Wayne Barrett that was going to be published in the *Village Voice* the next morning. Barrett had written several scathing articles blaming the Bloomberg administration and specifically the mayor for covering up and interfering with the Deutsche Bank building investigation,

Barrett's article was killed. The widely respected, award-winning journalist and senior editor, employed by the *Voice* since 1973, was fired. His last day was December 31, 2010. Why was Barrett fired? The

Voice's management said his position was being eliminated for budgetary reasons.

This was not the first time that Bloomberg was accused of having a journalistic thorn removed. Barrett was not the only top journalist to get the proverbial pink slip. *Daily News* investigative reporter and senior enterprise editor Brian Kates was also removed. Kates was part of the *Daily News* I-Team (Investigative Team) that covered the trial of the three construction supervisors. Kates wrote the story about DA Morgenthau's statement accompanying the indictments that said that 15 days before the fatal fire, the URS had warned the LMDC that the Deutsche Bank building "was an accident waiting to happen." Shortly after this story was published, the *Daily News* I-Team was disbanded, and veteran reporter Kates, after a long and distinguished reputation for hard-hitting reporting, was not heard from again.

Under the Bloomberg administration, negative news that couldn't be suppressed was deliberately released late Friday afternoon or early Saturday morning, so that it got scant coverage from the press and the public.

In the spring of 2012, I noticed that various media reports stopped naming the general contractor or subcontractors when they reported safety violations, accidents, lawsuits, or any other negative press against certain construction companies. When a worker was killed at a Columbia University worksite, a newspaper article mentioned that the contractor, which remained unnamed in the article, was hit with 59 building code violations but wasn't terminated. Nor was the company named on Columbia University's website. The general contractor was Bovis; the subcontractor, Breeze. Why no names? Was it to hide them from the public?

WABC News investigative reporter Jim Hoffa interviewed me in April 2012 in preparation for an upcoming broadcast on Bovis's abysmal safety record to air the following week. I told Hoffa it was a wasted effort because the powers that be would never let him air an interview that cast the mayor or his favorite contractor, Bovis, in a negative light. Hoffa assured me that his interview would be aired. Unfortunately, I was right. The interview never aired.

Nevertheless, Hoffa's reporting was excellent because it delved into Bovis's safety record (or lack thereof), which involved a long list of safety violations and crane accidents during the four-year non-prosecution agreement between Bovis and the Manhattan DA.

Bloomberg ruled New York City with a confident yet understated ruthless determination that was seldom questioned. The fearless reporters who eloquently exposed his behind-closed-doors deals and blatant cronyism were quietly and efficiently disposed of. And if there was a public outcry, it wasn't loud enough.

The Bloomberg Years in Retrospect

When Michael Bloomberg first ran for mayor in 2001, New Yorkers needed an astute businessman who could balance the budget and, at the same time, be fair to businesses and unions. Did he meet New Yorkers' expectations? I'll let you, my readers, answer that question. My job—better still, my mission—is to present facts and indisputable truths so that you can draw your own conclusions.

Putting Bloomberg's campaign promises aside, his three terms were pockmarked with problems that include cronyism, nepotism, frequent contract disputes, and links to organized crime.

Entrepreneur Turned Politician

Bloomberg effortlessly made the transition from successful businessman to politician. A quick study, he quickly learned how city and state politics operate. During his first term, Bloomberg scored kudos as a take-charge, no-nonsense leader. But problems surfaced by the end of his first term when he was embroiled in contract issues concerning post-9/11 construction and real estate development.

During his last term, many Bloomberg critics called his administration a dictatorship because he was more concerned with cementing big-business deals and pushing legislation that benefitted his wealthy constituents rather than meeting the pressing needs of the city's less fortunate majority.

Throughout Bloomberg's tenure, the City Council did his bidding with little pushback. Their actions included the removal of professional standards for commissioner positions and approval of the mayor's, his appointees', and the City Council's third term in office, against the public's wishes. With carte blanche approval they doled out big-salary jobs to friends and colleagues, regardless of qualifications. The City Council approved an 18 percent property tax increase and gave themselves a 25 percent raise with the mayor's blessing.

The City Council was just as responsible as the mayor for the erosion of safety standards in the city's buildings so profits of real estate and construction owners could increase.

In sum, Bloomberg had the City Council in the palm of his hand. As explained in the prior chapter, the press, which is supposed to represent the voice of the people, was powerless. His most articulate and vocal critics, notably investigative reporters Wayne Barrett, Tom Robbins, and a few others, were silenced. And the broadcast media either didn't report Bloomberg-administration mishaps or went out of their way to praise him.

Bloomberg's Checkered Scorecard

Meanwhile, monumental, costly mistakes; nepotistic deals; and major construction projects went to favored companies, without competition, throughout Bloomberg's tenure. The trial of the mayor's former campaign consultant for fraud and embezzlement brought out the unethical financial maneuvers that had poured money into his election campaign. It wasn't the first time Bloomberg had moved personal funds through the Independent Party's housekeeping account. He did it in the 2001, 2005, and 2009 campaigns by taking advantage of campaign-fund loopholes. The Independence Party, the NYC Board of Elections, and the state legislature should have been cited for unethical conduct because they stood by and allowed it to happen. During the mayor's campaign consultant's trial, DA Vance praised Bloomberg as the victim of embezzlement, asserting that he was not responsible for any violations.

There were other issues as well. As chief executive of the National September 11 Memorial & Museum, Bloomberg made sure that its top administrators were taking home six-figure salaries. From the onset, the project was fraught with problems, mostly budgetary. Senator Tom Coburn stalled legislation approving funding of $20 million a year, $200 million total. Despite partisan bickering and financial boondoggles, a decade after the project began; the museum was finally completed and opened to the public.

Regardless of the project, Bloomberg aggressively defended large staffs and huge salaries. At the same time, he stonewalled the city's unions over contracts. Some unions worked without a contract for five years. The mayor argued that the city lacked the funding to support union jobs and wanted them cut. The unions wouldn't budge. Bloomberg refused to back off and tried to change union job titles in order to slash salaries and benefits. The majority of unions won, but some agreed to take cuts. While this was happening, the mayor gave his staff a 21 percent pay raise.

Over Bloomberg's 12 years in office, there were constant battles with union heads. In the wake of several crane accidents, the DOB wanted to hire qualified, licensed crane operators from large cities to operate cranes in New York City. But Local 14 of the International Union of Operating Engineers fought back, refusing to recognize licenses from other cities. Their union president claimed that Bloomberg was trying to bust the union to reduce labor costs in order to benefit his development friends at the cost of New Yorkers' safety.

When Bloomberg left office in 2013, many of the construction projects he'd put in motion became the problem of the new mayor, Bill de Blasio.

Bloomberg's Legacy

Bloomberg is credited with revitalizing New York City. In 2013, more than 54 million tourists, highest number ever, visited the Big Apple, according to a *New York Times* story. Additional accomplishments include a reduced crime rate, a more efficient transportation system, a cleaner environment, a $2.4 billion budget surplus, and the opening 800 acres of outdoor space, along with new parks

On the debit side, the *New York Times* said that Bloomberg's worst mistake was "authorizing a police practice found unconstitutional by a federal court." Bloomberg and Police Commissioner Raymond Kelly "humiliated and alienated black and Hispanic communities by having stop-and-frisk turn into a generalized method of harassing law-abiding citizens."

The *New York Times* story went on to say that many New Yorkers thought Bloomberg was arrogant and "displayed few political skills" and that "his unscripted comments, especially about the poor, can range from thoughtless to heartless." And his "efforts to modernize the city payroll became a scandal ... eight people were convicted of cheating the city out of millions of dollars. And his donations to political parties to gain favor and ballot lines were an embarrassment, though not illegal."

A *Huffington Post* story evaluating Bloomberg's track record said, "Many New Yorkers thought Bloomberg was tone-deaf to people who were struggling." And Councilwoman Letitia James said that "the city's poor and underprivileged were a low priority during Bloomberg's three terms. There were 1.7 million people living below the poverty level, and approximately 52,000 people in homeless shelters—more homeless people than at any time since the Great Depression."

~ 15 ~

Non-Prosecution versus Deferred Prosecution Agreement

The potential problem to non-prosecution agreements and deferred-prosecution agreements is the top decision makers' perception of a particular case. Could that person be swayed or corrupted to prosecute or refuse to prosecute a case or deliberately sabotage the prosecution's case for conviction?

What is a deferred- prosecution agreement (DPA) versus a non-prosecution agreement (NPA)? Why are they used, and what makes them so popular among prosecutors?

NPAs are created before criminal charges are filed and have no court oversight. DPAs are created after criminal charges are filed with the courts. With an NPA, charges are not filed unless the charged corporation fails to uphold the agreement; with a DPA, the charges are deferred and then dismissed at the end of a specified time period if the corporation complies with the terms of the agreement.

The US Department of Justice created these agreements so that prosecutors could pressure corporations to pay large fines and change their business practices, have a measure of control over the corporations, and be able to fire top executives of corporations for alleged illegal acts. There is no trial and little, if any, court/judge supervision. The American judicial system started exercising these agreements in 1993, but they were rarely used.

In 2002, however, the federal indictment of the giant accounting firm Arthur Anderson on a single count of obstruction of justice made front-page headlines. A DPA was offered but declined because of stringent Department of Justice restrictions. Arthur Anderson was found guilty, but three years later the US Supreme Court reversed the verdict. In a case of too little too late. The firm went out of business, destroying thousands of employees' livelihoods and at the same time disrupting hundreds of businesses that had been clients of the firm. Since then, the DOJ has created methodologies and vague guidelines to assist prosecutors in these types of agreements.

Other federal agencies, such as the SEC (for civil issues) and state, county, and city prosecutors, have started using these types of agreements. Now prosecutors can attack major corporations on perceived law violations without going to court and have practically no oversight regarding the conditions they impose on the corporations. They can do whatever they want to modify company policy, make changes to business methodology, insert company monitors, impact costs, damage the companies' competiveness, remove top executives, and have a say in the running of the company—even though they know nothing about its business—with absolutely no repercussions.

Corporations are stuck between a rock and a hard place, because they can't afford a long court battle where they may be found guilty, even if they believe they are innocent. The repercussions of bad press are obvious. Clients run for the door, to be snatched up by competitors, and companies under indictment aren't able to win government contracts. And when their stocks plummet, obtaining credit will be difficult, if not impossible. If convicted of a crime, they'd lose their licenses and insurance. Fines levied by the DOJ against accused corporations have exceeded several billion dollars a year on the federal level and hundreds of millions of dollars on the city and state levels. There is no transparency or appeal right; prosecutors are literally the judge, jury, and jailer. The prosecutors regulate the business.

Over the past decade the use of these agreements has jumped dramatically. But are they reducing crime? And are they fair and ethical? As a former federal employee, I know it was governmental policy that employees' professional conduct must always be fair, honest, and ethical so that their character is above reproach.

We have government prosecutors who are no different than loan sharks. They muscle takeovers of companies they know nothing about and take billions of dollars in bribes (for the government) not to drag companies into criminal trials. What makes these actions legal? The prosecutor's word and badge. Where is the balance of justice? Providing prosecutors unlimited powers with few guidelines for control creates a breeding ground for corruption. NPAs and DPAs are tools that provide billions of dollars to the DOJ and to city, county, and state prosecutors. And the DOJ and prosecutors never want these agreements to end. The New York County DA's office has a memorandum that references the *US Attorneys' Manual*, title 9, chapter 9, the guidelines for "Consideration in Charging Organizations." An investigation into the allegations of criminal conduct can only be identified after the gathering of evidence and pertinent facts to establish individual and corporate criminal liability. The areas for prosecutors to evaluate are the following:

- *Harm:* What is the extent of harm to the public and people affected by the outcome or intent of the action? What is the potential future harm?
- *Percentage of employee participation*: Was it just a few people, or was the majority of the organization involved?
- *History:* Were there past incidents of misconduct, and how did the company address them? Were safeguards instituted to prevent existing and future incidents of wrongdoing?
- *Prosecution:* How might the public react to criminal charges being brought against individuals of the organization or the company to uphold the identity that the criminal justice system is fair?
- *Organizational efforts to correct misconduct issues:* Did the company start various programs to correct or retrain employees; adjust and evolve compliance programs to better correct past and present issues; reimburse those harmed via company misconduct; terminate, replace, or discipline individuals where warranted? Was the company proactive in cooperating with government agencies to correct the corporate attitude of misconduct?
- *Company's future:* How will prosecuting the company affect shareholders, employees, pensioned employees, and the public? Charges against a company may be enough to destroy a company. Will the harm of prosecuting the company be greater than the harm caused by the misconduct?

- *Victims' viewpoint:* The views of the victims can help the prosecutor determine to proceed or not with filing charges. Also the victims' views can have an impact on a judge's sentencing after a conviction.
- *Individuals' prosecution for company's wrongdoing*: Consideration must be given to file charges against the individuals of the company that created the misconduct. Other reasons and factors might exist that may determine non-prosecution as an alternative.
- *Non-criminal actions:* Could the organization's misconduct be corrected by civil lawsuit or regulatory actions? It's expensive to file criminal lawsuits. Options such as civil or governmental regulatory remedies may be better solutions.

The prosecutor should decide to charge an organization because it's in the best interests of the public and should make the decision without being influenced by prejudice or fear. The prosecutor must be aware of collateral damages to innocents before making a decision. The prosecutor must always be cognizant of the obligation to always reach fair and just resolutions. Let's review the unsigned version of the non-prosecution agreement with Bovis released to the public by New York County DA Robert Morgenthau:

> The New York County District Attorney's Office and Bovis Lend Lease LMB, Inc. entered into a Non-Prosecution Agreement. This agreement was approved by both sides so that the District Attorney would not seek criminal prosecution for the charges of manslaughter in the second degree, criminally negligent homicide and reckless endangerment in the second degree for the deaths and injuries of firefighters that resulted from a fire at the Deutsche Bank building located at 130 Liberty Street, New York City on August 18, 2007.
>
> Bovis Lend Lease agrees that it shall in all respects comply with its obligations in this Agreement. Bovis does not challenge the factual recitation of its conduct and that of its employees as set forth in the Statement of the District Attorney. Bovis Lend Lease agrees to

willingly acknowledge responsibility for its actions and comply with the following:

- Development of a safety program at 130 Liberty Street building and all other Bovis projects in New York City that includes fire prevention, first responder safety, smoking prevention and comprehensive standpipe.
- Management and staff changes to include hiring of a Senior Fire Safety Manager, approved by the DA, hiring a Regional Safety Manager, assigning executive responsibility for direct supervision, including safety to the Chief Operating Officer (COO) of Bovis Americas and the firing of four employees.
- Appointment of an independent monitor approved by the DA and paid for by Bovis to oversee safety initiatives at all Bovis projects in NYC. This is to include the integrity of Bovis subcontractors and Bovis compliance with all terms of this agreement for four years. The Monitor will prepare semi-annual reports and submit them to the DA.
- Create a Fire Safety Academy in collaboration with FDNY, for the training of NYC construction industry personnel and for research and development of fire safety initiatives. Bovis will pay $2 million to fund this and not use the money as a tax deduction or via insurance.
- Create a memorial fund for the families of the deceased firefighters. Bovis won't use these funds as a set-off against any civil liability that Bovis may incur.
- Bovis agrees that none of its attorneys, board of directors, agents, officers or employees will make any public statement that would contradict, excuse or justify any statement of fact contained in the Statement, except in connection with testimony or argument in any civil litigation or proceeding related to the events described in the Statement. If any Bovis employee did make such a contradictory statement, interpreted solely by the DA, Bovis would be subject to

prosecution to the crimes stated above. If the DA notifies Bovis of such a statement, Bovis will have three days to repudiate the statement. This agreement removes Bovis' rights from taking any legal, factual or administrative proceeding to which the DA is not a part. Bovis neither admits nor denies criminal or civil liability.

1) Should the DA determine that Bovis has committed any crime other than those stipulated earlier, at the sole discretion of the DA, Bovis would be subject to prosecution.

2) If Bovis violates the agreement in any material respect, as determined by the DA and hasn't started to cure the said breach within five days of written notice by the DA, Bovis agrees:

   a) DA may prosecute Bovis for any crime the DA has knowledge of including those set forth in this agreement.

   b) Bovis waives any claim that this agreement and any information contained in it are inadmissible against Bovis.

   c) Bovis waives any claim that such prosecution is time barred either on grounds of speedy trial, speedy arraignment or the statute of limitations.

   d) Bovis waives any rights to be charged via an indictment and any other rights it may have with respect to grand jury proceedings and consents to be charged and tried on Superior Court Information.

3) If Bovis sells its company or merges with another company its obligation continues to exist with the DA.

4) This agreement is not binding on any federal agency, or any state or local authority although the DA will bring the cooperation of Bovis and its compliance with this agreement to the attention of federal, state or local prosecuting offices or regulatory agencies, if requested by Bovis.

5) Bovis and DA agree that this agreement and its attachments shall be disclosed to the public.

Section 5, "Negative Air Requirements," in exhibit B, "Bovis Fire Safety Initiatives," was the first—and, I believe, only—time the DA mentioned the internal fans imposed by the EPA. Exhibit B was not part of the version originally released.

Firefighters' Lawsuits

Subsequent to the Deutsche Bank fire, injured firefighters filed civil lawsuits against Bovis. The firefighters stated they wanted to use the statement of facts agreed to by Bovis as part of the non-prosecution agreement with the NYC DA. The action in New York State Supreme Court was titled *Borst v. Lower Manhattan Development Corp.*

Bovis's attorneys argued that the NPA with the DA contained inadmissible settlement negotiations. This particular NPA was unique on many points and varied dramatically from the way a federal DPA or NPA would be structured. This NPA gave Bovis greater flexibility and latitude to argue major issues in civil actions, and Bovis did not have to admit any guilt, either criminal or civil.

In deferred prosecutions the company is criminally charged by the government, but the charges are withheld for a set amount of time and then dismissed if the company complies with the terms of the agreement. DPAs are filed with the courts and are public documents. In non-prosecution agreements criminal charges are not filed, and the terms do not have to be made public unless the DA wants to publicize the results of its investigation or the company is required to disclose the agreement. DOJ policy leaves the creation of DPAs and NPAs to each local office. With both DPAs and NPAs there is little, if any, judicial review.

In the injured firefighters' civil lawsuit against Bovis, the New York State Supreme Court ruled that the NPA was actually a settlement agreement because Bovis did not admit to any guilt.

In part of the settlement agreement Bovis stated that they would not contradict the DA's statement, except in connection with a civil case related to the fire. The injured firefighters argued that Bovis's agreement not to challenge the DA's statement was an admission of guilt. The court said that an offer to settle a claim is inadmissible as proof of liability under New York's evidence law; thus the agreement and any factual statements cannot be considered admissions by Bovis.

To support this conclusion the court did not distinguish between statements made in compromise negotiations and evidence provided to prosecutors in the course of a criminal investigation. The court also stated that the DA's statement was not admissible against Bovis because it was evident that the parties did not intend to bind Bovis to "admissions" outside of the criminal proceedings. The agreement explicitly stated Bovis's right to take legal and factual positions contradicting the DA's statement in any subsequent litigation to which the DA was not a party.

The agreement was treated as comparable to a consent judgment in civil litigation. Consent judgments, under which the respondent agrees to a sanction but neither admits nor denies the substance of the allegations in the prosecutors' complaint, are not admissible in a subsequent litigation to prove the truth of the claims described.

Most DPAs and NPAs include the following eight provisions:

1) Acceptance of a statement of facts describing illegal acts and/or an admission of wrongdoing
2) Agreement that the company and its employees and agents will not publicly contradict the statement of facts
3) Cooperation with the government for the duration of the agreement, including the provision of documents and efforts to secure employee testimony
4) Remedial efforts such as the enhancement of compliance programs, a corporate integrity agreement, and/or monitorship
5) Fines and penalties
6) Obligation to report future violations of the law
7) Waiver of the statute of limitations
8) Acknowledgment that the government has sole discretion determining whether the agreement has been breached and, upon breach, the agreed statement of facts shall be admissible in a prosecution of the company

Uniqueness of Non-prosecution Agreement between NYC DA and Bovis Lease

The NPA between the New York County DA and Bovis was unique for these reasons:

- The company did not admit to wrongdoing or make any admission of guilt.
- The agreement was manipulated to make the facts inadmissible in a civil lawsuit.
- The agreement was declared, in court, as a consent judgment.
- The NPA was structured so that Bovis could dispute key facts in a civil case.
- The DA's statement as to the cause of death for both firefighters contradicted the medical examiner's determination.
- The DA's statement never mentioned the instruments that caused the firefighters' deaths (internal fans / negative-pressure system) except in an amendment in the NPA.
- The DA never issued a breach of the Agreement when the US Attorney brought charges of fraud and other violations in Bovis's second trial.
- The DA refused to produce the independent monitor's reports of compliance even when Bovis and its subcontractors were being indicted for check-cashing schemes; for fire- and building-safety violations; and for workers being injured, maimed, and killed at unsafe construction sites.
- The DAs admitted that they omitted, in the official signed version, the prosecution clauses. Without the prosecution clauses the DA cannot return to prosecute Bovis for the crimes within the NPA and any crimes made during the four-year agreement time frame.

Why the significant changes from the public NPA to the secret NPA? The version released to the public had the standard and customary clauses below:

1. Should the DA determine that Bovis has committed any crime other than those stipulated earlier, at the

sole discretion of the DA, Bovis would be subject to prosecution.

2a. DA may prosecute Bovis for any crime the DA has knowledge of including those set forth in this agreement.

2c. Bovis waives any claim that such prosecution is time barred either on grounds of speedy trial, speedy arraignment or the statute of limitations.

2d. Bovis waives any rights to be charged via an indictment and any other rights it may have with respect to grand jury proceedings and consents to be charged and tried on Superior Court Information.

Why did the NYC DA deliberately extend such liberal leniency to Bovis? And why did the DA deliberately remove all the clauses to prosecute Bovis if they were to commit another criminal act, which they did? This raises another question: Why did the US Attorney for the Eastern District keep their NPA a secret?

The potential problem to non-prosecution agreements and deferred-prosecution agreements is the top decision makers' perception of a particular case. Could that person be swayed or corrupted to prosecute or refuse to prosecute a case or deliberately sabotage the prosecution's case for a conviction?

The DOJ states that the public's perception of the manner and methods used by its prosecutors matter, but its business practices are the opposite, as it hides behind secret agreements it refuses to release to the public.

What happens to the fines and conviction penalties in federal, state, county, and city DPAs and NPAs?

Several years ago Bloomberg and DA Morgenthau argued over who should get the funds generated by the fines. The mayor insisted that the money should go to the city, the way conviction fines do. The DA responded that he turns money earned from his office's convictions over to the city and the state.

In criminal cases after convictions and all appeals had been exhausted, the fines and assets of the convicted party are liquidated and go into a general fund. Critics believe there are some federal and state law enforcement agencies where agents get to share a percentage of those funds as either annual bonuses, arrest/conviction incentives, group/individual awards, or other type of stipends for their positions in that agency. Are prosecutors in this group?

Part V

Aftermath

~ 16 ~

March for Safety
June 21, 2008
130 Liberty Street to City Hall

In the wake of a long list of high-profile construction accidents following the fatal Deutsche Bank building fire, on June 21, 2008, my family and the Beddia family held a rally and March for Safety in order to draw attention to the urgent need for stricter fire-safety codes and tighter enforcement procedures. The rally also called attention to the inconsistencies in city, state, and federal building regulations.

Friends and supporters of the Beddia and Graffagnino families, along with firefighters, FDNY officers, and union officials marched alongside local politicians. The firefighters' unions' rank and file and the officers' union representatives spoke out against agencies that failed to abide by city regulations. Numerous local politicians—Senator Marty Golden, Senator Daniel Squadron, Manhattan Borough President Scott Stringer, and NYC Councilmen Tony Avella and Vincent Gentile—attended. Many delivered heartfelt speeches.

Some demonstrators held signs calling for the dismissal of city officials, and others criticized what they saw as a tendency by construction companies and the city to cut corners rather than commit to an investment in equipment and enforcement. UFOA President Jack McDonnell and Steve Cassidy of the UFA spoke eloquently and with conviction about losing a brother.

When my wife, Rosemarie, was asked why she participated in the march, she said, "We want to save other families from going through what we went through. We don't want anyone else to die."

At the same time, the mayor's office was drafting a 32-count edict to amend and add new laws to strengthen the city's building and fire codes. By the time our protest march and rally concluded, the mayor had added a 33rd.

For once, we were all on the same page.

Special thanks to civil rights attorney Norman Siegel for his help in planning and organizing this march.

Recommendations under Consideration

On March 18, 2008, I sent an e-mail suggestion to the Manhattan Borough president's office. With all the problems regarding building safety over the past several months, the public's attention was finally focused on building safety. One of my recommendations was to amend the regulations to include an updated architectural drawing of new and reconstructed buildings. This CADD drawing would follow completion of the permit work and DOB approval of a final inspection after a project was completed. A copy of these updated drawings, with the amended structure diagram that incorporated the windows, stairs, and doors (all on one page), would be sent to the FDNY and NYPD to keep in their databases, to be used at these locations for safety purposes. This would be a good start in sharing information between city agencies in order to help prevent loss of life.

Updated Building and Fire Codes

A new fire code, passed unanimously by the NYC Council, went into effect on July 1, 2008, replacing the outdated code created in 1913. The updated code, based on findings of a four-year study ordered by the mayor and modeled on the International Fire Code, was slightly different than New York State's fire code.

The revamped fire code was more in line with the new building code, which emphasized design, construction, and fire-safety systems. The new fire code stressed operations, building maintenance, and systems, including emergency preparedness. It also required a mandatory additional 10 weeks of training at the Fire Academy, which included hazardous material training and emergency-responder safety.

(See Appendix H.) The training also encompassed broader issues, such as rooftop access, comprehensive evacuation procedures, and safety programs for construction sites.

Several council members also introduced bills to improve building and fire safety throughout the city. Prior to these bills moving forward, I contacted Cas Holloway, an assistant to both the deputy mayor and Bloomberg. We discussed various scenarios where the fines the city imposes must be relevant to the violations. This was the problem when it came to construction safety rules. Fines for violations should be on a tiered system commensurate with the cost and size of the building being built or renovated.

The bills took into account the recommendations of the mayor's working group to establish better safety, oversight, and communications at construction, demolition, and abatement sites. Other bills introduced by council members Vincent Gentile, Alan Gerson, and others were combined into a dozen bills the mayor signed into law between June 29 and December 7, 2009. The new laws achieved the following:

1) Improved interagency coordination and information between the DEP, DOB, and FDNY
2) Established an asbestos-abatement permit program
3) Banned smoking at construction and demolition sites
4) Required the DEP to guide environmental contractors regarding maintaining entrances/exits at abatement sites
5) Prohibited smoking on any floor of a building where asbestos abatement is taking place
6) Required site-safety managers to check standpipes on a daily basis and trace the system on a weekly basis
7) Established a uniform code coloring of standpipe and sprinkler systems
8) Required contractors to obtain a permit to cut and cap standpipes or sprinklers during demolition
9) Required contractors to have a detailed plan for demolition when the project includes the use of mechanical equipment
10) Required air-pressured alarm systems for dry standpipes during construction or demolition

11) Required new or altered sprinkler systems to undergo successful hydrostatic pressure testing

12) Prohibited simultaneous demolition and asbestos–abatement activities within the same building

Sadly, good people died before the bureaucracy came to its senses and passed and enforced laws that protect both the people who've dedicated their lives to protecting us and the citizens of the city they swore to protect when they took office. And let's not forget that we pay their salaries. How ironic.

~ 17 ~

Building and Fire Safety for New Yorkers

Despite New York City's sudden concerted effort to formulate rules and standards that were applicable to all agencies—city, state, and federal—there wasn't a comprehensive fire-inspection enforcement for state properties.

In 2008, I struggled to understand New York State's building- and fire-safety laws. I met with Michael Balboni, NYS commissioner of the Office Public Safety; Floyd A. Madison, commissioner of NYS Office of Fire Prevention and Control; and John F. Mueller, acting state Fire Administrator, NYS Office of Fire Prevention and Control.

A problem area were agencies, such as the US Postal Service, semi–city/state agencies, and foreign embassies, including the United Nations building, that were in New York City or New York State but slipped through the cracks and accounted to no one. The commissioners and administrators I spoke with agreed that city and state building and fire-safety regulations need to be changed so that these exempted agencies and buildings were in full compliance. They pointed out that the Metropolitan Transit Authority and Con Edison complied with NYS codes, and while Empire State Development, the LMDC, and the LMCCC said that they will comply with state and city codes, they police themselves. The Port Authority of New York and New Jersey is in a gray zone and does not have to comply with the above city- and state-mandated safety regulations.

There are 885 buildings throughout New York City that are exempt from the building and fire codes and from city and state inspections. Regarding NYS safety issues, agencies are supposed to police themselves. NYS Office of Fire Prevention and Control agents are not allowed into those agencies' buildings to monitor or verify safety and building regulations unless they are invited by the agency.

All state agencies are responsible for conducting fire inspections (self-inspections) and for taking appropriate safety measures. It's the responsibility of each state agency to administer and enforce state building and fire codes. A state agency could voluntarily request and pay for the NYS Fire Prevention Bureau to inspect its offices or building. The Fire Prevention Bureau would, upon completion, issue a written report for the agency to voluntarily comply with the recommended changes. Currently there is no incentive to enforce or compel an agency to fix violations. Despite New York City's sudden concerted effort to formulate uniform rules and standards that were applicable to all agencies—city, state, and federal—there wasn't a comprehensive fire-inspection enforcement for state properties. A working model could be based on state universities; for state universities, the NYS Office of Fire Prevention and Control performs inspections and has state authority to give fines and enforce compliance for state safety compliance.

In early 2009, Manhattan Borough President Scott M. Stringer negotiated a major agreement with the Port Authority of New York and New Jersey. I attended the press conference when Port Authority (PA) Executive Director Chris Ward announced that the PA would release an annual report demonstrating compliance with safety codes. Ward said that the PA's compliance records dating back to 1999 are posted on its website. Anyone, taxpayers and officials, can monitor its compliance history to make sure that building and fire codes are being enforced. Accidents, for example, would be posted on the PA website weekly.

This agreement was a major point in Stringer's 2013 State of the Borough address. He stressed the importance of safeguarding the public's safety and the need for strict safety and fire standards since the Deutsche Bank building fire, frequent building collapses, and crane accidents.

Reporter Accuses Mayor Giuliani of Failing to Enforce Building and Fire Codes

Investigative reporters Wayne Barrett and Dan Collins lanced Mayor Rudy Giuliani and his top administrators in their 2006 book, *Grand*

Illusion: The Untold Story of Rudy Giuliani and 9/11, for not attempting to enforce fire and safety regulations at the World Trade Center.

Barrett wrote, "The public authority that owned the World Trade Center was encouraged to evade agreements binding it to comply with the building and fire codes."

Was this part of a concerted effort to dumb down building and fire codes in New York City?

My Frustrating Attempts to Initiate Building- and Fire-Safety Bills

My experience in trying to get bills for building and fire safety passed was frustrating and bizarre. It was an experience I'll never forget. If I thought I knew or even had an inkling how the political process worked, I was wrong. The facts and a long shopping list of events speak for themselves.

In the spring of 2009, I met with Senator Marty Golden and Assemblyman Peter Abbate in the hope of getting a bill passed that would make state-owned and rented buildings conform to NY State building and fire codes and regulations.

Golden and Abbate agreed that this was a good idea and said that not only would they draft legislation to this effect, but Abbate would seek the support of FDNY unions as well. My plan was to contact the state commissioner for public safety and the NYS Fire Prevention Bureau, along with upstate political groups that would be supportive of such a bill.

Shortly after our meeting I received a call from the mayor's office informing me the mayor planned on helping me get sponsorship for Golden's bill that would be for a statewide inclusion. It would be logical to simultaneously push for city and state reforms. NYC Council Speaker Christine Quinn told me to contact Rob Neuman and Andrew Doba. I called Golden's office and was told that they would be working with the mayor's office about the statewide bill.

I had just started to get the ball rolling, and I was pleasantly surprised that I had gotten off to a good start, a telling indicator that everything would fall nicely into place. How naive I was.

On May 19, 2009, assembly bill A8407, cited as the Graffagnino and Beddia law, was introduced by Assemblyman Richard Gottfried. This bill would amend the general city law by adding a new section, 20-H, that would place all buildings and structures located in New York City that were owned, leased, or operated by New York State under the jurisdiction of the DOB and FDNY to the same extent privately owned buildings and structures are under the jurisdiction of such agencies. All newly constructed and altered buildings would have to comply with DOB and FDNY codes. Existing buildings would be operated and maintained under DOB and FDNY codes. The bill further stated that the state's commissioner of labor and the city's DEP would continue to cooperate in providing notification of and sharing relevant information about asbestos-abatement projects in the city. The mayor urged the earliest possible favorable consideration of this proposal by the legislature.

However, this bill was not the bill I'd discussed with Golden and Abbate, and the legislators introducing and supporting it were not the legislators I thought were going to create and support the bill. The bill I wanted only addressed state buildings throughout NYS. The mayor's office intervened and amended the bill to include state buildings within New York City with fines and enforcement by city agencies. Buildings owned by the State are not subject to local city codes and regulations. Also, bill sponsorship was moved from Abbate to Gottfried and from Golden to Senator Daniel Squadron. I was not told about these changes or why the changes were made.

So why the change? At the time, I thought there must be a good reason for it. How wrong I was. During this long, convoluted process, I woke up and realized that I was stuck smack in the middle of an enormous and purposely complex political labyrinth with not even the slightest clue how to get out.

The next day senate bill S5597 was introduced by Squadron and Golden. This bill was exactly the same as assembly bill A8407. The senate and assembly bills were sent to the Cities Committee on May 20, 2009, and then to the Codes Committee on June 2, 2009.

On June 3, 2009, Manhattan Borough President Scott Stringer sent a memo of support to Squadron and Speaker of the New York

State Assembly Sheldon Silver for both the assembly and senate bills. The subject was "Closing a major loophole in NYS public safety." He stated that had the LMDC been required to comply with the city's building and fire code, it was likely that this tragedy would have been prevented. Two weeks later I received an e-mail from the mayor's office about rallying support for the bill's passage. The e-mail also included the names of the mayor's staffers in Albany, should I need them, and a local (NYC) staff member that could supply details about the bill.

In early September 2009, I continued to gain support for the amended state bill. My assumption was that to have a modified version for better building and fire safety was better than not having a bill passed. The bill progressed through the Codes Committee and was now being reviewed by the Ways and Means Committee. On the senate side, the bill hadn't moved. Now I was grilled with the following questions from the legislature, which I tried to answer:

Q: Which agency or department inspects NYS buildings for building- and fire-code violations?

A: The NYS Fire Prevention Bureau (FPB).

Q: Does this agency also have enforcement power such as issuing citations and closing buildings for serious code violations?

A: The FPB has enforcement power in state university buildings and could issue violations, enforce compliance, close down buildings, and take the college or university to state court if necessary.

Q: Which agency or department inspects NYS buildings within NYC and Long Island?

A: The FPB.

Because of FPB enforcement policies, building-safety violations were reduced by 25 percent. In the early 1990s, Governor Mario Cuomo dropped building and fire-safety code inspections. He gave state agencies the power to police and self-correct themselves. This could be likened to giving city architects the power to validate that their buildings were safe and complied with all city codes. Obviously, it couldn't work unless an agency checks on them and validates what they signed is true and accurate.

State law requires state inspectors to share inspection reports with city fire departments. Metropolitan Transportation Authority complies with state regulations and codes. The FPB inspects power authorities based on a mutual agreement. There would be some costs associated with state-performed inspections. The state, for example, inspects 55 Hanson Place in Brooklyn and the Adam Clayton Powell building in Manhattan. A thorough inspection of a high-rise building takes two days. Leased state spaces in cities are inspected by local building and fire departments because the state is a tenant in the leased buildings.

Snafu: Bill Stuck in Committee

I received a call from Abbate that my bill was stuck in committee and that I had better come to Albany to explain the bill and answer any questions. I was to meet with the various committee chairpersons and convince them to support the bill. Otherwise, it would die in committee.

The following morning I was in Albany and met with the various committee chairmen and even sat on a committee to explain the impact of the bill and how it would close the loopholes quasi-governmental agencies currently enjoyed by fence-sitting to avoid compliance with city or state regulations.

That afternoon the mayor's contingent in Albany, Abbate, FDNY Assistant Chief Richard Tobin, and I met with Assembly Speaker Sheldon Silver's group. There was a major problem with the bill, but with minor modifications the bills (assembly bill A8407 and senate bills S5597 and S5666) would be agreeable to both upstate and downstate legislators. NYC fire and Buildings Department people would be free to inspect state buildings in New York City, but NYC wasn't permitted to issue violations or fines to state entities, because it would violate state law.

After conferring with the mayor's people and Chief Tobin, I suggested that the FDNY and DOB inspect state buildings. If a violation was found, the state agency would get a written notification of the violation, and a copy would be sent to the state agency responsible for overseeing other state agencies for building- and fire-code violations.

This state entity would inspect and issue the violations, if necessary, and would share information and documentation with the DOB or FDNY. The FDNY would then return to validate that corrective action had been taken and report to that agency as well as to the state entity responsible for compliance. This way, the sovereignty of the city and state would remain intact. Sheldon Silver's group agreed that this scenario would work for the assembly side. Cost of implementation would be minimal.

On January 6, 2010, senate bill S5597A (amended) moved to the Cities Committee. On January 26, 2010, the bill moved to the Codes Committee, and then on March 23, 2010, the bill moved to the Finance Committee.

In April of that same year I was notified that the mayor didn't agree with the changes made to the bills. He felt that the state should be subjected to city rules if the state-owned building was in the city or if the state agency rented an entire building in NYC.

On June 22, 2010, I learned that Squadron had introduced senate bill S5597B. This version of the senate bill called for a NYC/NYS task force on building and fire safety in state-owned or -leased buildings. It would consist of dual co chairs appointed by the mayor and governor. In addition to the co chairs, the working group would have eight additional members, four from the city and four from the state. The bill set forth various areas the group should review related to fire and building safety and how NYC fire and building codes relate to NY State codes. It would include safety issues encountered by first responders in New York City when responding to emergencies in state-controlled buildings.

In early July, I sent an e-mail to Manhattan Borough President Scott Stringer about my thoughts on the changes to the bill that I, and others, had fought so hard to create. This bill troubled me for the following reasons:

- The mayor's office wrote the original bill knowing that it violated state law. A city cannot penalize its state in the same way the state cannot fine a federal-government entity; it is the right of sovereignty.

- I went to Albany to push for a modified bill that would pass the state's Codes Committee. The modified bill, S5597 part A, said the FDNY and DOB would inspect state buildings for violations and issue violation notices (not a fine or penalty) when a city violation was identified. This would be issued to the state agency where the violation was found, with a copy going to the state FPB and the governor's office. The state FPB might assert that the city code violation was not a state violation and that the agency was in compliance with state safety codes. If the violation was deemed valid, the governor's office would direct compliance with the city code and notify the agency commissioner in Albany. After the required time frame for repair, the FDNY/DOB would revisit the agency to verify compliance. If not fixed, the governor's office would penalize the agency and institute corrective action, billing the state agency in violation.

- The mayor gave the bill to Assemblyman Gottfried and Senator Squadron when the bill should have gone to Assemblyman Abbate, because he was in charge of the FDNY state issues and safety, and to Golden, the original creator of the bill.

- At the last minute I was told that there was a problem because of pushback from upstate senators and the governor's office. Because of this new wrinkle, Squadron and Gottfried sought counsel with the mayor's office (this was on a Thursday). On Monday part B was issued and quickly passed by the senate. A few days later the assembly gave it the green light. I was never consulted about part B.

Bill's Pros and Cons

The positive part of the bill was that the proper city and state agencies would interact in the hopes of securing a better bill. The negative part of the bill was the committee would take 15 months to make recommendations, and it didn't have to reach an agreement or push for a state law. The bill, basically stopped all action for 15 months, with no guarantee that anything would happen. (At this point, I was convinced this was a delaying tactic from the mayor so the bill wouldn't be passed into law.)

I was told that the governor would sign it because it costs nothing and doesn't force the city or state to do anything. I had hoped that something would be completed in the near future to make state buildings safer, but now all I can do is wait and pray that no one else dies due to building- and fire-safety issues and that the city and state people would realize that something must be done to protect New Yorkers.

The bill, signed by Governor Paterson on July 31, 2010, created, for one year, a joint city-state task force that would improve the building-inspections process.

The NYC-NYS Task Force on Building and Fire Safety issued its report in July 2012. The task force was chaired by FDNY Commissioner Salvatore Cassano and State Homeland Security and Emergency Services Commissioner Jerome Hauer. The report was an analysis of building- and fire-safety issues related to state-owned property in New York City. It included an updated inventory of state agency–owned buildings in NYC, and it provided recommendations for improvement. In sum, the report highlighted the significant dangers posed by discrepancies in fire and building codes and pointed the way toward improvements for safeguarding first responders and the public. The report's 19 recommendations also include time frames for implementation. Squadron urged relevant city, state, and affiliated entities to commit to implementing all recommendations within a year from the date the report was issued.

After not hearing anything from the task force for a year, I requested an update from Squadron's office. Mary Cooley, office director to the senator, sent an e-mail to me and to Community Board 1 Chairperson Catherine McVay Hughes:

> Hi Joe, Catherine – I wanted to pass this letter along that we got in response for a status update from Commissioner Hauer on the reform of state building codes and hiring of additional inspectors. I think you'll be pleased to see Commissioner Hauer's note to

Senator Squadron about additional hires and improved communication between the city and state fire agencies.

Regarding the update to codes, I want to be clear that when they met with Senator Squadron last year, Commissioner Cassano agreed that strengthening state codes was not as simple as just adopting the city codes. He and Commissioner Hauer believe a thorough update to the codes is needed, but that several standards need to be considered. Let me know your thoughts?

—Mary Cooley

The letter from Commissioner Hauer, dated June 6, 2013, to Senator Squadron as an update of the efforts related to implementation of the task force's recommendations read as follows:

I am happy to report that Office of Fire Prevention and Control staff has actively remained in contact with FDNY to serve as the State's liaison related to fire safety on state property. To date, FDNY has not reported any fire safety issues on state property. This past January, in an attempt to continue the efforts of the Task Force, my staff communicated to NYC Administration the need to identify top priorities for action. We are waiting to hear back regarding this prioritization. In response to your request for an update related to State and City codes, the State is currently undertaking the process to adopt the 2009 and 2012 International Code Council model codes, which should more closely align the State and City codes. It is important to note that the City code is based on the 2006 International model Codes, with enhancements, and with the State's adoption of the 2012 model code, there will be portions of the State Code which will likely provide greater fire safety protections than the City Code. We continue to work towards enhancing building and fire safety statewide.

Handwritten at the bottom, he added, "We are in the process of hiring several people, two of which will be stationed at FDNY HDQ. —NYS Commissioner Jerry Hauer."

Following a request for information, I received this e-mail from Cooley three weeks later:

> With apologies, the Assembly bill A05342 did not move this session and there is no state senate same-as, but Commissioner Hauer's office did respond to our letter about the status of hiring inspectors to ensure state buildings are inspected in collaboration with city personnel. They said that they are currently recruiting staff for active coordination, and should have people doing the work soon. I've asked my policy director to keep me posted as we will be continuing the conversation through the fall.

It seemed very strange that there was no equivalent state senate bill, since Squadron would be the one to create and introduce the bill. Why hadn't he?

The reason soon became clear to me when I listened to the runoff primary debate for public advocate between Squadron and Council Member Letitia James. The debate centered on personal attacks and how far removed from Bloomberg each candidate was. Squadron complained that James had voted for the mayor's bills 98 percent of the time. James counterpunched Squadron by saying that the senator had worked for the mayor, carried his water bottle in Albany, and sided with him about building housing in Brooklyn Bridge Park.

At this point of this seemingly endless political saga, I need to backtrack by saying that Abbate introduced bill A9368 on February 24, 2012. This bill would grant local and county governments the authority to inspect state-owned buildings for purposes of enforcing the NYS Uniform Fire Prevention and Building Code and the state energy-conservation code. This would permit localities to conduct inspections authorized by the current codes and to issue violation permits instead of having to issue premature fines automatically. This was the bill that was worked out between Silver's office and the various Albany committees. It had the support of both houses, upstate and downstate legislative representatives, and the UFA and UFOA unions.

This bill was referred to governmental operations. Months went by, and I heard nothing about it. When I asked Abbate about the bill's status, he said the legislature was waiting for the senate's version of this bill. He informed me that he had sent the bill to Golden over two months ago. I called Golden's office and spoke to his chief of staff about the senate's version of Abbate's. He told me that there was no version of a senate bill because everyone was opposed to it. Local governments were heavily opposed to it because it would cost too much. He said it was seriously flawed and would open the door to lawsuits because it encompassed so much ground. According to him, it needed to be renegotiated.

It took me a while, but by then I'd figured out how this poker-like game was played. Hands down, these men controlled the table; I didn't stand a chance.

When I look back on the long sequence of events, it seems more than apparent that this was the mayor's way of blocking and eventually shutting the bill down so he could continue to support his friends at the LMDC and in the real estate and construction industries. Now no one would have to worry about any safety laws slowing progress and increasing costs; instead profits could increase.

Bloomberg's Power Politics

Bloomberg spoke as if he wanted safer buildings and fire-code regulations. However, his actions said otherwise. He made sure that the past three governors vetoed training for firefighters and blocked giving the DOB additional powers to re-inspect buildings and increase penalties at construction sites, and he continued to allow architects to self-certify their own work.

Here's a list of Bloomberg's actions since he became mayor:

- In 2007, he pushed to have Governor Spitzer veto a bill that would have strengthened the Buildings Department and made

NYC buildings safer. The mayor argued that it would have cost the city $10 million.

- In 2010, he begged Governor Paterson to veto a bill that was supported by the city council, passed overwhelmingly by the Albany legislature, and supported by both FDNY unions. The bill was to provide eight hours of training in the recently passed, new FDNY codes and regulations manual. The mayor said it would cost $30 million and that it's not firefighters' job to inspect buildings. If it's not their job to inspect buildings, then why did he hold those seven FDNY officers up to ridicule, abuse, and public guilt for not performing the so-called "15-day rule to inspect buildings? How can you hold firefighters accountable if you won't train them?

- In 2012, he pressured Governor Cuomo to veto a training bill for the FDNY and DOB that would have cost, according to his numbers, $20 million.

Bill S2747 related to application of the state Uniform Fire Prevention and Building Code to certain premises owned or leased by the state or public authorities and directed the Office of General Services to create a staged plan for compliance. As of the start of 2015, this bill has gone nowhere.

~ 18 ~

Building and Fire Safety on the Federal Level

Nearly 900 state, federal, and foreign embassy buildings do not have to conform to NYC building or fire codes.

An item of great concern echoed by all city agencies was that there are close to 900 state, federal, and foreign-embassy buildings that do not have to conform to NYC building or fire codes. The rationale for this was political hierarchy where the federal government has jurisdiction over state governments, just as states have jurisdiction over city governments. And foreign-embassy buildings are considered extensions of the country they represent and cannot be controlled by federal, state, or city regulations. This political escape clause gave me an idea.

In September 2008, I went to the General Service Administration's (GSA) Director of Federal Technology Service, Kerry Blette, and discussed my idea. At the conclusion of our meeting, he suggested that I speak with the Assistant Regional Administrator, Patrick Donovan. I explained my plan to Patrick, and he agreed that I should present my proposal to the Northeast & Caribbean Regional Administrator, Emily Baker. At this meeting I discussed my thoughts about a change of protocol. The regional administrator agreed to set a precedent and allow a modification to structural protocol that would allow the FDNY and NYC Department of Buildings to inspect any federal building that GSA leased or owned throughout New York City.

This was a momentous first step in creating a universal building-and-fire-safety agreement. The regional administrator instructed GSA's legal department to contact the mayor's office to begin the authorization that would allow NYC agencies access to federal buildings. I contacted Deputy Mayor Holloway about this, and he agreed that this was a positive step and that he would be personally involved in making this happen.

At this point I opened negotiations with US Postal Service executive officers in an attempt to bring the same safety agreement to the Postal Service in the Northeast Region. I had worked for the Postal Service for 30 years and knew several executives. The postal executives wanted to wait until the pact was signed between the city and GSA and then would review it.

Virtually everyone I spoke with about creating a unique, one-of-a-kind agreement was positive and encouraging.

Approximately two weeks later a meeting was held at GSA's offices at 26 Federal Plaza, attended by GSA's attorneys, Patrick Donovan, and Regional Administrator Emily Baker, along with Cas Holloway, his staff, and the mayor's legal staff.

Prior to this meeting, I had sent a thank-you note to the executives of GSA. (See Appendix I.)

The meeting between the city and the federal government agencies was held, but an agreement was not signed. I asked GSA's legal staff why the agreement wasn't signed, because I had been under the impression that everything had been worked out. They told me that the mayor insisted that if any safety violations were found, the city wanted to have the federal government fined and made to pay the city for those infractions. This action would violate federal law. The federal government was willing to fix any violations if they were in violation of federal safety codes. The federal government agreed that there were differences between city and federal codes, but if the intent was there to satisfy a regulation by another method, then the infraction would not be a violation. The city disagreed and left the bargaining table.

The GSA regional administrator continued to hope that a reasonable agreement could be forged with NYC. The public-safety group within GSA could not believe that a minor issue embedded in federal law could not be modified so that it would be agreeable to both sides.

GSA continued to develop a draft of what the federal government can and cannot do and passed this along to the mayor's group and their legal staff to open negotiations. GSA continued to draft a Memorandum of Agreement/ Understanding for the city that would embrace and solidify an understanding that has enforcement parameters and site inspections as part of the terms that both sides could live with.

In January 2009, I sent an e-mail to Holloway explaining that I had spoken to GSA's Baker. She was taking a new position, and the Deputy Regional Administrator Steve Ruggiero would handle the memorandum of agreement (MOA) between the city and the federal government. My e-mail stated, "GSA will be happy to sign the MOA providing it does not violate federal mandates. I'm sure we can work around these issues. I know Emily spoke with you and that GSA is waiting for the next draft so our and your lawyers can have fun tearing it apart. If you need any help or anything I can do, just let me know."

Two days later I received a response from Holloway saying, "I'm working on the changes we discussed and hope to have a revised draft turned around by early next week. Will keep you in the loop —Cas."

Three weeks later I sent another e-mail to Holloway: "Mr. Holloway, Haven't seen or heard anything on the developing MOA draft between the city and GSA? Can you provide a status on it?"

GSA never received a response from city hall.

I wondered why the city would not take advantage of the opportunity to have a unique agreement with a federal agency over a minor issue and a federal-statute violation. The mayor used the same excuse with the state legislature on building-and-fire-safety bills. I could only conclude that the mayor never wanted it to happen.

Shortly afterward I met with Manhattan Borough President Stringer to discuss the lost opportunity between the city and the federal government. He believed that it was an excellent idea and that any opportunity to have closer and friendlier relationships between different political and governmental agencies should be pursued. Building and fire safety involves everyone. It is better to have a closer working relationship because it enhances productivity and cooperation between the various groups.

The only positive news on the federal level was OSHA's announcement of its new program, the Severe Violator Enforcement Program (SVEP), which would increase penalty violation costs. Effective in 45 days, SVEP administratively raised the dollar value on its penalties.

An OSHA news release explained how the program works:

The current maximum penalty for a serious violation, one capable of causing death or serious physical serious harm, is only $7,000 and the maximum penalty for a willful violation is $70,000. The average penalty for a serious violation will increase from about $1,000 to an average of $3,000 to $4,000. Monetary penalties for violations of the OSHA Act have been increased only once in 40 years despite inflation. The Protecting America's Workers Act would raise these penalties, for the first time since 1990, to $12,000 and $250,000, respectively. Future penalty increases would be tied to inflation. In the meantime, OSHA will focus on outreach in preparation of implementing this new penalty policy.

Replacing OSHA's Enhanced Enforcement Policy, SVEP requires that follow-up inspections must be conducted after the citations become final to determine whether the cases were abated or whether the employee was committing similar violations.

The OSHA news release went on to say, "When there are reasonable grounds to believe that compliance problems identified in the initial inspection may be indicative of a broader pattern of non-compliance, OSHA will inspect related sites of the same employer." In such cases there will be a SVEP nationwide inspection list, with all sites inspected if there are 10 or fewer, along with sites chosen randomly if there are more.

~ 19 ~

Civil Actions

The Beddia family and Linda Graffagnino (on behalf of her herself and her children) filed a lawsuit against New York City and the LMDC. The lawsuit blamed the contractors for being incompetent and inexperienced, the LMDC for ignoring its safety plan and for building and fire violations, and the city for gross negligence.

The initial civil action related to the Deutsche Bank building fire came November 2007 when five firefighters injured during the fire sued the city and state; the LMDC, as the building owner; and Bovis Lend Lease for negligence. The lawsuit sought millions of dollars because the firefighters suffered career-threatening injuries.

In April 2008, the Beddia family and Linda Graffagnino (on behalf of herself and her children) filed a lawsuit against New York City and the LMDC. The lawsuit blamed the contractors for being incompetent and inexperienced, the LMDC for ignoring its safety plan and for building and fire violations, and the city for gross negligence.

In June 2008, DA Morgenthau sought an injunction to stop the civil suit the Beddia and Graffagnino families filed. The DA's office said the civil suit should be delayed until the criminal investigation was concluded. A court-ordered stay would stop any depositions in the civil suit indefinitely.

The Graffagnino family went to court to have the DA's civil-case delay canceled. John Meringolo, the family attorney, argued the following points:

- The DA had presented only conclusory and speculative allegations that the continuation of the civil trial would hinder the grand jury investigation.

- The DA's office had failed to meet its burden of asserting particular and specific reasons why the stay is necessary.
- The DA had not identified any member of the defendant class herein as a specific target.
- The DA had failed to represent that any indictments would come out of the grand jury investigation.
- The DA had not identified any particular subject of discovery or any specific individual deponent in this matter that might be introduced as evidence.
- Four of the defendants were public defendants and thus were not subject to criminal prosecution.
- The DA sought a stay of unlimited scope and indefinite duration based solely on the conclusory and speculative allegations that the continuation of the civil action might jeopardize the grand jury investigation.

Under ordinary circumstances, a normal term of the grand jury is four weeks. Although a grand jury may be extended beyond four weeks due to incomplete business, such as unavailable witnesses or subpoena issues, no new matters can be presented during the grand jury's extended term.

Judge Eileen Rakower's ruling concurred with the DA's request and stated, "This court is mindful that any extension of the Special Grand Jury impaneled to investigate this matter can only be obtained after application to the court which impaneled that Special Grand Jury with good cause shown for such extension. The investigation has been ongoing since August 2007 and is being supervised by the court to ensure that such investigation does not continue indefinitely based solely on the whim of the DA."

The motion to intervene was granted, and the motion for a stay of the civil proceedings was granted until the termination and disbanding of the special grand jury impaneled for this investigation. However, the court allowed the investigation to continue indefinitely based solely on the DA's unilateral assertions.

Around December 2008, the DA called the Beddia and Graffagnino families in for a meeting. Dan Castleman, Morgenthau's assistant, headed the assembly. With him was Patrick Dugan, who was in charge of the investigation, and other members of their staff.

The DA's office asked us how we would feel if they did not prosecute Bovis, the city, or the state. At that time, the families immediately rejected any agreement that would not seek to prosecute those groups or individuals whom we believed played a major part in our family members' deaths.

Castleman suggested that if we would agree with the DA's decision, each person at this table, representing the families of Robert Beddia and Joseph Graffagnino, would leave the table with over $1 million each. Again, both families rejected the offer. The DA said that we should take a week or so to think about the offer made by Bovis. After that time, the offer would be dropped. Michael Barasch, attorney for the Beddias, asked why the DA would negotiate with the families of the deceased firefighters on Bovis's behalf and not Bovis directly who would pay the settlement. The DA brokering a deal for the company he was supposedly seeking criminal charges on had the appearance of impropriety.

Prosecutors quickly countered, saying that it wasn't a bribe but simply an expression of remorse and regret without conceding liability. If accepted, this money would not be part of any civil action the families might win. The prosecutors were continuing to seek indictments against the John Galt Corporation and 14 workers from Bovis and Galt. My family believed that if this were true, Bovis could have simply offered the money with no strings attached.

I asked what had happened since the previous time I was in this office when Morgenthau had told me, "We will follow the money trail, no matter where it leads." Well, it led to the steps of city hall, where it all came to a screeching halt.

Later, it was found that the DA's rationale was that Bovis employed hundreds of people in NYC and that an indictment against them could cause government agencies and other companies to drop their business dealings with Bovis, possibly putting the company in bankruptcy. Also, the maximum penalty against Bovis would be $10,000. The prosecutors thought that they could extract much more through negotiations with the city and Bovis. A week or two later the Beddia family accepted a $5 million settlement, with New York City adding another $1 million later. To my knowledge, the settlement was listed as a luxury payment.

The estate of Joseph P. Graffagnino rejected the offer of payment, stating that it was blood money. Castleman said that this was the best deal for everyone, and he couldn't understand why we wouldn't accept it. I told him that it was the best deal for him, Bovis, New York City, and New York State, but it was certainly not the best for us.

In February 2010, the estate of Joseph P. Graffagnino made a motion to lift the stay order imposed by Judge Rakower at the request of the DA so that we could proceed with the civil case. Our attorney argued that the grand jury had handed up indictments against Galt and three individuals. But the grand jury still remained impaneled. The defendants—the LMDC, the LMCCC, Galt, and Bovis—objected on the grounds that being deposed in the civil action might be self-incriminating for the criminal case. They said they couldn't be deposed until the criminal case was over. The DA stated that they would allow for document discovery only. Meringolo argued that there was evidence that the LMDC, the LMCCC, and Bovis were not to be prosecuted; that Galt had been indicted on a minor offense; and that the other indictments were against only three employees.

Judge Barbara Jaffe ended the stay on the civil case. A normal grand jury investigation lasts one month and with extenuating circumstances perhaps a couple of weeks more. This grand jury lasted 17 1/4 months.

Money Settlements Only Assuage Guilt; They Don't Fix Problems

In May 2012, the estate of Joseph P. Graffagnino accepted a settlement from Bovis of $9 million with an additional $1 million from NYC. This basically ended the Graffagnino family's civil actions. I wasn't in favor of accepting the offer, because it ended our family's chances of pursuing legal action to bring those we believed to be guilty to justice. I understood my daughter-in-law's position and that she had to consider her children's future. But I never believed that throwing money at a problem ever solved anything. All it did was cover up and mask the real issues. It never fixed the problem; it just made it more complicated.

I continued to push for state investigations into the Deutsche Bank building fire. I asked Governor Cuomo to appoint a special prosecutor or special investigator to look into the actions taken by the DA, the mayor, the LMDC, and the LMCCC, along with those of Spitzer and Bloomberg's political appointees. I unofficially inquired to have the Public Integrity Commission conduct an independent investigation. I asked NYS Attorney General Cuomo and Schneiderman to open an investigation based on the evidence that I had acquired over the years. All my efforts were rejected.

I then sought to open a civil rights case against the city and state. In order to proceed with a civil rights case you need to have *standing*. According to New York State law, *standing* is the capacity of a party to file a civil suit. At the heart of these statutes is the requirement that plaintiffs have sustained or will sustain direct injury or harm and that this harm is redressable.

As the father of the deceased firefighter, I was not considered to have *standing*. The Beddia family and my daughter-in-law, Linda, had settled with the relevant parties; thus they could no longer become involved with anything involving the Deutsche Bank building fire. The criminal-liability time limit expired on August 18, 2012.

In June 2012, I contacted civil rights lawyer Norman Siegel because I believed I had found a way to file a federal civil rights claim. I had researched several civil rights actions and found an area that was directly related to the actions taken and not taken by city and state agencies that had caused the fire and to the apparent cover-ups that stemmed from the criminal investigation of that fire.

Stuart Goldman, a dentist friend, suggested a qui tam action (an individual can bring suit with knowledge of past or present fraud committed against the government on its behalf or if the bringing of this suit is in the public interest).

The statute for redressing constitutional- and federal-statute violations is 42 U.S.C. Section 1983. I concentrated my research on the areas I believed were directly related to the actions of city and state agencies and their officials that had led to the deaths of two firefighters and injuries to 105 others. Those areas are as follows:

- *Deliberate indifference:* The LMCCC and the LMDC, along with city hall and Albany elected officials, showed deliberate indifference in keeping safety people away from the Deutsche

Bank building. Safety violations were rampant because the priority goal was to demolish that building by year's end.

- *Lack of training:* Firefighters said that they were not trained in fighting hazmat fires. Also, DOB inspectors repeatedly stated that they were not trained to identify a standpipe or other safety controls within that building.

- *State-created danger:* The LMCCC and the LMDC were repeatedly told by the DOI that Galt was not qualified to deconstruct buildings or hazard removal. The LMDC signed a contract with Bovis stating that they both would obey all city and state fire- and building-safety codes, yet they repeatedly ignored all of them. And political interference kept safety engineers and local subcontractors who witnessed safety violations (OSHA, the EPA, the FDNY, and the DOB) from reporting them.

- *Municipal and supervisory liability:* The combination of untrained workers, incompetent supervisors, and the removal of anyone who voiced disapproval created death trap conditions.

The statute of limitations to file a federal civil rights investigative claim was three years from the date of the Deutsche Bank building fire.

~ 20 ~

Similar Catastrophes

Safety-enforcement funding took second place to other financial needs, such as real estate, city infrastructure, and construction. Deaths and injuries were soon forgotten in the course of business expansion.

Many of the circumstances surrounding the Triangle Shirtwaist Factory on March 25, 1911, are similar to the Deutsche Bank building fire.

The Triangle Shirtwaist Factory fire has been described as the deadliest workplace accident in New York City's history because most of the deaths were preventable. The fire killed 146 workers, 123 women, and 23 men. Located in the top three floors of the Asch Building, on the corner of Greene Street and Washington Place in Manhattan, the Triangle factory was a sweatshop that employed mostly immigrant teenage girls who spoke no English and worked 12-hour days in a cramped space, hunched over sewing machines. There were four elevators to the factory floors, but only one was fully operational. To reach the elevator, the workers had to walk down a long, narrow corridor. There were two stairways to the street, but one was locked from the outside to prevent stealing; the other opened inward. There was a fire escape, but it was so narrow it would have taken hours for the women to use it.

The fire reportedly started by a dropped match in a rag bin. A manager tried to extinguish it with a fire hose. It was a wasted effort because the hose was rotted and its valve was rusted shut. As the fire grew and quickly spread, panic ensued. Like the firefighters trapped in the Deutsche Bank building, the workers were entombed in a death trap.

The owners of the factory, Max Blanck and Isaac Harris, had had multiple fires in the building, had insurance on all merchandise, and had a long history of ignoring government safety regulations. The owners retained shrewd lawyers and, with the help of biased judges, walked away with minimum fines.

Safety marches and political speeches promising improved building and fire regulations followed the disaster. Despite front-page investigative stories, protests, and public outcry from workers and unions throughout the United States, the partners never repaired the building and continued to ignore mandatory fire-prevention regulations, such as a sprinkler systems and functional fire escapes.

Mike Wallace, a professor at John Jay College of Criminal Justice, said the safety initiatives that were instituted after the Triangle Shirtwaist Factory fire—mainly initiated from public outcry—were eventually reversed because of the lack of funding and enforcement intent. Safety-enforcement funding eventually took second place to other financial needs, such as real estate, city infrastructure, and construction. Deaths and injuries were soon forgotten in the course of business expansion. Wallace pointed out the similarities between the Deutsche Bank building fire and the Triangle Shirtwaist Factory fire, including faulty standpipes, inoperable sprinklers, blocked exits, a failure of the city to inspect the factory for building and fire violations, lack of qualified inspectors, and a failure to heavily fine and penalize the builders' owners and the City of New York for gross negligence. The indictments were for second-degree manslaughter, criminally negligent homicide, and reckless endangerment.

Following the Deutsche Bank building fire, Bovis's top managers faced a 20-year prison term after their second trial yet only received a fine. Galt's maximum fine was $10,000, or $5,000 per life lost.

Lack of adherence to safety protocols has resulted in many deaths and injuries, including the following events:

- 2005, Texas City, Texas: BP refinery explosion—15 dead, 170 injured
- 2006, Upshur County, West Virginia: methane explosion at Sago Mine caused by lighting blast—12 dead.

- 2006, Harland County, Kentucky: Darby mine gas explosion—5 dead
- 2007, New York City, New York: Deutsche Bank building fire—2 dead, 105 injured
- 2008, Savannah-Chatham County, Georgia: sugar-refinery explosion—13 dead, at least 40 injured
- 2010, Middletown, Connecticut: power plant explosion—6 dead, at least 50 injured
- 2010, Comfort, West Virginia: explosion at Upper Big Branch Mine—29 dead
- 2010, Gulf of Mexico: Deepwater Horizon (BP) oil spill—11 dead

~21~

Positive Actions

Over time tragedy unites people to perform positive actions for the betterment of humanity.

While most of my book focuses on the need for improved and consistent building- and fire-safety regulations and just penalties for offenders, a great deal of good has come out of the catastrophes and tragic accidents that have resulted in the loss of hundreds of lives. Here are a few of the efforts worthy of mention.

George Steinbrenner College Scholarship Fund

Yankee baseball team owner George Steinbrenner created scholarships to attend a city or state college for the children of police and firefighters who died in the line of duty.

Joseph B. Cavallaro Intermediate School

The students of Joseph B. Cavallaro Intermediate School in Brooklyn honored the tragic deaths of firefighters Joseph Graffagnino and Robert Beddia by collecting funds to plant a tree in their memory. They worked closely with Susan Gooberman of the NYC Department of Parks, who was in charge of NYC Going Green to help the environment. A fund drive, Fallen Heroes Memorial, for the FDNY and NYPD raised money for planting a tree near Ladder 5/Engine 24 on Houston Street following a ceremony on March 20, 2008.

Students of Cavallaro Intermediate School also adopted Ladder 5/Engine 24 and planned to honor the lives of Graffagnino and Beddia on the eighteenth of every month. Special thanks to Linda Mollo-Holmes,

Joy Simoes, Kim Viglione, Anna Maria Comuniello, Lorraine Biondo, and Theresa Cardazone for their efforts in remembering both firefighters and the other members of the FDNY and NYPD who have given their lives to protect others.

The bond between Cavallaro Intermediate School and the firefighters of Ladder 5/Engine 24 continued. Firefighters visited the school and spoke to students about fire safety, and the students in turn made gifts for the firefighters and dedicated a song to them, which was sung by the school's choir. Prior to the Super Bowl, the students made a Giants Super Bowl basket of chips, dips, and football paper goods for the firefighters of Ladder 5/Engine 24.

There were other celebrations and events as well, all of which were heartfelt demonstrations of love and support for the fallen firefighters and police officers.

Fort Hamilton High School, Brooklyn

In 2007, teachers that attended Fort Hamilton High School with my son received approval to have the gymnasium renamed the Joseph Graffagnino Memorial Gymnasium and to have the bodybuilding training room dedicated to Joey. My son was an avid bodybuilder who won a trophy in the Mr. Fort Hamilton Lightweight Division 1991.

Starting in May 2008, the bodybuilding-contest scholarships were given in my son's name. Also educational scholarships—Joseph Graffagnino Profiles in Courage Scholarships—were given in Joey's name to students who had overcome adversity and couldn't afford to attend college. The presentation of these bodybuilding and educational scholarships became annual events, which I always attend. Special thanks to former Principal Jo Ann Chester, Assistant Principal Susan Russo, and teachers Tanja Larsen and Kristen Brehm. My son was inducted into the Fort Hamilton High School Hall of Fame on February 13, 2016.

William McKinley Junior High School (IS 259) Scholarships

At William McKinley Junior High School, educational scholarships are presented in my son's name to hardworking students who strive for good grades and perform optional school-related work. The scholarships are awarded annually. Special thanks to Kathy Molfino for organizing the scholarships and fundraising.

New FDNY Training Manual

An updated FDNY training manual with new codes and regulations was published in July 2008. The new regulations and safety laws are for building and fire safety in construction, demolition, and abatement sites. New and veteran firefighters are being trained in these procedures at the FDNY Training Academy on Randall's Island and at the Bureau of Training at Fort Totten, New York. This new training manual is dedicated to the memories of firefighters Graffagnino and Beddia.

Radio Frequency Identification Devices (RFID)

A few weeks after my son died, I decided to identify the reasons why my son and Bobby Beddia were not found in time to save their lives. I researched other fires where firefighters had died to find out whether better technology could have saved them. I learned that many firefighters and first responders who never made it out of buildings died because they became disoriented and lost and fellow firefighters and rescuers couldn't find them in time. The victims were trapped, had depleted air supplies, and died from suffocation or smoke inhalation.

A good example was a fire at a 99 Cents Store in the Bronx. A firefighter on the scene tripped and fell to the floor, knocking over shelves of products, which covered him. He called out a mayday, but brother firefighters couldn't find him in the dense smoke of the dark building, even though they were only a few feet from him.

I wanted to know what technology was being used to find firefighters in similar scenarios. I learned that the FDNY has been using Global Positioning Systems (GPS) technology on FDNY vehicles. GPS was tested to find firefighters within buildings but without success.

Having been a telecommunications engineer for more than 20 years, first with the US Postal Service and later with the US General Services Administration, I had a working knowledge of various types of wireless technology. I knew that GPS technology was most effective in outdoor, open environments. Once inside a building, however, it becomes almost useless. Knowing this, I felt that radio frequency technology would be a better alternative in an enclosed or interior environment.

I had a representative of an RFID company give a presentation at FDNY headquarters to explain how radio frequency technology can be used to find firefighters trapped inside buildings. Another demonstration of RFID technology took place at the FDNY Training Academy on Randall's Island. Battalion commanders from every borough attended. Chiefs controlled laptop computers that followed firefighters into training structures where controlled fires were started and fire hoses were used to put out the fires. The chiefs were able to follow the firefighters throughout the structure. The field test did well.

Starting on December 11, 2008, the FDNY successfully field-tested RFID tags in Queens. The field tests were engineered and developed by the US Navy Research Laboratory in Washington, DC. I was invited to meet with the researchers and review the variables of the system. I pointed out different methodologies to increase the output in order to get optimum benefits from the tags. I am pleased to report that the FDNY is continuing its research to develop an operational RFID system to track first responders in varied interior locations, such as subways and high-rise buildings.

I would like to be present when the first firefighter is saved using RFID technology. I can't think of a better reward.

St. Ephrem's Church's Chapel of Remembrance, May 3, 2009

The Chapel of Remembrance at St. Ephrem's Church in Brooklyn was dedicated to honor fallen firefighters Joseph Graffagnino and Robert Beddia and all firefighters who died trying to save others. The chapel is not just for firefighters but for the community of St. Ephrem's.

Joann Altieri, my son's aunt, came up with the idea for the chapel. It started with a small plaque in an unused area of the church but evolved into a beautiful side chapel. The chapel area was renovated by firefighters from Joey and Bobby Beddia's firehouse, Ladder 5/Engine 24, and firefighters from local firehouse Engine 284/Ladder 149, along with friends, cousins, and family. A statue of Saint Florian, patron saint of firefighters, was created by Reto DeMetz of the DeMetz Art Studio in Ortisei, Italy. Facing Saint Florian is *Saint Michael Archangel Guides Souls to Heaven*, a stained glass built by Henry Garguilo in Mount Vernon, New York. The statue and stained glass were coordinated by John Chiarelli.

Saint Anthony of Padua Church's Annual Memorial Mass, August 18, 2009

On the anniversary of Joey Graffagnino's and Bobby Beddia's deaths, a mass is held every year at Saint Anthony of Padua Church in the SoHo section of Manhattan.

Joey Graffagnino Place

In the winter of 2009, Council Member Vincent J. Gentile and Carlo Scissura, former chief of staff to Brooklyn Borough President Marty Markowitz and current president and CEO of the Brooklyn Chamber of Congress, were responsible for renaming the street on the southwest corner of 77 Street and 13 Avenue in Brooklyn to Joey Graffagnino Place.

The Joey "Botz" Day Party, Fall 2010

Held annually on a Sunday afternoon, Joey "Botz" Day includes rides and bounce houses for children and food and drink for families and friends. The event is the brainchild of Joey's close friends Vincent Guifferdo, Chris Auletti, and Steve Fadel. They host it and supply the food and drink. My daughter-in-law and grandchildren are always there to help out. James Romeo, another close friend of Joey, donates the frankfurters and hamburgers.

Plaque on Exterior Wall of Engine 10 and Ladder 10, 124 Liberty Street

The FDNY and Lower Manhattan's Community Board 1 recognized and honored the memory of firefighter Robert Beddia, Engine

Company 24, and firefighter Joseph Graffagnino, Ladder Company 5, with a plaque. The location was chosen because it is directly across the street from where these men died. Community Board 1 pressed for the creation of this plaque. Our thanks go to Catherine McVay Hughes of CB1 and FDNY Commissioner Salvatore Cassano.

~Epilogue~

Those who cannot remember the past are condemned to repeat it.
—George Santayana

I want to sum up and clarify facts that support the premise of *The Fix Is In*, all of which prove that the eight years spent writing this book were not in vain. The meticulously documented chain of events and the large cast of players—which includes New York's top decision makers, city, state, and federal agencies; global corporations; powerful unions; and convicted criminals—prove that the Deutsche Bank building fire should have been prevented. I didn't want any doubts in my readers' minds about what happened on the worst day of my family's life, along with the families of the two other men who lost their lives, and the 100-plus firefighters who suffered injuries, many of which they'll never recover from.

I want to restate facts, share observations and lessons learned, and, describe the impact the fire had on my family. For starters, the Lower Manhattan Development Corporation (LMDC) purchased the damaged Deutsche Bank building at 130 Liberty Street for the city and state in 2004. JP Morgan Chase Bank agreed to have their headquarters built on that site, but only if the LMDC could have the building leveled by December 2007. Larry Silverstein, chairman of Manhattan-based real estate development firm Silverstein Properties Inc., also had an agreement that the area would be ready for rebuilding within specific time frames. If LMDC failed to meet a specified deadline, severe financial penalties would be imposed.

The LMDC gave the general contractor's job to Mayor Bloomberg's and Deputy Mayor Daniel Doctoroff's favorite contractor, Bovis Lend Lease. LMDC had Regional Scaffolding create the John Galt Corporation. Both Bovis and Galt were hired without competition. The contractors insisted on using Safeway Environmental Corporation's officers and equipment. They refused to consider anyone else. They even defied New York City's Department of Investigation (DOI).

Because of strict Environmental Protection Agency (EPA) mandates, Bovis and Galt demanded more money in December 2006. At a Gracie Mansion meeting, the city and state approved more money for the project but demanded the building be torn down by December 2007. If the deconstruction goal was met, there would be millions in incentives. If it wasn't met, there would be costly penalties. At the same meeting, in order to save time, it was decided to simultaneously combine abatement and deconstruction procedures. Eventually, an additional $220 million was added to the original $80 million for the project. Not once was this outrageous increase challenged by any city or state administrator.

When the new strategy was employed in February–March 2007, everything changed. The Department of Buildings (DOB) pulled its Buildings Enforcement Safety Team (BEST), which was responsible for inspecting high-rise construction sites, and replaced it with DOB volunteers. The DOB issued alteration permits instead of demolition permits. LMDC personnel were pulled from the building. Their safety contractors—URS and Site Safety LLC—remained but were ignored. Whistle-blowers were removed, along with a DOB inspector who tried to do his job. The FDNY was kept out of the building and provided no updates regarding the building's contractors. The DOB, the EPA, the Department of Environmental Conservation DEC, OSHA, and scores of other safety teams were blind to the many obvious fire and building violations.

Bovis and Galt Underestimate Project's Complexities

Bovis and Galt quickly realized that they'd underestimated the project. It was impossible to have the building demolished by year's end. The LMDC pushed relentlessly, and the EPA continued to verify compliance. No matter what they did to speed up the deconstruction project, it wasn't fast enough. Bovis and Galt had to come up with another way to get the Deutsche Bank building down—and quickly.

By mid-August, they were on the 26th floor (the building originally had 41 floors). It had taken about 18 months to remove 15 floors. They had four months to remove 26 floors. You do the math.

Enter the FDNY

On August 18, 2007, one of the contractor's employees smelled smoke. Nine minutes later, she called 911. Prior to that, the firehouse across the street from the Deutsche Bank building was notified about the fire by an anonymous person.

Firefighters were at the Deutsche Bank building three minutes before the employee called 911. At about the same time the employee called 911, the FDNY, already in the building, called in a second fire alarm. Less than 10 minutes after the FDNY arrived, the fire was out of control.

This was the only time the FDNY received an emergency fire call from anyone in that building.

FDNY Lied to—Firefighters Walk into a Death Trap

Building engineers swore three times that the building's standpipe system and both internal water pumps were operational. But none of these systems worked, and they'd been that way for years.

When FDNY units arrived, they found that street fire hydrants had been removed or covered with debris. Access points to the building's standpipe system were behind locked and barricaded doors, with plywood boards covering the Siamese building connections. When the FDNY finally gained access and hooked up fire hoses to the building's Siamese connections from three different sides of the building, the water—the only thing that could put out the fire—was being emptied into the basement because both standpipes were broken in multiple places throughout the building.

The firefighters faced bizarre conditions. The fire burned up on the outside of the building, but inside the building it burned down. The stairwells' fireproof walls had been removed, and alternate-floor staircases were covered in combustible wood, plastic sheeting, and glue, which added more fuel to the fire. The fireproof floors and ceilings had been pierced, allowing the melting, burning combustible items to drop to lower floors, further fueling and spreading the fire. If windows and stairwells were sealed tight with plastic, wood and glue so that no toxic material could escape, why create holes in fireproof floors?

Was an attempt to burn off the toxic material from inside the building a calculated strategy so only a non-toxic shell remained?

The placement of the internal fans on every floor violated the approved implementation plan. The fans were supposed to contain toxic materials inside the building; instead they quickly spread the fire to multiple floors. The fan locations on floors 13–17 dragged the fire, smoke, and hot gases across the entire floor, propelling the smoke and hot gases down both stairwells and through holes in the floors such that the smoke and hot gases hugged the floor below. When the smoke and hot gases reached the fans and received fresh air, the hot gases ignited, causing a flashover across the floor, burning everything in its path—equipment, debris, plastic sheeting, wood, diesel fuel, gasoline cans, propane and acetylene canisters.

The DA misled the grand jury, dragging out its investigation for 39 months with inaccurate information and at the same time deliberately failing to mention top government officials responsible. The DA removed any clause in the non-prosecutorial agreement that would have allowed him to prosecute Bovis for their original crimes. The Supreme Court ruled that the agreement was a settlement and not admissible in a civil case, because Bovis never pleaded guilty to anything. After almost four years of investigation and court hearings, the DA created the path that allowed the arrested scapegoats to walk. The Eastern District US Attorney followed the DA's example by allowing Bovis to pay a fine and avoid prosecution. Not one federal, state, or county prosecutor voiced any opposition.

Elected Officials Abuse Power

The way corrupt elected officials abused their power, manipulated the press by distorting information, and then covered up their actions by blaming others is deplorable.

An apathetic public made it easy for Bloomberg to run New York City unchecked. His loyal minions were afraid of him, and the city's taxpaying voters, who put him in office, hardly protested. Having powerful friends who own newspapers and radio and television stations practically guaranteed positive press.

It's no surprise that Gallup polls over the past decade have found that Americans neither trust, respect, nor have much confidence in their elected officials. We're so used to their boasting, false promises and deceiving antics that we'd be amazed if they acted otherwise. But let's assign blame where it belongs. Politicians continue to lie, cheat, and deceive because we allow it. We ought to hold them accountable, but we don't.

The Public Is Partially to Blame

Deservingly, I blame Bloomberg and his legions of gutless suck-ups and all the city, state, and federal agencies that played a part in the Deutsche Bank building fire. Eliot Spitzer, NY governor at the time, was equally to blame. Not only was he complicit in all the deceptive antics, lies, and distortions, but he also turned a deaf ear, giving Bloomberg carte blanche to do whatever he wanted. In a democratic government and a capitalist economy, where checks and balances are built into our system, Bloomberg changed the rules. He ran New York City with immunity. If he felt he had to break rules and bend laws, he did so, and no one objected.

The Fix Is In is not just a New York story. The political involvement and manipulations surrounding the Deutsche Bank building fire are not unique. They're a variation of similar incidents happening throughout the nation. The players—powerful politicians—are playing to a similarly apathetic and impassive audience.

News Media's Impotent Role

The small group of investigative reporters who had the guts to write scathing stories taking Bloomberg to task and holding him accountable paid a heavy price for doing their jobs. They were fired.

Pulitzer Prize–winning journalist Jimmy Breslin attacked the media for its sloppy reporting of 9/11, especially the death of 343 firefighters. Writing for the *Daily News* at the time, Breslin blamed Rudy Giuliani, then NYC's mayor, for failing to get the FDNY radios that worked and for failing to fix the archaic communication problem between the police and fire departments. In one column, Breslin wrote, "Three-hundred-and-forty-three firefighters die and nobody says anything."

In several columns, Breslin blamed a new generation of journalists for coverage lacking passion. When interviewed, Breslin said, "The big thing in the press is total absence of anger. They're the best-educated people we've ever had, but there's nothing inside them to get mad. They're sheep. Name one person at a newspaper or on TV who got mad about firefighters dying by city negligence."

History as Teacher

Philosopher and poet George Santayana wrote, "Those who cannot remember the past are condemned to repeat it." And they do so with predictable frequency.

Lessons learned from 9/11 are a good example. Since then, there have been many improvements in FDNY communication systems. I mentioned a couple of them in earlier chapters, and there are more on the drawing board. Similarly, positive changes in FDNY procedures following the Deutsche Bank building fire have been slow in coming. But I'm confident that many of the suggestions I proposed about comprehensive safety and enforcement procedures for firefighters and first responders during fires and similar catastrophes will one day be standard procedures.

Impact on My Family

The pain my family and I suffer, along with the anguish other families of firefighters who died or were injured during the Deutsche Bank building fire, will never go away. All the firefighters who fought the fire are heroes. If my son, Joey, and his brother firefighter Bobby Beddia were alive today, along with the 100-plus injured firefighters, they'd do the exact same thing again. Knowing that, however, is small consolation, because the pain of my family's loss will never go away.

Holidays will always be painful for my family. My daughters still cry over the loss of their brother, and my wife still expects to hear my son's footsteps as he races up our stairs. And when the telephone rings, she still expects to hear his voice when she answers it. For all of us, every happy event is tinged with sadness because he is not with us.

I vividly remember the day after Joey died. His wife, Linda, could not bear to tell their daughter, Mia, that her father was dead. Their son, Joseph, was only nine months old, but Mia kept asking where her daddy was. "Why isn't he home?" she asked. The next day was his birthday, and she wanted to help set up the birthday preparations.

Linda thought it best to bring Mia to our house so that Mia would be in familiar and comforting surroundings and would have us for support. After bringing Mia over, Linda sat her down on the living room couch and told her that her daddy wasn't coming home anymore. The little girl had such a scared look on her face. Mia and her daddy had been best friends.

Mia wanted to know why her daddy wasn't coming home. Was it something she'd done? If he couldn't come home, why couldn't she speak with him over the telephone? All of us cried. What do you say to a four-year-old whose father was killed because of corporate and political greed?

While there is a sense of satisfaction in completing this book, I need to believe that some good will come out of my work, such as new, updated safety and enforcement laws and procedures, along with a greater public awareness of their importance. Hopefully, New Yorkers will be more vigilant and not be complacent and assume the people they put in office will do their jobs.

I am ending my book with an appropriate quote from the Old Testament:

> "Moreover, the arrogant man seizes wealth without halting. He widens his gullet like Hell and like Death he never has enough."
>
> —*Habakkuk 2:5*

Appendix A

LMDC Board Minutes of February 14, 2007

In attendance

Directors: Kevin Rampe, Chairman
Robert Balachandran
William C. Rudin
Carl B. Weisbrod
(via telephone) Robert Douglass
Robert Harding
Thomas Johnson
James Kallstrom
Edward J. Malloy
Joshua Sirefman
Martha E. Stark
Madelyn Wils

Staff Attending: For Lower Manhattan Development Corporation:
Irene Chang, General Counsel and Secretary of the Corporation
Daniel Ciniello, Senior Vice President – Operation
Eileen McEvoy, Assistant Secretary
Robert Miller, Chief Financial Officer
Other staff

Counsel to the Board:
Elizabeth Condren, Esq., Fulbright & Jaworski

For Speaker Sheldon Silver:
Judy Rapfogel

For the Lower Manhattan Construction Command Center:
Charles Maikish, Executive Director
Daniel McCormack, First Deputy Director
Robert Harvey

For Empire State Development Corporation:
Avi Schick, Downstate President and Chief Operating Officer Designee

Also Present:
The Public

The chairman then asked Director Johnson to provide the Audit and Finance Report. Director Johnson opened the report by stating that the Committee met twice since the last Directors' meeting. First, to review the HUD action plan resolution and the other financial resolutions on today's agenda, and after considering the purpose, the cost justification and availability of funding for these projects, the Committee recommends the approval of those resolutions.

The second meeting, Director Johnson explained, allowed for a careful discussion of the nuances of how the increases in the cost of the deconstruction of 130 Liberty affect the overall financial plan. He noted that the Committee is satisfied with the approach being taken and recommends that the Board go forward on that basis.

Lastly, Director Johnson noted that in accordance with LMDC's Emergency Authorization Procedure, the Committee's Chairmen were notified and concurred with three small contract amendments that were acted on in January and are being considered for ratification by the Board today.

The Chairman then presented a request for funding for additional costs associated with the 130 Liberty Street deconstruction. Following this presentation of the specifics of this request, the Chairman read the relative resolution into the record. The Chairman then called for any questions or comments with regard to the request. Director Malloy asked for verification that he is correct in his interpretation that this action will allow for the job to be finished without disruption or delays, and further that any money issues will be resolved after the job has been completed.

Chairman Rampe stated that that was correct.

There being no further questions or comments, upon motion duly made and seconded, the following resolution was adopted (It was noted for the record that Director Harding recuse himself from voting with regard to the following resolution.):

Authorization to Amend or Supplement Contract with
Bovis Lend Lease for 130 Liberty Street Deconstruction

RESOLVED that the Corporation is hereby authorized to amend or supplement its agreement with Bovis Lend Lease for the cleaning and deconstruction of 130 Liberty Street, to increase the authorized expenditures thereunder by an additional $30,000,000 to an amount not to exceed $129,000,000 in the aggregate, as described in the materials presented to this meeting; and be it

FURTHER RESOLVED that the expenditures approved hereby shall be allocated from funds included in Partial Action Plan 7, as amended, and from the recovery or reimbursement of such costs under the 130 Liberty Street Memorandum of Understanding with Deutsche Bank and its insurers of 130 Liberty Street, Allianz and AXA, and the Deconstruction Funding and Settlement Agreement with Allianz and AXA; and be it

FURTHER RESOLVED that the proper officers of the Corporation are hereby authorized to take any such action and to execute such instruments as may be necessary or appropriate to effect the foregoing.

Appendix B

Summation of Deutsche Bank building Contracts

The first contractual document for the Deutsche Bank building project that I was aware of was the LMDC Emergency Action Plan (EAP) for 130 Liberty Street dated September 5, 2005, that stipulated the phases of the deconstruction project. The EAP mentioned the use of negative-pressure containment, which was later identified as internal fans. Also mentioned was a three-floor and then a two-floor buffer zone for abatement, cleanup, and deconstruction. Copies of the EAP were to be provided to the LMCCC; the FDNY; and all the city, state, and federal health and safety agencies.

The contractors named in the document were Regional Scaffolding and Safeway Environmental Corporation. Per the EAP, if any emergencies occurred, 911 must be called. The EAP went on to state that the contractor was to have a system where every employee and visitor was placed on a list when on the project site. For site evacuation, the GC emergency contractor coordinator was responsible for retrieving the daily visitor and workers-on-site logs and for controlling entries and exits. The subcontractor emergency coordinator was responsible for safely stopping the work and securing all operating equipment.

Under Appendix D, "Emergency Egress from Building," was a diagram that showed the floor layouts. From the roof through floor 25, the A staircase was designated as the emergency egress with a note that the standpipe location was in stair A. For floors 24 through 1, emergency egress was via both stairwells A and B.

Appendix A, "Emergency Response Communication Chart," had contact phone numbers, including the number for the Regional Scaffolding Emergency Coordinator, Paul Mazzucca. Regional Scaffolding would call 911 and the subcontractors, the LMDC owner's representative, and URS (the LMDC's subcontractor for safety) as well as the LMDC and the LMDC Community Liaison.

The Regional Scaffolding and Safeway Environmental Corporation phone contacts were Mitch Alvo, Safeway president; Don Adler, Safeway VP; Ted Tworzydlo, Safeway project manager; Larry Blinn, Regional president; Gregg Blinn, Regional VP; Paul (PJ) Mazzucca, Regional project manager; and James Kane, Regional project supervisor.

The next contractual document was the trade contract between Bovis Lend Lease and John Galt Corporation, dated February 13, 2006. The contract started as every normal construction contract with the owner LMDC's approval of the contract with general contractor Bovis Lend Lease and its agreement with subcontractor John Galt Corporation. The agreement stated that the contractor [Bovis] was responsible for all coordination and that there were to be two separate contracts for the entire deconstruction and abatement work for bonding purposes. It was the contractor's responsibility to complete the project within a 15-month schedule, as if there were only one contract for abatement and deconstruction. The agreement stated that Galt was entitled to all proceeds from salvageable materials (this would include cut and broken pipes). The contract between the LMDC, Bovis, and Galt was amended the following year when the plan was changed to simultaneous abatement and deconstruction. The contract also had a "time is of the essence" clause that stipulated time frames and financial penalties if the project was not completed on time.

The agreement also included a five-floor buffer zone (an additional two floors from the EAP) and stated that the approval process performed by the LMDC would include, but not be limited to, review of all safety and health issues and regulatory agency requirements by federal, state, and local entities and LMDC procedures. (Thus, the LMDC was responsible for approving the interior conditions of the building, which were blatantly unsafe and failed to meet mandatory safety regulations.)

Section 13 stated:

> ... to further minimize the effects of the work on surrounding areas, the Contractor shall:
> - Provide the maintenance on fire protection and standpipe systems.

- Provide temporary fire protection 24 hrs/day, 7 days per week as required.
- Contractor shall insure that the dry standpipe system is fully operational during demolition work.
- Contractor includes a full-time on site safety manager, as required, for the proper completion of the demolition operations.

Another section included this contradictory clause: "Contractor includes all labor, material and equipment rate increases for the duration of the project. Rate increases will not be entertained. Rates provided shall be effective through the end of the Contractor's work, contractual and additional. Rates shall also be all inclusive."

On the subject of adequate workers and overtime, the contract said:

> Sufficient manpower shall be provided at all times to maintain progress of the Work. A shortage of labor in the industry shall not be accepted as an excuse for not properly manning the job. Also the Contractor understands and agrees that time is of the essence, and in the event overtime is required to maintain pace with the construction schedule due to Contractor's lack of progress or to keep up with other trades, it will be performed at no additional cost to the Construction Manager.

Shanties, storage rooms, field offices, etc. shall be equipped with fire extinguishers and shall be of fireproof material only, such as concrete, gypsum block, rated drywall or sheet metal.

> There were multiple sections that stated that the contractor was responsible for anything that went wrong at the work site, including injury and death. The owner and general contractor were not to be liable for anything. (Why would Bovis have this clause in the contract unless

it anticipated major problems, such as absence of safety precautions causing injuries, death, and lawsuits?)

Other sections stated that rubbish and debris must be removed daily from the work floors.

Another section stated, "That the contractor must comply in full with all applicable environment, health and safety ('EHA&S') local and national legislation, including all OSHA regulations ... In circumstances where there is a conflict between local or national legislation and this Article 15, the higher (more protective) requirement shall prevail."

Galt had a performance bond of $25,000,000 with Arch Insurance Company to Bovis and a labor-and-material-payment bond with the same insurance company to Bovis for $33,500,000.

The next contractual document was the Implementation Plan between Bovis and John Galt Corporation dated September 19, 2006. This plan was created to protect workers and the public from airborne contaminants. Its purpose was to comply with the requirements of the NYC DOB, US EPA, NYC DEP, and NYS DOL. (This plan included procedures for removal of toxic contaminants and for sealing the environment. It also included procedures for managing negative air pressure, like sealing floors, exits, windows, and so on.) The project had three sections, covering interior abatement, external abatement, and deconstruction of the building. Project procedures had to conform to DOB, DOS, FDNY, and OSHA requirements. The DOL sections stated that the contractors were to comply with all federal, state, and local codes and regulations. Permits and notifications required for the project included EPA, DOL, and DEP permits for asbestos; a DOB work permit for building demolition (which did not include alteration of building) and sidewalk bridges; NYC cranes and derrick permits; and an FDNY certificate for "Fitness for Burners."[Official title is "Torch Use for Flammable Gases, Fitness #G-60] The contract required a fire watch for torch use [building demolition of cutting steel and other metals] and a safe place to store air and gas containers on site.

The contract also mentioned that utilities would be disconnected and capped prior to deconstruction, with the exception of temporary water, sewer, and electric to be maintained by the GC along with the water rises and drains. Any deviations or changes were to be submitted to the LMDC for approval.

Stairwell Requirements

In section 2, under the paragraph for "Waste and Equipment Deconstruction," were the stairwell requirements:

> The two (2) existing stairwells shall be maintained free of obstructions and shall be used to provide access between floors within the containment areas. All interior stairs shall be accessible in the event of an emergency. At work areas containment boundaries, stairwells shall be isolated using minimum 2x4 studs at 16" on center, sheathed with 3/8th plywood and two layers of 6 mil polyethylene [earlier sections cited that the wood and plastic must be fire retardant and comply with federal, state, and city codes], secured with duct tape. Kick out panels [no dimensions given] shall be installed, containment barrier walls and within stairwells to maintain emergency egress throughout the duration of the project. Kick out panels shall be clearly marked with adequate signage.

Section M provided the details for the negative air units (internal fans) and their quantity.

Section V, "Phase II Structural Deconstruction," stated that there would be a four-floor buffer for abatement. It also stated that the deconstruction would comply with all federal, state, and city regulatory requirements, as well as requirements in construction documents and permits. Building pipes and equipment were to be removed by torch cutting, and a fire watch and burner (with FDNY certificates of fitness) were to be present.

Section E, "Fire Protection," stated that a dry standpipe was to be maintained within the building throughout the duration of the deconstruction process.

The final contractual document I saw was the Supplemental Agreement, dated February 5, 2007, between LMDC and Bovis, which addressed the disputes for the Deconstruction Contract dated October 20, 2005. The reason for the agreement was to determine if the LMDC should pay Bovis for additional costs for "gross cleaning" above the "base gross cleaning amount."

Both parties agreed that it was of critical importance that the Deutsche Bank building be completely demolished and the area cleared no later than December 31, 2007. Gross cleaning covered abatement and decontamination, which included work related to human remains, above the initial contract amount of $35 million.

The main terms of the contract were that the LMDC would pay $9.7 million for actual costs above the originally contracted-for amount, in installments. Bovis must submit documentation of actual costs incurred for work completed prior to February 3, 2007. The $9.7 million amount was nonrefundable but subject to audit. If the audit proved a lesser amount, then the total amount would be reduced as per dollar amount, but the remainder of the $9.7 million would be kept by the contractor. For costs incurred after February 3, 2007, the LMDC would pay the next $6 million of actual costs on a nonrefundable basis but subject to audit. The contractor could bill up to $1.5 million of actual costs completed prior to February 3, 2007, separate from the $9.7 million work, and the LMDC would pay that as part of the $6 million, which would not be increased. If the contractor failed to complete the terms of the contract by December 31, 2007, no excuses would be permissible; the $6 million would be deemed as an advance, instead of a nonrefundable payment. From $15,700,001 to $30 million, the LMDC would pay actual costs as an advance. From $30,000,001 to $32 million, the contractor was to pay actual costs without reimbursement or any litigation. From $32,000,001 to $40 million the LMDC would pay actual costs as an advance. Costs over $40 million would be shared, divided equally. Actual costs did not include profit; off-site costs; or off-site personnel costs, compensation, or administrative costs but would include labor, material, permits, salaries, bonuses, material, and related costs. This agreement was subject to review and approval by the LMDC

Board of Directors, scheduled for the meeting of February 14, 2007. (As expected, the LMDC board approved the agreement.)

The contracts also stated, *in multiple places*:

> The work of this Contractor shall be performed in accordance with the most stringent of applicable current codes and standards whether or not said codes or standards are indicated in drawings and/or specifications. In the event that there exists, for any aspect of the work, conflicts between applicable codes, the plans and specifications and industry standards, the most stringent shall prevail and are included. Contractor is aware that the work performed within the building line shall be subject to all DEP, DOL, DOB approvals and/or sign offs. [Note: The FDNY was not included.] The Contractor will provide all services which would meet or exceed these requirements and this Contractor shall be required to comply with said requirements prior to final acceptance and payment.

It's important to point out that prior to the "Scope of Work" section, paragraph 7 stated, "… and for the Contractor's assumption of all risks of all foreseen and unforeseen conditions, hazards and difficulties in connection with the performance of the Work and for Contractor's assumption of credit risk regarding the Owner as provided herein."

Based on my 40 years of government service, 26 years of which I worked with contracts that involved buildings and construction, in typical government contracts the general contractor assumes all the risks for its subcontractors encountering foreseen conditions. The owner takes responsibility for unforeseen conditions and then issues a contract modification, which allows the GC to correct it. It is very odd that a contractor would assume all liability for a contract of this magnitude, considering the dangerous toxins inside the building and the subcontractor's minimal experience in this type of project.

Section 71 of the "Scope of Work" stated, "Contractor shall ensure that the dry standpipe system is fully operational during abatement work."

There was a subsection titled "Time Is of the Essence," which stressed the importance of completing the project within 15 months. If not completed in that time frame, financial penalties would be applied. There were other sections that offered incentives if the project was completed prior to the end date.

The "Separate Special Condition of Trade Contract" was inserted to allow Mitch Alvo and Don Adler approval via the LMDC to work on this project as John Galt employees. They were not allowed to hire any other senior people of Safeway Environmental Corporation, Dynamic Equipment Corporation, or Big Apple Wrecking Corporation nor rent, lease, or buy equipment from any of these companies. In addition, all subcontractors must be approved by the LMDC and Bovis prior to working and Galt must comply with the LMDC's integrity monitor and allow all of the above to cooperate with the NYC Department of Investigation. (It was rumored that an LMDC executive and Deputy Mayor Doctoroff inserted this paragraph to appease the DOI and other state/city LMDC executives to provide a legal safeguard buffer against unprofessional, unqualified, and criminal involvement for this project.) Reference to the DOB was exhibit B, "General Deconstruction #47 Project and Worker Safety," subsection page: "Contractor is responsible for providing protection for any openings required in the performance of this work. If this Contractor removes such protection in order to perform his work, he will provide whatever safety planking and temporary protection necessary to protect all openings in accordance with the regulations of all govt. agencies having jurisdiction."

Appendix C

Letter to State Attorney General Andrew Cuomo

Hon. Andrew M. Cuomo
Attorney General
New York State
120 Broadway
New York, N. Y. 10271   April 7, 2010

**Re: Criminal investigation into the deaths of firefighters Joseph
Graffagnino and Robert Beddia**

Dear Mr. Attorney General:

On August 18, 2007, my son, New York City Firefighter Joseph
Graffagnino and Firefighter Robert Beddia passed away in a seven-
alarm fire at the Deutsche Bank building.

You should be aware that the Department of Investigation warned
LMDC and Bovis Lend Lease, the general contractor, that they
should not hire subcontractor John Galt for alleged mob-ties and lack
of experience.[1] After the numerous warnings by the Department of
Investigation, LMDC and Bovis completely disregarded these warnings
and hired John Galt even though John Galt had no prior experience in
demolition, deconstruction or decontamination. (See Attached Letters
from the Department of Investigation) I believe that high-ranking city
and state officials set the stage for a demolition project that sacrificed
safety in order to expedite the deconstruction of the building.

---

[1] Be advised that John Galt did not have any experience whatsoever in
deconstruction or decontamination.

284

Shortly after the start of the deconstruction and decontamination of the Deutsche Bank building Bovis and John Galt walked off the "job" demanding an increase in monies, which clearly breached the contract to deconstruct and abate the building. On January 29, 2007, after Bovis and Galt walked off the "job" there was a meeting at Gracie Mansion regarding additional payment. Mayor Bloomberg and Governor Spitzer supposedly hosted the meeting, and according to the New York Times, an agreement was reached that Bovis would receive an additional $40 million if the contractor met a December 31, 2007 deadline. The $40 million incentive caused LMDC and Bovis to sacrifice the safety of all first responders.

After a 16-month grand jury investigation, on December 22, 2008 New York County District Attorney Robert Morgenthau concluded a lengthy report of his findings with these words, "In summary, everyone failed at the Deutsche Bank building."

Morgenthau did single out the Fire Department and the Buildings Department for repeated failures that "contributed to the conditions that led to the deaths of Firefighters Robert Beddia and Joseph Graffagnino and the injuries to approximately 105 other New York City firefighters who were injured in the blaze of August 18, 2007."

But strangely missing from his abbreviated list of agency failures were the officers and directors of the Lower Manhattan Development Corporation, the owner of the building, who after being warned by the Department of Investigation completely disregarded said warnings.

Everyone failed, the District Attorney said, but no public official was ever named or held accountable for either of the two deaths. The grand jury indicted three construction executives and the company that served as a subcontractor, but those most responsible were never publicly identified or censured.

On September 7, 2005 the LMDC published a 55-page Emergency Action Plan. Numerous city and state agencies participated in the year-long drafting of that plan, which was designed to ensure the safe demolition of 130 Liberty Street. But between the beginning of demolition in March 2007 and the fatal fire in August, the plan was violated as if the document didn't exist.

The FDNY had insisted that the Emergency Action Plan include a mandate that any fire or explosion in the building had to be reported to 911. Shockingly, nine fires in the building prior to the fatal fire on August 18, 2007 were never reported. After the seventh such unreported fire on August 3, 2007 the LMDC's site safety consultant, URS, warned the agency that "Bovis should no longer be trusted to ensure building safety," Morgenthau said. "The LMDC was notified that the building was 'an accident waiting to happen,'" the District Attorney added. And to this day, virtually no one in New York City knows why LMDC ignored this warning. (See District Attorney submission to the press heretofore attached).[2]

High-level city and state officials, to my knowledge were never investigated for nonfeasance, misfeasance, malfeasance, gross negligence and/or reckless endangerment of lives and property. Three individuals from Bovis and John Galt were arraigned on charges of second-degree manslaughter, criminally negligent homicide and reckless endangerment. There should have been an investigation into the potential racketeering acts of city and state officials who deliberately abandoned their sworn duties and responsibilities at the site to keep it safe for all first responders.

Ironically, Joseph F. Bruno, the head of the Office of Emergency Management, is never mentioned in the Morgenthau report. His agency was in charge of coordinating every emergency response. Did he not know of the nine unreported fires in the building? Was his first inkling of anything wrong at that job the day of the fatal fire? Did he and his agency make sure the FDNY had a fire plan for the building? Did he make sure the Fire Department had a plan to regularly inspect that toxic building?

---

[2] We do know that on August 9, 2007, the eighth unreported fire in the building occurred. "Bovis, Galt and the LMDC were notified," Morgenthau said, "but no notification was made to the FDNY by calling 911." The next day, August 10, 2007 another slag fire occurred on the 23rd floor. There were no fire guards or fire extinguishers on that floor. Again, the FDNY (and no one else) was not notified of the fire. Fifteen days after the URS warning that the building was an accident waiting to happen, and only a week after two more unreported fires occurred.

The FDNY had participated in an effort to recover hundreds of human remains and objects of identification on the roof of the building in 2006. Deputy Mayor Edward Skyler supervised the successful operation. The firefighters needed special passes to get into the building. They wore Tyvek suits; they were escorted to the roof by LMDC personnel and they were decontaminated after every shift.

By law, the Buildings Department must inform the FDNY when DOB issues a Demolition Permit. The FDNY was never notified of a Demolition Permit for the Deutsche Bank building. DOB decided it would issue a series of Alteration Permits for each floor. Nothing in the law requires DOB to notify the FDNY when it issues an Alteration Permit, thereby circumventing the system.

Morgenthau said the LMDC told the Department of Environmental Protection that the city/state agency was exempt from local laws. The District Attorney said the LMDC brought in the State Department of Labor to replace DEP inspectors, but on occasion, DEP did manage to visit the building. In any event, the personnel from both agencies never saw anything amiss.

I remember that the Attorney General's office early on announced that it would be offering its assistance to the Manhattan District Attorney. The ones most responsible for the death of my son and his fellow firefighter have never been identified. I am requesting that you commence a new and more thorough investigation of the deaths of Joseph Graffagnino and Robert Beddia.

Respectfully,
Joseph Graffagnino

Appendix D

Letter to State Attorney General Eric Schneiderman Requesting an Investigation into the NYC DA's Safety Reports from Bovis's Independent Monitor

Attorney General Eric T. Schneiderman
120 Broadway
New York, New York 10271-0332   March 29, 2012

Dear Sir,

I have attached a report from WNYC News Blog involving a legal agreement between Bovis Lend Lease and the Manhattan District Attorney's office. After reading the report I am very disappointed in the negative replies and lack of action from the Manhattan District Attorney's office in its pursuit of compliance to its own legal agreement with Bovis regarding the safety of New Yorkers.

As the father of one of the fallen firefighters at the Deutsche Bank fire in August 2007, I am disgusted at the appalling lack of legal redress from Cyrus Vance's office. The non-prosecution agreement created by Robert Morgenthau, the Mayor's office and Bovis Lend Lease certified that Bovis would create a better and verifiable safety record and improve safety standards in all of their construction sites. This has not happened. In fact there have been 40, yes 40 safety violations after the agreement was signed at the Deutsche Bank site alone. These were not trivalent violations, but serious enough to have stop work orders produced by the FDNY and the Buildings Department. These notifications of safety violations were brought to the Manhattan District Attorney's office by the Buildings Department, the Fire Department, and the various media outlets and still nothing was done by the District Attorney's office.

I am requesting that your office become involved in order to produce these safety reports, produce verifying proof of safety reforms or if Bovis never kept their part of the legal agreement; revoke the agreement and issue criminal prosecution indictments against Bovis Lend Lease.

The Manhattan District Attorney's Office must be held accountable to the citizens of New York. It's believed that the District Attorney works for the taxpayers and not for construction companies, or am I mistaken?

Any questions please contact me at my information above.

Respectfully yours,
Joseph Graffagnino

Appendix E

Letter to Governor Cuomo Requesting an Investigation by NYS Inspector General or a Special Prosecutor into the Actions of City and State Officials

Hon. Andrew M. Cuomo
Governor, State of New York
Executive Chamber
State Capitol
Albany, New York 12224   May 14, 2012

Dear Governor Cuomo:

I am respectfully requesting that your office conduct an investigation into the criminal conduct of City and State officials. On August 18, 2007 my son Joseph Graffagnino died in a fire at the Deutsche Bank Building. He died because of the criminal acts of city and state officials who were responsible for the safe demolition of that building. In December, 2008, a New York County Grand Jury returned criminal indictments of three construction supervisors. While then-District Attorney Robert Morgenthau said "everyone screwed up," his grand jury did not indict any city or state public official. Recently a Bovis executive pled guilty to fraud conspiracy.

Many of the people who caused the death of my son and his fellow firefighter Robert Beddia are still in high places of authority and influence. They should not be. They should have been in the dock, along with the construction supervisors.

Recently, new information on the appalling criminal neglect has surfaced that requires me to ask you to request the appointment of a

Special Prosecutor, or a referral to your State Inspector General, for a new and thoroughly honest investigation.

Newly discovered evidence was posted on web site [www.evesmag. com/j'accuse.htm] and there is a link under J'ACCUSE on www.IAFF. org (International Association of Firefighters)] since April 24, and it includes excerpts from an FDNY Safety Command report that was finished in August of 2008. The new discovered evidence also includes the contents of an E-mail from the URS Corporation to its client, the Lower Manhattan Development Corporation. The E-mail was dated August 3, 2007, just 15 days before the fire that killed my son and firefighter Beddia. The E-mail detailed numerous safety complaints about General Contractor Bovis Lend Lease, and its sub-contractor, the John Galt Corporation. URS noted that Bovis had an $80 million contract. It was unlawful to not haul away garbage or debris that caused the death of the two firefighters. It added that the sub-contractor Galt did not comply with the New York City codes and willfully, intentionally failed to perform necessary duties that proximately caused the death of the two firefighters. Fifteen days later, the two firefighters were killed and another 105 were injured, in a seven-alarm fire that started when a worker intentionally threw a lit cigarette violating the Rules and Regulations of the applicable codes.

The reason that I write this letter is after the "newly discovered evidence" proved that the urgent, anguished warning from URS could not have been more prescient. URS had warned their client that the building was "a serious accident waiting to happen" outing City and State officials on actual notice that a serious incident could occur. The consultant had stressed one of the ways it would happen---piles of garbage or debris left lying around.

There is, I am certain, more to be discovered and made public. The FDNY Safety Command makes it plain that the New York City Fire Department was excluded from the planning or execution of the demolition. It was deliberate, and those who participated in the exclusion of the FDNY must be thoroughly investigated.

I am certain that scores of high-ranking Deputy Chiefs and Battalion Chiefs would testify under oath that if the Fire Department was allowed into that building at any point in the demolition, they would tell your investigators that the FDNY could have, should have, and would have kept that demolition within the laws that prohibit blockage of egress, laws that prohibit the reckless destruction of stairway enclosures, laws that mandate sprinkler systems in a demolition or alteration, and laws that demand that a standpipe system remain operative throughout a high-risk demolition project.

I am certain those veteran FDNY chiefs would tell your investigators Joseph Graffagnino and Robert Beddia would still be alive if the Fire Department was not deliberately excluded from the premises.

I am enclosing several documents to prove that there was a criminal act committed.

Governor, I'm asking you to honor the memories of my son and firefighter Robert Beddia. I'm asking to open a new investigation because of the newly discovered evidence of those responsible for the deaths of two New York City firefighters, and the injuries to 105 more.

Respectfully,
Joseph Graffagnino

Appendix F

"J'ACCUSE" ("I Accuse") by Martin J. Steadman

URS, the safety monitoring agency hired by the LMDC, sent an urgent written memo to the president of the LMDC 15 days before the fatal fire, stating that the general contractor, Bovis, was not paying attention to general housekeeping, fire watch, and overall management. It's appalling that Bovis had an $80 million contract and no one on staff to remove garbage or debris. Why did Bovis have to beg its subcontractor Galt to perform this work? Why was it only performed sporadically? URS mentioned that Bovis should withhold payment if necessary and/or take legal action if needed to correct those safety issues.

- On June 19, 2007, URS sent a four-page memo to the president of the LMDC about its concerns with Bovis. "In the past month alone URS communicated 54 emails on safety observations that needed immediate attention by Bovis … Our earlier recommendation was to have a separate environmental abatement contract in order to eliminate the deconstruction activities overhead." At the beginning of the project URS told the LMDC to drop the flawed plan to abate and deconstruct simultaneously.
- The FDNY Fatal Fire Report detailed shocking illegalities at the Deutsch Bank building that were ignored by the District Attorney, the mayor's office, and the reporters and editors of the skeletal remains of the New York City press corps. The FDNY Fatal Fire Report was released four months before Morgenthau ended his grand jury indictments. There were several portions of this report that were completely ignored, such as the fact the

130 Liberty Street building did not meet NYC building code requirements for buildings undergoing alteration or demolition, including the following code violations:

o The sprinkler systems were out of service.
o The standpipe system was out of service.
o The means of egress were blocked.
o The fire-rated construction comprising the stairway enclosures was either compromised or completely removed at many locations.
o A demolition permit was never filed nor issued, because it would have required working standpipe and sprinkler systems, enclosed stairways, an unobstructed means of egress, and fireguards. In addition, the DOB would have to notify the FDNY under demolition-permit regulations.

The FDNY Fatal Fire Report handed the Manhattan District Attorney a blueprint for the indictment of every public official who allowed that project to proceed in violation of numerous laws of New York City that govern demolition or alteration. The DA had it in enough time to present the findings to the grand jury, but instead it was buried and forgotten.

Steadman cited the following elements in "J'ACCUSE":

• Detailed 2005 memos from three veteran FDNY chiefs, never made public, outlined plans for ensuring the safe demolition of the Deutsche Bank building as early as January 2005. The suggested plans hit a stone wall at the highest levels of the Fire Department.
• The New York City Fire Department was not consulted and was never involved in the planning or execution of the John Galt Corporation's new implementation plan.
• A *New York Times* story on October 3, 2007, quoted former chairman of the LMDC Kevin Rampe as saying that New York City had insisted that information about the Deutsche Bank

building, including communications to the Fire Department, had to be routed through the mayor's office.

- Something happened at the NYC Department of Buildings when the John Galt Corporation applied for and was issued a series of alteration permits for each floor, instead of a demolition permit for the entire building. The difference was that demolition permits had to be reported to the Fire Department by the DOB. There was no such requirement applied to alteration permits. Who told the DOB that under no circumstances should they notify the Fire Department? Who in the DOB issued those alteration permits knowing that doing so was wrong on so many levels?

- NYC building code demands that, before a building is either demolished or altered, the sprinkler system must be back in operation.

- Every day for five months, safety coordinators working for Bovis certified the Deutsche Bank building standpipe system was operational. Bovis supervisors reported it to be operational on August 18 as firefighters raced into the building at the start of the seven-alarm blaze. But in fact, since before the demolition began, the standpipe system was never in operation, and Bovis, Galt, and others knew that and falsified documents to support their lies.

- The illegal destruction of at least 10 floors of fireproof staircase enclosures was the most critical failure to protect both everyone working in the building and the firefighters.

- The 25 large exhaust fans operating, with no remote shutoff switches, on the 13th to the 17th floors continued to bring smoke and flames lower into the building, creating fires on numerous floors above and below where firefighters battled the blaze that raged around them until they collapsed and died.

- Illegal wooden slabs over the stairwell were wrapped in polyurethane plastic sheeting. Firefighters could not get out, and help could not get in.

- Garbage and debris were not removed from the building. There were piles of metal studs, ductwork, piping, conduit, and other materials, along with tanks of propane and acetylene torches for cutting through metal on multiple floors.

- There were no fire extinguishers on the day of the fatal fire and no fire watches around to prevent the fire from growing out of control.

- Many veteran fire officers believe that the Fire Safety Report was sanitized and edited down by city lawyers.

- On August 3, 2007, URS sent an urgent e-mail to the president of the LMDC regarding Bovis's safety problems and lack of action. A slag fire started in a pile of garbage and debris on the 24th floor, and the DOB issued a stop-work order because the Fire Department permit for acetylene torches had expired. These three actions all happened on the same day, a Friday. The Fire Department renewed the burning permit, no questions asked, and Bovis/Galt was working again on Monday morning.

In his article Steadman questions why veteran commanders of the FDNY accepted their exclusion from the planning and execution of the demolition of the Deutsche Bank building. When the pipe crashed through the roof of firehouse 10/10 and the commissioner and top echelon of the FDNY visited the site, why didn't they demand to see what had happened to cause this accident within the Deutsche Bank building? Why didn't the FDNY ask about a fire plan for that building or even a fire-inspection plan? Why didn't they ask, based on the 15 day rule, when the building was last inspected?

The FDNY participated in the Office of Emergency Management's emergency Action Plan (EAP) from its start in early 2005 to its finalization in September 2005 for the Deutsche Bank building but was not heard from after that.

There were 10 fires in five months in that building, yet none of those fires were called into 911 or the fire department. This lack of notification was in direct violation of the LMDC EAP as well as the Bovis/Galt EAP.

The Strakosch memo of January 30, 2005, reviewed and edited some finer points of the EAP, which stipulated that only the FDNY should put out any fires that occurred in that building and not the building's workers. In addition, any fires, no matter how small, must be called into 911; FDNY Division 1 was to schedule a walk-through of the EAP and know how the work was progressing at the Deutsche Bank building. The problem was that the memo fell on deaf ears and blind eyes. No one in Division 1, Battalion 1, or the firehouse across the street from that building ever saw the EAP—they were deliberately excluded! FDNY headquarters was forced to admit that it didn't have a plan to fight a fire in a toxic building and didn't have a plan to inspect the building under demolition either. No one from the FDNY set foot in that building, and no orders from the FDNY were issued to ensure a presence in the project. Instead the Mayor dumped the blame for that horrible fire onto field officers; their careers were destroyed, and they have since retired.

Appendix G

Community Board #1—Manhattan Resolution
Date: September 18, 2007
Committee of Origin: WTC Redevelopment

Committee Vote: 9 In Favor 0 Opposed 0 Abstained 0 Recused

Public Member Vote: 0 In Favor 0 Opposed 0 Abstained 0 Recused

BOARD VOTE: *37 In Favor 0 Opposed 0 Abstained 0 Recused*

RE: 130 Liberty Street (a/k/a Deutsche Bank Building)

WHEREAS: CB#1 expresses its deep and sincere condolences to the families of the two firefighters, Robert Beddia and Joe Graffagnino, who died needlessly on August 18, 2007, while fighting a major fire at 130 Liberty Street (Site) that would never have occurred if the government agencies and contractors overseeing the demolition of that building had performed their jobs adequately, and

WHEREAS: CB#1 also hopes for the complete and speedy recovery of the two firefighters who were seriously injured at the Site on August 23, 2007, when a worker for John Galt Corporation (Galt), the demolition subcontractor for the project, lost control of a pallet jack that fell from the 23rd floor, and

WHEREAS: The members of the Board of Directors of the Lower Manhattan Development Corporation (LMDC), which owns the Site and has the primary overall responsibility for the safe and efficient decontamination and demolition of this WTC-contaminated building, are directly appointed by Governor Spitzer and Mayor Bloomberg, and

WHEREAS: CB1 appreciates that Governor Spitzer recently met with New York State Assembly Speaker Sheldon Silver, U.S. Representative Jerrold Nadler, Manhattan Borough President Scott Stringer, New York State Senator Martin Connor, New York City Council Member Alan J. Gerson, and members of CB#1 to discuss how to move forward constructively, and we hope that this signifies a much better line of communication with the current management of LMDC than existed under the prior administration, and

WHEREAS: CB1 appreciates the meetings that Speaker Silver has organized with the community, elected officials and LMDC on these issues, as well as the efforts of Borough President Stringer, Congressman Nadler, Senator Connor, Councilman Gerson and Assembly Member Glick, and

WHEREAS: CB#1 unanimously passed a resolution on April 18, 2006, expressing its serious concerns about Galt's lack of relevant experience and the poor safety record and questionable business integrity of Safeway Environmental – a company with close ties to Galt – and calling on the LMDC only to use companies with appropriate qualifications and experience to safely and effectively conduct abatement and demolition at the Site, and

WHEREAS: CB#1 unanimously passed a resolution on July 27, 2004, emphasizing that the safety and well-being of local residents and workers must be given the utmost consideration during the lengthy demolition process; calling for full and open consultation among all interested parties; requesting that the demolition of the building "be undertaken in an open and transparent manner insuring that all applicable City, State and federal health, safety, environmental, and counterterrorism laws are fully observed and enforced," and recommending that "contingency plans ... be developed and enforced in conjunction with the Fire Department of New York, the New York City Police Department, and any other relevant emergency management agencies in the event that any emergency arises, such as fire, on-site injury, contaminant release, or other disaster," and

WHEREAS: CB#1 unanimously passed a resolution in December 2005 urging LMDC to appoint Julie Menin, the sitting Chairperson of CB#1, to sit on the Board of Directors of the LMDC. That request went unheeded and the Chairperson of CB#1 was not appointed until June 2007, and

WHEREAS: Through both written and verbal communication (including directly with prior LMDC officials), CB#1 repeatedly urged the adoption of a codified emergency and community notification plan, such as expressed in the letter from Julie Menin, Chairperson of CB#1 dated October 27, 2005, to the then LMDC President Stefan Pryor, which included a series of very specific suggestions including phone trees, e-mail blasts, two-way handheld radios and building captains, and

WHEREAS: For reasons that we cannot begin to understand but that we hope will be publicly revealed through one or more thorough and competent investigations, LMDC and/or its general contractor, Bovis Corporation (Bovis), in a process totally lacking in transparency, selected Galt as the demolition subcontractor for the project over other qualified bidders including North American Site Developers, LVI Services Inc. and Bedroc Contracting (New York Times, August 30, 2007), completely ignoring the unequivocal and insistent warnings from CB#1 and other concerned groups and individuals in the local community regarding Galt's lack of qualifications and other serious concerns with respect to the demolition project, and

WHEREAS: Many other red flags were ignored including: numerous safety violations; a 10-page letter from the Department of Investigations dated January 2006 (according to the New York Times, August 25, 2007); multiple reports of debris falling from the Site including a 22-foot pipe that fell into the fire engine house immediately across the street last May; an incident wherein a worker fell 40 feet from the building scaffolding in March, 2006; an earlier fire that according to

WABC occurred at the Site in July, 2007 but was not reported; and prominent media coverage, and

WHEREAS: An investigation of the fire is currently being carried out by the Manhattan District Attorney's Office, and is reportedly focusing not only on the firefighters' deaths, but also on the actions of several contractors and government agencies, and

WHEREAS: There was minimal community notification on the day of the fire, August 18, 2007, and

WHEREAS: CB#1 has now had three emergency meetings (August 22, August 28, and September 5, 2007) concerning the recent events at the Site but there remain many unanswered questions (including the process by which the contractors and subcontractors for the work were selected, and the division of regulatory and oversight responsibilities at the Site among the agencies involved), and

WHEREAS: In response to some of the expressed concerns of CB#1 and the public, assurances were given at numerous meetings regarding remedial actions being taken including:

- The development of an Emergency Action Plan including firefighting at a September 14, 2004 meeting (minutes at http://www.renewnyc.com/content/pdfs/130liberty/advisory_committee_mtg_transcript_9-14-04.pdf),
- Steps including the following, taken by Bovis as described by Mr. Abruzzo to the Community Advisory Committee of 130 Liberty Street on March 28, 2007, in response to questions about an emergency plan and the issue of emergency first responders (minutes at http://www.lowermanhattan.info/extras/pdf/032807_130LibertyStreetAdvCommittee01.pdf)
  o Orientation training for all construction workers on the Site,
  o A public address system being established and a PA system for workers on and around the site,
  o An Emergency Plan developed in conjunction with the unions, the public sectors and private sectors,

o   Direct communication with the NYC Office of Emergency Management,

o   Trained professions providers on call,

o   Four (4) Bovis Safety Engineers on jobsite full-time,

o   Additional supervision by URS and the BEST Squad, and

WHEREAS: Subsequent to the fire, including in letters addressed to LMDC dated August 29, 2007 (http://www.epa.gov/wtc/lmdc_letter_epa_concerns.pdf) and September 7, 2007 (http://www.epa.gov/wtc/demolish_deconstruct/130liberty_streetletter910.pdf), EPA expressed concern that LMDC would consider leaving the building at 130 Liberty Street unsealed and concern that LMDC would engage in a new sampling plan to gather new data for the building and revisit abatement procedures with the objective of supporting an LMDC decision to leave the building unsealed, and

WHEREAS: In these same letters to LMDC, EPA has expressed its strongly held position that the building at 130 Liberty Street be resealed as quickly as possible and has further stated that "EPA has participated, and continues to participate, in meetings to understand the concerns of the FDNY and to address them expeditiously" with respect to the fire safety in the building. In addition, "on August 27 and August 28, 2007, dioxin was detected at levels below the established target and trigger levels for this project. Dioxin was not detected in any of the existing ambient air monitoring stations at 130 Liberty Street before the fire and the subsequent work with the building. Such detections are a reasonable indicator of the ongoing potential for release of contaminants to the outdoor environment during periods of activity within the building. This can be mitigated by resealing the numerous breaches in the building's façade," and

WHEREAS: EPA further stated that "our primary environmental concern at this time is the need for LMDC to implement all necessary measures to seal the building to control potential releases of contaminants into the environment," and

WHEREAS: CB1 acknowledges that LMDC entered into an agreement last week with the relevant agencies to seal the perimeter openings as part of the preliminary work required to prepare for the restart of decontamination and deconstruction of 130 Liberty Street (as per TRC's letters to the New York State Department of Labor dated and approved September 12 & 14, 2007). We understand that this process will begin tomorrow and take approximately three weeks and it will be done simultaneously with the construction of the two fire-safe staircases, and (http://www.lowermanhattan.info/extras/pdf/091207_Approvedvariancere opening.pdf & http://www.lowermanhattan.info/extras/pdf/091407_05-0427-reopeningapproval.pdf), and

WHEREAS: In a resolution passed at a meeting on June 20, 2006, CB#1 urged the Mayor and the Department of Education to permit the principals of individual schools to fashion their own policies regarding cell phones, and opposed any blanket ban on cell phones in the New York public schools; and

WHEREAS: CB#1 in this resolution supported Intro 351, which was passed recently by the City Council, amending the Administrative Code of the City of New York to permit school children to carry cell phones in school, and City Council Resolution (Resolution 342) calling on the Department of Education to place a moratorium on the confiscation of students' cell phones, now

THEREFORE

BE IT

RESOLVED

THAT: LMDC must adopt and enforce a completely open and transparent process, including competitive bidding, for the selection of any additional subcontractors in connection with future work on the Site, and

BE IT

FURTHER

RESOLVED

THAT: To ensure that community concerns and safety are of paramount importance and are given the consideration that they require, we expect Governor Spitzer and Mayor Bloomberg to use their authority to ensure that the LMDC creates a workable mechanism whereby resolutions, letters and other written or oral communications directed to the LMDC by CB#1, as the principal voice of the broader downtown community on public issues, are responded to in a timely manner and not simply ignored or even treated with disdain, as has happened too often in the past, and

BE IT

FURTHER

RESOLVED

THAT: CB#1 agrees with EPA's position that the 130 Liberty Street building should "be sealed as soon as practicable to protect public health and the environment" as expressed by Pat Evangelista at the CB#1 public meeting on August 21, 2007, and that LMDC's "preliminary position" is unacceptable, as stated by Mr. Evangelista at the CB#1 public meeting on August 28, 2007 meeting, and with which "a representative of the NYCDEP concurred" (http://www.epa.gov/wtc/lmdc_letter_epa_concerns.pdf), and

BE IT

FURTHER

RESOLVED

THAT: CB#1 supports the EPA working cooperatively with the FDNY, NYSDOL, NYCDEP, OSHA, NYCDOB and other agencies and make necessary "modifications to some plans … to address concerns expressed by city emergency responders" (as stated by Alan Steinberg, EPA Regional Director, as reported in the New York Times, September 1, 2007), and

BE IT

FURTHER

RESOLVED

THAT: Both an updated and approved Health and Safety Plan and an Emergency Notification and Evacuation Plan must be rapidly developed and put in place before decontamination and demolition can proceed, and such plans must be shared with the public in a public meeting and posted on-line and approved by all the relevant agencies, and

BE IT

FURTHER

RESOLVED

THAT: The community should not have to choose between safety and speed and CB#1 calls on both Governor Spitzer and Mayor Bloomberg to make certain that the proper oversight, accountability and transparency are in place to guarantee that 130 Liberty Street is taken down safely and efficiently, and

BE IT

FURTHER

RESOLVED

THAT: All contracts and subcontracts entered into by LMDC should be available to the public and should not include provisions permitting a contractor or subcontractor to invoke confidentiality or other restrictive provisions to avoid answering legitimate questions posed by CB#1 and other members of the community whose health and safety depend on the quality of the work done by that contractor or subcontractor, and

BE IT

FURTHER

RESOLVED

THAT: No government agency should hinder in any way the investigation currently being carried out by the Manhattan District Attorney's Office, and

BE IT

FURTHER

RESOLVED

THAT: The lessons learned from the tragedy at the Site must be implemented going forward, at that location and also at Fiterman Hall, 130 Cedar Street, and any other relevant site(s), and

BE IT

FURTHER

RESOLVED

THAT: CB#1 recommends that the government and private entities responsible for emergency community notification protocol at the time of the 130 Liberty fire, be immediately reassigned, and

BE IT

FURTHER

RESOLVED

THAT: If the City implements a procedure whereby parents are notified of emergencies via cell phone, it would be entirely consistent with this procedure to permit parents to use cell phones to remain in contact with their children during emergencies as well, and

BE IT

FURTHER

RESOLVED

THAT: The specific next steps to assure that the 130 Liberty Street building is taken down in a manner that is safe for the workers, the first responders and the people who live and work nearby should include the following:

☐ Secure the fire-damaged, World Trade Center-contaminated building so that debris will not fall out and injure someone,

☐ Determine why the fire occurred and put in place a plan so that it will never happen again, such as enforcement of basic safety construction codes. Such a plan should mandate that the water main and standpipe that supply water to the building and various floors would be functioning during the remainder of this difficult project,

☐ Develop an Emergency Action Plan with a contingency plan for various emergencies – including fighting fires – and make sure that as work proceeds in this building the response team is given the floor plans as they change. Make sure that all the relevant agencies (including FDNY, OSHA, and OEM) meet regularly and address these plans and that dates and results of inspections and reports by FDNY, OSHA, OEM and other agencies are publicly posted,

☐ Clearly specify and publicly post the role and responsibilities of LMCCC in relation to overseeing activities at the Site,

☐ Create an Emergency Notification and Evacuation Plan – an effective communication plan from city agencies to neighborhood residents and businesses – consider reverse 911, text messaging, a phone tree, televised announcements, sirens coupled with loudspeaker or emergency frequency radio announcements and email blasts in real time. Such communications should include guidance as to whether residents/workers should evacuate or stay in their homes or at work, whether they need emergency breathing apparatus and if a building is in danger of collapse,

☐ Determine whether the fire re-contaminated previously decontaminated areas at the Site and require any contaminated areas to be re-cleaned and re-inspected prior to demolition,

☐ Review the impact of water damage from putting out the fire to ensure that mold does not become an issue again,

☐ Test residential and workplace areas in the immediate neighborhood for contaminants that may have been released during the fire and require any contaminated areas to be cleaned,

☐ Hire a responsible subcontractor to replace Galt – one that, as required by the Procurement Policy Board Rules of the City of New York, is capable "in all respects to perform the contract."

Develop a timetable and share it with the public to ensure that work is done in a safe and expeditious manner,

In order to make the process more transparent as possible, LMDC must continuously update its website (www.renewnyc.com) with all relevant information and documents. We note there appear to be gaps in the information currently on the website relating to the period 2005 and 2006 (http://www.renewnyc.com/plan_des_dev/130liberty/public_documents_chrono.asp),

Create a Whistle Blower Protection Program that works. The LMCCC Fraud Prevention Program and other layers of accountability and integrity that were in place to report safety violations and abuses did not work,

Require LMDC/LMCCC to work with each of the regulatory agencies, including EPA, FDNY and OEM, to make sure that all safety measures are in place, and to establish and make public clear lines of accountability for contractors and staff working at the Site,

Disclose details relating to the supervisory role of United Research Services (URS) so that the public knows what their responsibilities are in general and in particular in relation to Bovis. A recent New York Sun article (August 27, 2007), stated, "a construction firm [URS] involved in the demolition of the former Deutsche Bank building is the same company that assured Minnesota officials a highway bridge was safe before it collapsed this summer;"

Implement tests of the various types of Emergency Notification and Evacuation Plans as described by Deputy Mayor Skyler before and after demolition begins again, and perform such tests on the regular basis during the demolition process,

Include appropriate information and actions for special needs, disabled, and deaf persons in the Emergency Notification and Evacuation Plan,

As Deputy Mayor Skyler noted in his opening statement that Civilian Emergency Response Teams (CERT) will play an important role in responding to future emergencies, take steps to ensure that funding for CERT is included in the City's annual budget instead of being dependent upon yearly grants, and

Require vigilant enforcement of city building, construction, safety, and fire codes and regulations – including enforcing a smoke-free, drug-free and alcohol-free policy at the construction site, and

Post a sign outside the Site stating on each day how many prior days have passed without an accident at the Site, and

Implement a process to properly vet all workers at the Site, including those employed by all involved contractors and subcontractors.

The Community Board #1 – Manhattan, Resolution, of Sept. 18, 2007, proves the local Community Board was originally against LMDC as the organizer for the destruction of the Deutsche Bank building. After the fire it states, very plainly what they want and expect from LMDC and others in order to have a safe operation both inside and outside that building.

Appendix H

Abatement, Demolition, and 33 Safety Recommendations

Abatement was regulated by the DEP under their Asbestos Control Program, pursuant to state and federal regulation. Per these regulations, abatement must take place in a controlled work area, and large jobs require the establishment of a containment area, including decontamination enclosure systems, negative air pressure, isolation barriers, and sealing with plastic sheeting. Large or complex jobs can impact fire safety, and the report recommends that the DEP should formally notify the DOB and FDNY of any abatement jobs of a certain size or complexity.

The report also recommends that the DEP establish a permit requirement for large or complex abatement jobs, to ensure that the work plan is reviewed for public-safety and construction issues. The report also recommends that the materials used for partitions, wall surfaces, and plastic sheeting in abatement jobs be fire retardant and that negative-air-pressure systems (required at large job sites to ensure that no asbestos fibers escape) be equipped with a central cutoff switch so the systems can be turned off quickly in an emergency. Under certain fire conditions, negative air units can change the dynamics of normal fire and smoke movement and can pull fire and smoke to floors below the fire.

The working group also found that DEP inspectors, while highly skilled and expert at locating violations that could threaten the integrity of a containment area are not trained in enforcing the fire and building codes. Accordingly, the report recommends that DEP inspections should include inspection of egress and other fire-safety requirements. Also the inspectors should have the power to enforce the fire and building codes at abatement sites, strictly limit simultaneous abatement and demolition work, and have strict criteria before such work is allowed. The DEP,

DOB, and FDNY should be jointly responsible for monitoring these operations.

Under current law, demolition activity requires a DOB permit, and the FDNY is required under its rules to inspect construction and demolition sites every 15 days. Until last year the FDNY did not receive formal notifications from the DOB that a construction or demolition permit had been issued at a particular site. The report now recommends that the DOB formally notify the FDNY whenever a demolition permit is issued and provide a second notification when the DOB is alerted that demolition will commence.

Currently the FDNY, DOB, and DEP perform independent inspections with the FDNY concentrating on fire-safety concerns, the DOB focusing on building and construction-site issues, and the DEP monitoring air-quality concerns at asbestos-abatement sites. To integrate their work and make this process more effective, the report recommends that all three agencies prioritize their inspections according to certain risk factors, such as contractors' history of violations or the size and occupancy of a construction site.

The report recommends that the DEP, DOB, and FDNY incorporate each others' primary safety concerns to create a baseline set of common protocols for all inspections, regardless of which agency's inspector is at a particular site.

Post–Deutsche Bank fire the FDNY made significant changes to its uniformed inspection program. In November 2007 the FDNY decided that it was not operationally effective to meet that requirement, and those buildings under construction or demolition that are less than 75 feet in height are now inspected every 30 days.

The report recommends that the FDNY develop an automated, computer-based system that facilitates the sharing of inspection data throughout the agency as well as with the DOB and DEP. The Fire Department is redesigning its inspection systems to create a single, comprehensive database containing all FDNY-related information about each individual building in NYC.

The working group also reviewed safety issues in so-called "non-jurisdictional" properties that are neither privately owned nor city owned, such as New York State, federal government, and international entities. The report recommends that the city pursue a single standard of safety for all property owners within NYC, including those mentioned above. At the same time that this single standard is pursued, the report recommends the city work with the non-jurisdictional entities to establish a process to enable inspections and enhance code compliance.

The report recommends that the DOB, DEP, and FDNY update their websites and publications to provide thorough descriptions about these processes, including links to the other agencies' websites.

The report recommends the following thirty-three regulations:

Abatement Operations

1. DEP should regularly notify FDNY and DOB about large and/or complex abatement jobs that meet thresholds to be determined by DEP, FDNY, and DOB.
2. DEP should establish a permit requirement for certain large and/or complex abatement jobs based on thresholds to be determined by DEP, DOB, and FDNY.
3. DEP should require building owners and/or air monitors on abatement jobs to notify DEP when abatement work at a particular site is complete.
4. DEP should promulgate clear guidance to contractors about how to maintain proper egress at abatement sites and enforce this requirement in the field.
5. DEP should require that egress conditions be recorded daily in the abatement contractor's logbook and kept on site.
6. DEP should require that all materials used in the construction of temporary enclosures for abatement work be non-combustible or flame-resistant.
7. DEP should require the installation of a central negative air "cut-off switch" or similar mechanism at abatement jobs that meet thresholds to be established by DEP, FDNY, and DOB.
8. DEP should develop written protocols, such as a checklist or other guidance, to ensure that its inspections are comprehensive and consistent at all abatement jobs.

9. DEP inspectors should be trained to inspect and address egress and other safety requirements at abatement sites.

10. DEP should have the authority to enforce provisions of the Fire and Building Codes at abatement sites, including issuing Notices of Violation and other penalties.

11. DOB should make permanent its capacity to have inspectors and other personnel respond to abatement sites—based on criteria to be established by DOB, DEP and FDNY—to augment DEP and FDNY inspections at a particular site. DOB inspectors and other responders must have proper training and personal protective equipment to do this job.

12. DEP should formally establish a policy that strictly limits simultaneous abatement and demolition work, and requires a variance—including review by DOB and FDNY—to undertake it.

Demolition Operations

13. DOB should issue full demolition permits only after an applicant certifies that the site does not need to be abated, or that abatement is complete.

14. DOB should amend its rules and/or seek legislation to increase permitting requirements for all building demolitions using hand-held mechanical devices, including the submission by an engineer of means and methods used and detailed mechanical equipment calculations and details.

15. DOB should notify FDNY whenever a construction or demolition permit is issued.

16. DOB should amend its rules and/or seek legislation to require additional site safety coordinators at certain stages of the demolition process for buildings that are 25 stories or more, and at demolition jobs over 500,000 square feet, regardless of height.

17. DOB should require that Site Safety Managers conduct daily checks of standpipe connections and valves, and a weekly tracing of the standpipe to verify that it has not been breached.

18. DOB should amend its rules and/or seek legislation to require uniform color-coding of standpipe and sprinkler system lines.

19. DOB should amend its rules and/or seek legislation to require a plumbing or fire-suppression license and a permit to cut and cap standpipes or sprinklers during full demolition.

20. FDNY and DOB should study the feasibility of requiring the installation of a pressurized standpipe alarm system (or other security measures) on new building and full demolition jobs.

21. DOB should amend its rules and/or seek legislation to require pressure testing by a licensed plumber or fire suppression contractor of every 75 feet of standpipe in buildings under construction.

22. The Citywide smoking ban at construction, demolition and abatement sites should be strengthened and enforced with a zero-tolerance approach.

Inspection Processes at DOB, DEP and FDNY

23. DOB, FDNY, and DEP should review their inspection criteria and make changes to ensure that, to the extent possible, inspections are prioritized on the basis of risk.

24. DOB, FDNY, and DEP should create common safety protocols incorporating high-priority safety issues within the inspection capacity of all three agencies, and should cross-train inspectors to address these common safety issues.

25. DOB, FDNY, and DEP should implement a system to share relevant results of inspections of buildings that meet agreed-upon criteria. As part of this effort, FDNY should develop a computer-based process to share inspection data internally and with DOB and DEP.

26. DOB, FDNY, and DEP should review their inspection programs to ensure that they have sufficiently robust quality assurance controls in place.

27. DOB should identify "high-risk" alteration sites and develop an appropriate inspection program; FDNY should determine

whether and how frequently these high-risk alteration sites should be inspected.

FDNY Demolition Inspections

28. FDNY should amend Rule 11-01 and other inspection requirements to establish the appropriate frequency and scope of demolition inspections by the Department.
29. FDNY should incorporate inspections of buildings under demolition that take place every 30 days or at any higher frequency into its Building Inspection Safety Program ("BISP") Tracking System.
30. FDNY should develop an automated, computer-based system that facilitates the sharing of inspection data throughout the agency, as well as with DOB and DEP. The Department should also accelerate its transition from paper-based to computer-based data collection and storage for inspections and other processes.
31. FDNY should streamline its process for referring non-emergency conditions to DOB.
32. DOB, DEP and FDNY should update their websites and publications to provide comprehensive and coordinated guidance about the construction, demolition and abatement processes, including how to file for and conduct these operations safely, and the regulatory schemes that are triggered by these operations.

Non-Jurisdictional Buildings

33. The City should pursue state and federal legislation to require that any building built or demolished in New York City is subject to the City's Building and Fire Codes, regardless of owner. Until that requirement is in place, the City should seek to enter into agreements with Federal, State and international building owners to allow DOB and FDNY to conduct inspections and assure code compliance so that these agencies have critical information about conditions at these properties that could affect public safety.

Appendix I

Thank-You Note to the General Services Administration October 24, 2008

I want to thank you for approving the idea of having NYC Fire & Building Department inspectors verify that the Federal government is compliant with NYC code and regulations. I have discussed this with Louis Locito and Eric Marriman (PBS safety people). A meeting is set for Monday at 10:00 AM so that within GSA we can verify all code compliance issues. Eric believes that we are even more compliant, in several areas, than the NYC code requires. As per your direction we shall verify these issues to be factual prior to proceeding outside of GSA.

I have been working with the Mayor's Office, Manhattan Borough President and with NYS Fire Prevention and Public Safety to try and close the loopholes the "quassi" govt. agencies slip through. Agencies like Lower Manhattan Development Corp. and Empire Development Corp. are allowed to police themselves. It is obvious that this does not work.

I am very grateful that I have found so much support in this and other endeavors that I am involved with in order to bring a greater measure of safety to our citizens and first responders. Having your active support and the support of the ARA's (Assistant Regional Administrators) in this personal battle of mine gives me hope. In this new found hope I will continue to fight because it is the "right thing to do." Having the support of GSA makes me very proud and very humble at the same time. I greatly appreciate this, not only for me but for my family and for every person who works or enters and leaves these buildings.

I'm sure that my son and every other fireman, EMT, and police officer who perished while performing their job in buildings that are unsafe, send their thanks as well.

Printed in the United States
By Bookmasters